To the 21st century Crewe family

Acknowledgments

First and foremost I would like to thank Colin Crewe for his interest, support and encouragement over many years. The British Library, besides holding the manuscript of Mrs Crewe's diary, has been the major resource for background and unique information on the people, incidents and geography of the book, for which much thanks. The Corporation of London's Guildhall Library has been a wonderful supplement to The British Library and it is always a pleasure to work there. Thanks also for the facilities at The National Archives, Kew, and to the staff for their help and expertise. I'd like to thank my colleague Alan Lewis for his interest in my research on the Crewe family and his assistance with elements of this book. Thanks also to Ray Gladden who first showed me round the magical Crewe Hall, and shared his own research with me. Sadly, Ray died in 2010. I'm grateful to The Lord O'Neill for unique information on the family background. Finally, thanks to my wife Barbara, the most important member of my crew!

AN ENGLISH LADY IN PARIS

Also by Michael Allen

Charles Dickens' childhood. Macmillan, 1988.

As contributor to:
Oxford Reader's Companion to Dickens; edited by
Paul Schlicke. Oxford University Press, 1999.
Paperback edition, 2000.

A Blackwell Companion to Dickens; edited by
David Paroissien. Blackwell Publishing, 2007.
Paperback edition, 2011.

TO BE PUBLISHED 2011

Charles Dickens' childhood. 2nd revised edition. Oxford-Stockley
Publications, 2011.
Also Kindle edition, 2011

Charles Dickens and the Blacking Factory. Oxford-Stockley
Publications, 2011.
Also Kindle edition, 2011

Frances Anne Crewe
By Sir Joshua Reynolds

frontis

An
English Lady in Paris

the diary of
Frances Anne Crewe
1786

edited and introduced by
Michael Allen

Oxford-Stockley Publications

Published by
Oxford-Stockley Publications
17 Heather Close, St Leonards BH24 2QJ
United Kingdom
email: oxfordstockley@btinternet.com

First edition 2006
reprinted 2011

ISBN   978 0 9552490 2 0

CONTENTS

LIST OF ILLUSTRATIONS

Introduction

The world of Frances Anne Crewe

Anyone reading accounts of the second half of eighteenth century Britain – biographies, diaries, social histories – would be struck with the role women played: as confident leaders of society, as participants in the social sides of politics and the arts, and they might pick out a dozen or so women with the highest profiles and the most influence. Georgiana, Duchess of Devonshire might head the list, followed perhaps by Elizabeth Montagu, Fanny Burney, the Lennox sisters, Mrs Thrale, Mrs Fitzherbert, Elizabeth Villiers and so on. One name that appears in a great many accounts but rarely with a high profile is that of Frances Anne Crewe. But 'twas not always so. If the views of Richard Brinsley Sheridan, Sir Joshua Reynolds and Fanny Burney are anything to go by then Mrs Crewe – and Mrs was a title she wore with a flourish until made Lady Crewe at the age of 64 – was one of the most beautifully stunning women of her time. With a wealthy husband she lived in great style, at the apex of London's bon-ton, welcoming over the threshold of her London home – as well as at Crewe Hall in Cheshire – the rich, aristocratic, influential and intellectual cream of society, including the Prince of Wales. In the winter of 1785 she travelled with her husband from London to Brussels and Spa before eventually arriving in Paris on Christmas Eve. From the day she arrived in Paris till her return to England halfway through March she recorded her visit in letters to a friend, which were eventually re-written to form the journal that is at the centre of this book.

Letters, diaries and journals

"Letters are valuable and entertaining in proportion to the wit and ability, and above all to the imprudence, of those who write them. For the merit of a really good letter is always colloquial; it is full of news or gossip, it is personal, unstudied and indiscreet. It shows the writer without his guards or defences, uncovers all his thoughts and feelings; and that is why honest letters are more informative, more amusing, more pathetic, more vital than any considered autobiography. Of all documents these are the most essentially human. They bring us into a curiously intimate relation with men and women of the past, a relation sometimes exhilarating, sometimes nearly painful. Even when literary skill is absent, a passionate or vigorous expression, a trick of humour, is enough to produce an immediate sense of living personality." (C.E. Vulliamy: *English letter writers*)

From a viewpoint at the beginning of the 21st century it's not easy to understand how pervasive letter writing was in the eighteenth century (and into the nineteenth), certainly at the level of society being dealt with here: business letters, government letters, letters to relatives and friends. *Georgiana: extracts from the correspondence of Georgiana, Duchess of Devonshire*, though it contains a range of letters, is a good example of the extent and depth of correspondence between a daughter (Georgiana) and her mother, much of it the sort of advice and admonishment that might have been expected from a parent in the second half of the eighteenth century. On the other hand *The life and letters of Lady Sarah Lennox, 1745-1826*, is made up mostly from a lifetime of correspondence between two friends, Sarah Lennox and Susan Fox Strangeways, a correspondence that inspired the high-profile book *Aristocrats* by Stella Tillyard as well as a television series of the same name. Both sets of letters give the impression of people talking to each other: often, though not always, they resemble conversations written down. Mrs Crewe's letters bear the same stamp: "I write down what occurs to me just as I should venture to speak to you, were you present" (p107) and "my chief Motive for Scribbling as I do is for the Pleasure of conversing with you"(p145). The 12 volume Pilgrim edition of the Letters of Charles Dickens, though written more than 40 years after the Crewe diary, gives an excellent insight into the pervasiveness of letter writing, of the everyday minutiae of life recorded in letters and, certainly in London, of the speed of letter delivery. Two instances from Dickens will suffice: firstly, when he writes to his friend Henry Kolle in 1832[1] saying he has that morning received a note from a young lady, as a result of which he would like Kolle to take the enclosed letter to her the same afternoon; secondly, when he writes to another friend, Henry Austin in 1833[2], at 8 o'clock in the morning saying he hopes to see him on the Thames before 9 o'clock. In both of these letters we have speed, immediacy and detail. Now we would use the telephone, text or e-mail – none of which, it may be presumed, will survive – then, they sent a letter. Of course, most letters from the eighteenth century haven't survived either, but a great many have, some held in libraries and archives, some privately held and some published. Of the most voluminous survivals Horace Walpole's amount to 48 volumes, Fanny Burney's to 10 volumes, Edmund Burke's to 10 volumes. There are other examples.

At the same time that letter writing was endemic the keeping of diaries or journals was also widespread. For the purpose of this book the terms diary and journal will be used synonymously. The pursuit of

---

[1] *The letters of Charles Dickens.* The Pilgrim edition, Oxford University Press, 12 vols, 1965-2002. vol 1, p8, Summer 1832

[2] *The letters of Charles Dickens*, op cit, vol 1, p22, Spring 1833

diary-keeping was considered to have an improving effect on the writer, the writings reflecting, as they did, their thoughts and views, their attempts to understand culture and taste; they encouraged, particularly through re-reading, a self-consciousness and self-examination. Attention to culture is particularly marked in eighteenth century diaries and Mrs Crewe's is typical of her time, drawing attention throughout to books, poetry, theatre, music, painting and language. There gradually developed a cross-over between letter writing and journal writing, which became known as letter-journals – Mrs Crewe's Paris journal is such an example; another is *The Letter journal of George Canning, 1793-95*. There was also a cross-over between letter writing and novel writing, a genre that became known as epistolary novels – for example Smollett's *Humphry Clinker*, Fanny Burney's *Evelina* and Richardson's *Clarissa*, the last of which is referred to in the diary (p129). Novels were, of course, written for a wide public but for the most part letters and diaries were not written for publication, though some people with literary or political aspirations or achievements undoubtedly did keep half an eye on a wider audience. But even Pepys' diary, written 1660-1669, remained a personal document for 150 years and was not transcribed until the early nineteenth century; John Evelyn's diary, completed in 1706, took the same course and didn't appear in print till 1818. In order to maintain the confidentiality of what he wrote the letter journal of George Canning was prefaced with a set of 4 "general rules" specifically restricting access: "1. That the nature and intent of the said letters be not talked of before any other than the family… 2. That they be never read out by or before any other persons…. 3. That as… it may often happen that they will be days or weeks behind hand – it be not supposed therefore that there is any neglect or forgetfulness…. 4. That a little portfolio be assigned to them, in which they shall be laid orderly and smoothly, without crease or confusion, and preserved for the inspection of the writer of them, when he shall come to Ashborne in the summer."[3]

Mrs Crewe's diary is held at The British Library as part of its Windham Papers[4], a collection purchased for the British Museum in 1909. The Crewe diary is bound in half-leather together with two other diaries. The first of these three is a travel journal written by William Windham, dated June 1779, covering a trip through Surrey, Wiltshire, Dorsetshire, Devonshire, Somersetshire, Wales, and Worcestershire – it's written in Latin and covers 18 pages, the last three of which are mostly torn out. Mrs Crewe's Paris diary starts at page 19, the pagination having been added at a later date by a librarian, and runs to page 129. It is

---

[3] *The letter-journal of George Canning, 1793-1795*; edited by Peter Jupp. Camden fourth series volume 41. Royal Historical Society, 1991. pp23-4
[4] It is held in The Manuscripts Library under the title *Travel diary of Frances Anne Crewe*; shelfmark: Add.37,926

written on individual sheets of paper 18.5cm x 23.4cm, for the most part using both sides of the paper, and these sheets have then been bound together. The handwriting, which is not Mrs Crewe's – apart from the very first page, beginning "A Paris journal…" – is clearly written and the ink is clear on the page, black, and very little faded. The third diary is also by Mrs Crewe, probably in her own handwriting, and describes a trip through Wales in 1795. It runs from page 130 to page 156. This Welsh diary indicates at the top that it is "Addressed to the Honble Miss Fox".

The Paris diary is described by Mrs Crewe as a journal written in the form of letters to a friend. Since the letters were written in Paris and sent to England she did, at some stage, retrieve them from her friend and have them, in her own words, "copied fair"(p73). She suggests they might be united with similar journals she had written at Brussels and Spa, which she had visited prior to travelling on to Paris.[5]

The language used by Mrs Crewe is remarkably modern – it flows easily, and uses many words and phrases that would fit comfortably into 21st century conversation. She describes a ball room as "brilliant", is "amazed" at a book, discerns a "buzz" in the air at the Royal Academy; she spends time "dipping into" a book, is able to "pop in and out" of the Luxembourg Gardens, and likes "winding up the day with a few people"; she wanted to be well dressed without aiming at "the pink of taste"; she talks of little affectations which are "absolutely necessary" to correct behaviour; and how people have to "puzzle" over anagrams; family parties are "pretty large", people speak "pretty freely" and get "pretty well acquainted". Phrases like these demonstrate powerful links between the language of today and that of 200 years ago. At the same time she uses words that have now dropped out of common use: there are many but a few examples will suffice: "tags" meaning loose ends, "tantivy": at full speed, "coxcomical": the amusing behaviour of a conceited dandy, "umbras": shadows, "prate": to chatter, talk foolishly and too much, "encomiums": praise, and "tiff": to get dressed up. Perhaps the aspects of the writing that jar most to the modern eye concern spelling, punctuation and use of capital letters, all of which seem a little eccentric to modern taste. The spelling of names, particularly French names, is often inaccurate. There is extensive use of the long s, as in Bruſsells, Permiſsion, etc., and regular use of the ampersand. Mrs Crewe is keen to underline words or phrases that she feels need emphasising. All such

_____

[5] A letter from Richard Burke in Paris to his father in England, written on 25th December 1785, gives the information: "I have just been at Mrs Crews who came the night before last. She has been ill at Brussels but is quite recover'd." – *The correspondence of Edmund Burke*. Cambridge University Press and Chicago University Press, 10 vols, 1958-78. vol 5, p246

punctuation and spelling is transcribed just as it appears in the handwritten copy.

The writing does not have any pretence at being literary but flows in a conversational way, as she notes herself: "I write down what occurs to me just as I should venture to speak to you, were you present"(p107). At the same time she peppers her pages with quotations, mostly from the stage, and with references to books. Of prime importance to her is Shakespeare, with quotations or references to no fewer than nine of his works and of those nine *Hamlet* is referred to five times. Many of the other authors she refers to are well known to us today, authors like Milton, Dryden, Pope, Sterne, Richardson and Moliere; others less so: Prior, Barbauld, Delille and Dyer for example. Her memory serves her well, most quotations having a high degree of accuracy.

The Crewe family

The earliest document to record a Crewe is dated 1150, though there is evidence to show that the family was derived from an earlier time, and from one of the eight Norman Barons of Cheshire. The first recorded member of the family, Henri de Criwa, built a Manor House about the year 1170: a timber-framed building that survived, just, until the early 17th century. It was located in eastern Cheshire: the town of Crewe did not then exist, it being a product, primarily, of the 19th century railway boom.

The Crewe Manor House and the estates surrounding it passed through five more generations of the family - until, in the 14th century, there was no male heir, and everything passed, through marriage, into the Praers family. Then two generations later the estates passed, by marriage again, into the Fulleshurst family. The property stayed with the Fulleshursts through eight generations, though during that time the old Manor House deteriorated badly, and a second house was built adjacent to the first. In 1579 Queen Elizabeth's Lord Chancellor, Sir Christopher Hatton, bought the Crewe estates, from whom they passed to his nephew, and then to his nephew's wife. The Crewe family, though not in possession of their ancestral home and property from the 14th to the 16th centuries, nevertheless continued to maintain a proud record of their family line, and continued to hold an important social position in Cheshire.

In 1559 was born a member of the family, Ranulphe Crewe, who was to turn their fortunes. He chose to enter the profession of Law, at a time when its members first began to grow in status and in wealth. He also married well, his wife bringing money and property to the match. In 1597, still in the reign of Elizabeth, he became a Member of Parliament. So successful was Ranulphe Crewe in his law practice that in 1608 he was able to buy back from the Hatton family, the ancient Manor House and its estates. In 1615 he pulled down the dilapidated old house at Crewe and laid the first stone of a brand new mansion, which took him 21 years to build. Ranulphe Crewe went on to become Speaker of the House of Commons, Attorney-General and eventually Lord Chief Justice, serving first under King James and then Charles 1. Unfortunately for Crewe, his tenure as Lord Chief Justice proved a short-lived one. From the very beginning of his reign Charles and his Parliament were at loggerheads over their rights and privileges. So when Parliament refused to grant the King money, in 1626, and when the King responded by trying to force a "loan" from the population, it was to the law, and to the Lord Chief Justice, that people turned for protection. Sir Ranulphe's pronouncement was that: "...by the law of England, no tax or talliage, under whatever name or disguise, can be laid upon the people without the authority of Parliament; and the King cannot imprison any of his subjects without a warrant specifying the offence with which they are charged."[6] The reaction was swift: the King dismissed Sir Ranulphe from office. Political wrangles continued for some years and eventually the country slipped into Civil War. Crewe Hall did not escape the conflict. It was held first by the Parliamentarians, then by the Royalists; Cromwell's men seized it once again, and then in December 1643 it was lost back to the King's men, after a bloody battle, with sixty Royalists killed, and 136 Parliamentarians taken prisoner. The last battle came two months later, when the Roundheads regained it, and this time held it. Crewe Hall was not structurally damaged during these battles, but Sir Ranulphe wrote to a friend: "If you saw the counties - how devastated, how impoverished, how defaced, it would grieve you...I myself receive nothing of my revenue, and have been plundered to a great value."[7] Sir Ranulphe Crewe died in 1646, aged 88, having to a great extent restored his family's fortune and property.

From the time of Sir Ranulphe through to the John Crewe who married the author of this diary there were many other members of the family who took their part in public life. A brother of Sir Ranulphe, Thomas Crewe, was also Speaker of the House of Commons and he had a son, John, who became the 1st Baron Crewe of Steane in Northamptonshire: this John Crewe features a great deal in Pepys Diary, since he was father-in-law to Pepys' master the Earl of Sandwich; he also featured as one of the Parliamentary Commissioners negotiating with King Charles to end the Civil War. This first Baron Crewe had two sons, the youngest of whom, Nathaniel, was a great favourite at the court of

---

[6] The lives of the Chief Justices of England by Lord John Campbell. Murray, 4 vols, 3rd ed., 1874. vol 1, p441
[7] Barthomley by Edward Hinchliffe. Longman, Brown, Green, and Longmans, 1856. p237

Charles 2nd, and was made Bishop of Durham in 1672, a position he held through six reigns, his death coming in 1721. He was also, by then, the 3rd Baron Crewe of Steane, a title that died with him.

Crewe Hall and the Crewe estates were passed from Sir Ranulphe, to his son, and to his grandson; but then the family ran out of male heirs, as it had in the 14th century, and the property passed instead to a daughter, Anne Crewe. Her marriage was to John Offley, Lord of the Manor of Madeley in nearby Staffordshire. The name of Offley was a proud one, boasting not only the land and property in Staffordshire, but also an Elizabethan Lord Mayor of London. Anne Crewe's father-in-law had been a great friend of Isaac Walton, and was proud to have had Walton's famous book *The Compleat Angler* dedicated to him. Nevertheless, the Crewes had an even longer and prouder history than the Offleys and were determined that their name should not lapse. With urgings from an uncle of Anne Crewe's, who also had substantial property in Cheshire, which would be left to them, the family agreed to change their name from Offley to Crewe, and to continue the line. Her son, John Offley Crewe, became a Member of Parliament; so too did two of her grandsons; and so too did the great-grandson who found himself in Paris at the beginning of 1786.

There are a great many John Crewes in the family tree but the John Crewe we are interested in here was born 1742. He was the heir to Crewe Hall, Madeley Manor and extensive estates in Cheshire and Staffordshire, inheriting those estates when he was just ten years old. The young Crewe was educated at Westminster School in central London, and Trinity College Cambridge, though he did not graduate. When he came of age in 1763 he was rounding off his education on the fashionable and obligatory Grand Tour of Europe. His tutor on the Grand Tour was an ex-master (and, later, Headmaster) from Westminster School, John Hinchliffe, who later went on to marry one of John Crewe's sisters and to make a career in the Church as Bishop of Peterborough. The Bishop's nephew, Edward Hinchliffe wrote a history of the Crewe family (among others) in his book *Barthomley*, published in 1856. In 1764, at the age of 22, John Crewe took a town house in London's highly-fashionable Grosvenor Square. That same year he was made Sheriff of Cheshire; and the following year, at the age of only 23, he entered Parliament, sitting for three years for the Stafford constituency and then holding the Cheshire seat from 1768 until 1802: it can have done him no harm to have as a next door neighbour in Grosvenor Square, the Prime Minister, the Marquess of Rockingham. In fact, the whole square bristled with the wealthy, the aristocratic, and the influential. Horace Walpole dismissed dandified John Crewe at this time as "young rich Mr Crewe, a Macaroni".[8] Lady Sarah Lennox wrote in a

---

[8] *Horace Walpole's correspondence.* Oxford University Press and Yale University

letter that he was a fine catch for any Miss, being very rich, and a very good kind of a man. "He is very amiable", she wrote, "and there is no harm in his having £10,000 a year"[9] - an annual income, it's worth noting, that would amount in 2006 to about £850,000[10]. Though Sarah Lennox describes him as rather shy - a man prodigiously afraid of being married, who wouldn't speak to the ladies - nevertheless, on 4th April 1766 he took to the altar at St. George's Church, in London's Hanover Square, a 17 years old bride, reported by many people to be the most beautiful woman of her age, Frances Anne Greville.

Looking back through accounts of the late eighteenth century we can see that Mrs Crewe was a shining star whilst her husband was but a shadow. His nephew, Edward Hinchliffe, described him as a man of no great talent or acquirement but with a clear head and strong common sense. He was fond of politics and parliamentary life, yet in his 37 years in the House of Commons spoke only a dozen times, mostly on a bill with which his name is associated, to prevent revenue officers from voting at elections. This bill, passed in 1782, sought to curb the influence of the King and is indicative of Crewe's political outlook, always supporting liberal Whig policies.

He voted for Shelburne's American peace preliminaries, and for Charles James Fox's East India bill in 1783, but when the King dismissed Fox as joint secretary of state at the end of 1783 Crewe followed him into opposition. With a great deal of support in the House of Commons Fox expected an immediate return to office, in anticipation of which he drew up a list of supporters who would be installed in the House of Lords – John Crewe was among them. That it didn't happen was a great disappointment to Crewe as well as Fox, so that he had to remain in the Commons for a further 22 years. During that time he brought before Parliament, on a number of occasions, a bill for the repeal of salt duty, seeking to protect the interest of the important cheese industry in Cheshire and although he didn't achieve the measure himself he laid the ground for eventual abolition in 1825. He remained loyal to Fox and was rewarded with the title 1st Baron Crewe of Crewe in 1805 when Fox was once again called to share in a coalition government. Fox died the next year but Crewe sat in the House of Lords for 24 years more, until his death in 1829. There is in the National Portrait Gallery, London, a

---

Press, 48 volumes, 1937-1983. vol 38, p394
[9] *The life and letters of Lady Sarah Lennox, 1745-1826.* 2nd ed., Murray, 1902. p188
[10] throughout this book price comparisons are based on "Equivalent contemporary values of the pound: a historical series 1270 to 1998 taken from The national wealth: who gets what in Britain, by Dominic Hobson, published by HarperCollins in 1999.

group portrait including Crewe and other colleagues standing round a bust of Fox.

Crewe's attachment to Charles James Fox was financial as well as political. Crewe was a founder member of Brooks's Club where gambling was heavy and losses great. Not that Crewe was known as a great gambler, but Fox was and a great loser, too, wasting a great part of his family's considerable fortune. Crewe's admiration for Fox led him, rather foolishly we might think, to provide a financial safety net, settling on him an annuity of £1200. Others did the same. Unfortunately for Crewe his brother Richard and his own eldest son, John, also accrued debts and proved to be serious drains on his resources.

Sorting out other people's profligacy cost him some of the property portfolio built up by his predecessors, which was a great pity since he was generally recognised as a good and progressive landlord. He had a great interest in agriculture, encouraging experimentation and the invention of new implements. Not surprisingly farmers were keen to lease his farms. He spent much of the year among them, becoming personally acquainted, working with them to achieve good results. He was similarly a good employer to the servants who worked for him (one of the few times he spoke in Parliament was against a tax on maidservants). Hinchliffe reported that a number of servants' gravestones in the local churchyard at Barthomley boasted the number of years spent in his service, quoting 43 years and 50 years as examples. There is a fascinating instance of his kindness as an employer. In 1781 his butler, William, married another servant, in itself unusual since employers preferred not to employ married couples. The butler was aged 58 and his wife 36 and over the next four years they had two children, both boys. A small family might have seemed a large encumbrance for the Crewe family but it appears not since the circumstances didn't interrupt the employment of the couple. This demonstration of generosity on the part of John Crewe was tested further in 1785 when the butler died. Still his wife remained with the Crewes, bringing up her children and eventually rising to the position of housekeeper. She remained with them till she reached an age when she had to retire, remembered by the Crewe grandchildren for the time spent with her listening to the wonderful stories she told. It's an example of Crewe loyalty, the crowning piquancy of which is that the butler and the housekeeper were the grandparents of Charles Dickens.[11]

---

[11] see The Dickens/Crewe connection by Michael Allen IN *Dickens Quarterly*(USA), December 1988

The mother of John Crewe's wife, Mrs Greville, features a great deal in the Paris travel diary which is at the centre of this book, and is a character of great interest in her own right, so let's look first at Frances Macartney and then the man she married, Fulke Greville.

Frances Macartney was one of four daughters of Irishman James Macartney and 3rd cousin to George, created Earl Macartney in 1794. (see Appendix Ten) The relationship with Lord Macartney, however distant, was kept up by the junior branch of the family and he is mentioned in the diary. Frances Macartney was vivacious, aggressively bold, and very attractive. Her features were small and fine, and a slight croak in her voice added to the manner in which she stood out from other young women. There was a sharpness about her that often stung people with its sarcasm and satire, and all the more effectively because of a sharp sense of humour. She intimidated many people. She was loud and commanding and could ruffle feathers with her criticisms, as she did Mrs Thrale, who protested to Dr Johnson: "You never told me she was so Lofty a Lady".[12] Mrs Thrale complained to Johnson that Greville put people down, a characteristic of Mrs Selwyn in Fanny Burney's novel *Evelina*, who Rizzo claims was certainly based on Greville. Such brusqueness upset her friend Lady Spencer[13] who, when they were together in France in 1773, refused to talk in her daunting presence; she challenged the indomitable Mrs Montagu[14], whose own manner was described by Wraxall as dictatorial and sententious.

Mrs Greville complemented her conversational wit with an ability to write. She attempted a novel that she failed to finish but was more successful with verse. Her *Ode for indifference*, referred to in the diary, was first published in 1759 and thereafter frequently reproduced and widely known (see Appendix One); it continues to appear in modern compilations[15]. In the year dealt with in the diary Mrs Greville achieved the age of 61 and wrote the following lines:

My sixty years are roll'd away,
Nay more, alas! I'm sixty one
Yet not in darkness ends my day
Some light still gilds my Horizon
And to the last expiring spark
I'll gaily steer my little bark.

---

[12] Companions without vows: relationships among eighteenth-century British women by Betty Rizzo. Georgia University Press, 1994. p241
[13] Margaret Georgiana Spencer, 1737-1814, mother of Georgiana, Duchess of Devonshire
[14] Elizabeth Montagu, 1718-1800
[15] The new Oxford book of eighteenth century verse; chosen and edited by Roger Lonsdale. Oxford U.P., 1984

To Tyrant age I must submit
But O avaunt ye hideous crew
Detested followers of it;
Think not I'll be a Slave to you;
Time to my form may be unkind
But he shall ne'er debase my mind[16]

A note in Walpole's Correspondence[17] suggests she may have written much of her husband's own book *Maxims and characters*, which enjoyed some favourable attention in the latter half of the eighteenth century. Her intelligence, confidence in society and ability to write may well have been seen, as the marriage progressed, to be a challenge to his rather prickly character, since the two separated just prior to the 1786 visit to Paris. Following the breakdown of the marriage she seems to have retained the loyalty of her children, most of whom were with her in Paris. She was particularly close to her daughter, who had travelled with her parents to Italy when she was eight years old (just as, on this trip, Mrs Crewe took her 5-6 year old daughter Emma). It was Mrs Greville who took her teenage daughter out into society, introducing her to all the right people including, no doubt, her future husband. She took her also to Paris in 1773 and was there with her again in 1786. Mrs Crewe inherited her mother's confident, out-going character, her ability to converse and mix in society, but not her sarcasm or sharpness with people. Frances Greville died in 1789, three years after the Paris diary.

The youthful vivacity of Frances Macartney met its match in the person of Fulke Greville – he was the grandson of the fifth Lord Brooke, and had hopes of inheriting that title, together with the seat at Warwick Castle and a vast fortune (see Appendix Nine). As a young man he had been a popular figure in fashionable society, described as the finest gentleman about town. He was exceptionally handsome: tall, well-proportioned and commanding; his face, features and complexion were striking; his general air and carriage noble and dignified. He excelled at all the fashionable exercises: riding, fencing, hunting, shooting, dancing, tennis, and so on - and worked at hem with a fury for pre-eminence. Another passion was for racehorses, which he owned and trained; and a slightly less healthy passion, which he shared with so many of his contemporaries, was that of gambling. Though he was a wealthy man, and this, together with his other attributes, dazzled and attracted a great many possible brides for him, nevertheless his recklessness at the card tables alarmed and deterred the parents of prospective partners. Horace Walpole recorded in 1741 that Greville had lost £15,000 at cards. A less expensive interest was music, which brought him into contact, in 1746,

---

[16] Rizzo, op cit, p254
[17] Walpole's correspondence, op cit, vol 37, pp460-1

11

with a twenty-year old musician called Charles Burney. So impressed was Greville with the young man that he sought to immediately employ him as a domestic musician and companion, and took him back to his splendid country seat at Wilbury House, at Newton Tony near Amesbury in Wiltshire. Greville's style of life in the country was every bit as enthusiastic and extravagant as it was in fashionable London or at Newmarket races. Burney described it as "princely; not only from his equipages, outriders, horses, and liveries, but from constantly having two of his attendants skilled in playing the French horn. And these were always stationed to recreate him with marches and warlike movements, on the outside of the windows, where he took any repast."[18] Frances Macartney and Fulke Greville were a romantic couple, determined to add a spice of excitement to their wedding by running away together to marry in secret. Charles Burney was persuaded to act as father to the bride, to give her away, since she was still under age, and he was pledged to silence. On their return the elopers sought the forgiveness and blessing of the bride's father, but he was clearly unimpressed by the adventure: "Mr Greville," he said, "has chosen to take a wife out of the window, whom he might just as well have taken out of the door."

It was not long after, in the summer of 1749, that Burney also married, and since Greville had decided to set off on a trip to Italy, the two parted company. Two years later Burney was advised to move from London to the countryside, and he took a job as organist at St. Margaret's church in Kings Lynn, Norfolk. It was there in 1752 that his third child was born, a girl who was to achieve wide recognition as one of the very earliest women novelists in English literature and a pre-eminent diarist, the famous Fanny Burney. Both she and her father were central characters in the life of Frances Anne Crewe.

Fulke Greville never really found his niche in life. From his early high hopes of becoming the next Lord Brooke he became a disappointed man, serving just one term in Parliament, representing Monmouth from 1747, and later serving for six years as an Envoy Extraordinary to Bavaria. After the excitement of its early years his marriage was not a happy one. He lost the affection of his wife, Rizzo claiming that her *Ode for indifference* was a "personal declaration of the severance of her identification with her husband, of her independence, which thereafter she maintained as much as possible by living as separately from her husband as she could"[19]. Fanny Burney wrote that he became angered and disgusted with life and in a gloomy sullenness retired from public view, living a rambling, unsettled sort of life, ill at ease with his family and with the world, frequently inflicting wounds on himself and others

---

[18] *Memoirs of Doctor Burney* by his daughter Madame d'Arblay. Edward Moxon, 3 vols, 1832. vol 1, p47. Madame d'Arblay was the married name of Fanny Burney
[19] Rizzo, op cit, p247

through irritability and argument[20]. He receives no mention in Mrs Crewe's diary but lived on to 1806, dying in Wandsworth near London – his last will and testament was a scrappy letter written to one of his servants.

Frances Anne Greville

Mrs Crewe was born Frances Anne Greville in 1748 and was baptized on November 28th at Newton Toney church, Wiltshire, close to the family home. Charles Burney, father of Fanny Burney stood proxy for the Duke of Beaufort as godfather to the child. Little is known of her childhood but in the diary she does recall time spent at the family home and on a visit to France: "…the fine open Downy Country We passed through filled my Head with a thousand pleasing Reveries, and recalled to my Mind my Youthful Days in Wiltshire and Hampshire"(p209); and then also: "The Gentleman and Lady of this House are very old Friends of my Mother's, and talked to me about my Brothers and myself when we were Children in Loraine"(p147) – this was in 1756, when she was about 8 years old. Time would also have been spent in London. There is no denying the recognition of Miss Greville's good looks. Some indication of that developing beauty can be seen in a portrait of her painted by Joshua Reynolds in 1760, when she was just twelve years old. The painting has a curious history: it featured Miss Greville as Psyche, and included, standing beside her, her younger brother William, representing Cupid. At the time of its creation the painting is said to have attracted a great deal of attention, since with it Reynolds introduced a new style of poetic full-length portraiture, a style that rapidly caught on, and was adopted by the fashionable people who flocked to him. Some years later Fulke Greville had a terrible argument with his son William, and cut the child out of the painting, replacing his figure of Cupid with a tripod. However, the cut out portion was preserved, and after passing through several hands was eventually bought back in the 1860s, and sewn once again into its place on the original canvas. An engraving was made from the painting and printed as early as 1762[21] In 1764 Mrs Greville took her 15-year-old daughter to Spa in Belgium where Stephen Fox, the eldest son of Lord Holland and four years her senior, had fallen in love with her. Sarah Bunbury, an aunt of Fox, wrote in September of that year: "I had a letter from Mrs Greville from Spa. She says Ste. and Miss Greville go on just as she wishes, nothing particular, but yet seem to like one another very well; she seems to dread her taking an aversion to him, which I think as well as her Miss G. will certainly do the moment she finds out he is a lover, which notwithstanding Ste.'s violent love she

[20] *Memoirs of Doctor Burney*, op cit, vol 1, p136
[21] *Reynolds*; edited by Nicholas Penny. Royal Academy of Arts/Weidenfeld and Nicholson, 1986. pp200-1

does not yet suspect. I own I don't think Ste. will remain in the same mind long, & hope he won't, for I don't like it, but must not say so."[22] The attraction continued for more than a year but by January 1766 she was writing: "Miss Greville's match with him is quite off, why I don't know; but he never proposed, tho' he liked her."[23] In the same letters she wrote: "Miss Greville is vastly improved & is prettier than ever; she and her mother go to Munich next spring; Mr Greville is Envoy there, & goes immediately. I hope she marries tho', for if once she goes abroad, nobody knows how long she may stay, & if her beauty goes off her money won't get her married. The D[uke] of Beaufort I forgot to name; he is an admirer of Miss G.'s"[24] In the end, though, it wasn't Stephen Fox or the Duke of Beaufort who won the hand of the lovely Miss Greville but John Crewe.

The way she lived

There is no doubt that, though it was John Crewe who was a rich landowner, who had an illustrious pedigree, and who was a Member of Parliament, it was his wife, Frances Anne Crewe, who was to glisten and shine, to draw about her the famous and the talented, and to leave her mark in the letters, diaries and memoirs from the second half of the eighteenth century. Her looks were said to be flawless, and exquisitely perfect. "The most completely a beauty of any woman I ever saw"[25], wrote Fanny Burney. Sheridan wrote, towards the end of his life, "She was in truth the handsomest of the set"[26]. Sir Joshua Reynolds painted her before her marriage, when she was only 12; then twice more when she was Mrs Crewe.

The Crewes' pattern of life was dictated principally by the society seasons: broadly speaking, the winter months at Crewe Hall and the summer months in London; with regular visits to spa towns such as Bath or Tunbridge Wells, or less regularly to fashionable continental spas, or to Paris. From London, weekends were also frequently spent at Mrs Crewe's villa, in the earlier years at Richmond and later at Hampstead.

At the centre of London society were established a group of some 300 people known as the 'ton', derived from the French word for tone: style, fashion, distinction. Though essentially controlled by, and comprised of, titled and aristocratic families, invitation and acceptance

[22] Lennox, op cit, pp144-5
[23] Lennox, op cit, pp180-1
[24] Lennox, op cit, p182
[25] *The journals and letters of Fanny Burney* (Madame d'Arblay); edited by Joyce Hemlow and others. Oxford University Press, 10 vols, 1972-82. vol 1, p193
[26] *The letters of Richard Brinsley Sheridan*; edited by Cecil Price. Oxford University Press, 3 vols, 1966. vol 3, pp202-3

into this elite company was spread a little further: to the wealthy, the beautiful, the powerful, and the talented. The beauty and wealth of Mrs Crewe may have been enough to ensure her a place as a leading light of the 'ton', but the fact that she had character and personality to match, established for her a position at the very pinnacle of society. It was Mrs Crewe's irresistible charm that bound people to her. She had a spice of devilry in her character, a bohemian dash of unconventionality, and a quick wit. She was daring and flirtatious with men, encouraging admirers, not always discreetly. But despite her daring she wore a look of baptismal innocence. She warmed the hearts of friends and acquaintances, and won their unhesitating appreciation. And though her position in society was one of high standing, her character made her, nevertheless, the good-hearted friend rather than the grand lady.

Mrs Crewe was one of the most successful society hostesses of the day, firstly at Grosvenor Square, then at a house just round the corner in Grosvenor Street. It was part of the routine of a hostess to hold a regular 'salon', where good conversation could be listened to, and participated in: the success of a salon was judged by the eminence of the people attracted to it. To the home of the Crewes flocked all members of the ton: politicians, writers, artists, musicians. Only one other person with her salon rivalled Mrs Crewe's position in society: Georgiana, the Duchess of Devonshire. Their relationship, though, was not one of rivalry, but of complement. Outside of their own immediate family circles the Duchess and Mrs Crewe were probably closer to each other, in friendship, than to any other members of a close-knit set. They moved in the same circles, of course, attending the same social events, receiving the same people to their salons; but they were drawn closely together also because they were equally regarded by the population at large as eminently beautiful, and as the epitome of style. Their complementary sparkling characters sealed the relationship: as Frances Anne was daring and devilish, so was Georgiana broad-minded and tolerant; as the former was warm and friendly, so was the latter described as having an enthusiasm of affection. The Duchess was said to have had "something" shining within, a happiness of nature, a warmth and affection. Mrs Crewe had Charles James Fox write some charming lines about her, printed in 1775:

"If then for this once in my Life I am free,
And escape from a Snare might catch wiser than me,
'Tis that Beauty alone but imperfectly charms;
For though Brightness may dazzle, 'tis kindness that warms.
As on Suns in the Winter with Pleasure we gaze,
But feel not their Force, though their Splendour we praise,
So Beauty our just Admiration may claim;
But Love, and Love only, our Hearts can inflame."[27]

---

[27] For complete version see Appendix 5

John Crewe's staunch support for Fox was re-inforced by his wife, at no time more so than the famous and critical election of 1784, when Fox stood for the Westminster constituency in the heart of London. The Whigs were trying to wrest power back from Pitt's Tories: King George the 3rd supported Pitt, and to his great fury his son the Prince of Wales supported Fox. A contemporary record relates: "On the 22nd April I find Sir Joshua Reynolds attending at Covent Garden, no doubt to record his vote for Fox in that famous election which was now filling the neighbourhood of the hustings with fighting mobs, through whose greasy ranks the brilliant Whig ladies, headed by the Duchess of Devonshire and Mrs Crewe, moved like beings of another sphere, courting, cajoling, and canvassing."[28] Fox won the election, and a celebratory banquet was held at the Crewe home in Grosvenor Street, many of the participants decked out in the party colours of buff and blue. The toast of the evening was given by the Prince of Wales, who proclaimed "Buff and Blue, and Mrs Crewe", which evoked tremendous applause, and to which she rose and responded with great panache "Buff and Blue, and all of you!"[29]

Another great friend of the Crewes was the influential Edmund Burke, a visitor to Crewe Hall and frequent correspondent of Mrs Crewe. Despite their friendship he was often frustrated at the ease with which she changed her mind: for instance, in the early stages of the French Revolution opinion in England was divided as to whether it was a good or a bad thing; Burke was vehemently against the Revolution, Fox was for it. Burke spent much time persuading Mrs Crewe to his view, with seeming success; to his great annoyance, though, she would go away and be equally persuaded by somebody holding the exact opposite view, so that when they next met he had to go over the whole argument with her again. Nevertheless, they remained great friends throughout.

Of all the politicians, however, there was one other to whom she was particularly close. In 1773 a 22-year-old unknown son of an actor arrived in London from Bath, unsure how best to make his way in the world. His wife was as beautiful as Mrs Crewe, but more importantly was a singer of exquisite quality, for which she began to receive invitations to social events. Mrs Crewe was foremost in introducing the couple to prominent members of society, and to Whig politicians. The couple were Richard Brinsley Sheridan, and his wife Elizabeth. Though Sheridan's reputation is sustained today through his prowess as a playwright and the continued production of such classics as *The school*

---

[28] *Life and times of Sir Joshua Reynolds* by Charles Robert Leslie and Tom Taylor. Murray, 2 vols, 1865. vol 1, p433
[29] *Fox: the life of Charles James Fox* by Stanley Ayling. John Murray, 1991. p137

16

for scandal and *The rivals,* he achieved as much fame in his own day as a politician. He sat in Parliament from 1780 to 1812 and held office as Under-Secretary for Foreign Affairs (1782), Secretary to the Treasury (1783) and Treasurer to the Navy (1806). Always noted for his oratory performances in the House of Commons he received particular praise for his role in the impeachment of Warren Hastings, which commenced in 1787. Outside of politics he became a theatre owner as well as a playwright, buying the Drury Lane Theatre from David Garrick between 1776 and 1778. His financial situation, which was never secure, was damaged when the theatre had to be closed because it was declared unfit to hold large audiences; a new one was opened in 1794 but it burned down in 1809, a financial calamity from which he never recovered.

Sheridan moved in the same social and political circles as Mrs Crewe and she played some part in obtaining his acceptance into that society when he first came to London in the 1770s. He was also a great friend of Charles James Fox and confidante of the Prince of Wales. Sheridan's acceptance into high society served him well when he wrote *The School for Scandal,* a sharp comedy of manners that has proved to be the most enduring of his work. On the first night, 8th May 1777, Mrs Crewe and the Duchess of Devonshire were in the audience, together with all the most fashionable members of society, waiting to see themselves imitated on the stage. The satire could have proved offensive to those who were the objects of Sheridan's wit, but instead they delighted in it, and Sheridan's reputation was greatly enhanced, as was the demand for his presence in the dining and drawing rooms of the ton.

As a playwright and theatre owner Sheridan was one of the great representatives of a major aspect of 18th century entertainment. But if theatre was one of London's great attractions, so too were the public balls and assemblies staged for the ton. Foremost in the development of these entertainments was Theresa Cornelys who took a lease on Carlisle House, a large building in Soho Square, where she instituted a variety of entertainments. At first they seemed innocent enough – 'Society' evenings of music and card-playing. Admission was to 'subscribers' only – an exclusive pre-selected section of society: the wealthy, the fashionable, and the interesting. With a flair for promoting such exclusivity, Cornelys struck a highly sensitive vein of snobbishness: once the word was spread, those who considered themselves to be part of such a set were determined not to be left out. She advertised, addressing herself to 'the Nobility and Gentry', and encouraged word-of-mouth recommendations. Within just a few months the somewhat sober gatherings were developed into something much more exciting: wild masquerades and balls, which were seized upon by the ton as a wonderful outlet for their energy. They started to scandalise some of the more sedate citizens of the Square, but the sheer weight of numbers wishing to attend swept all resistance before them.

It was clear she had a tremendous success on her hands: money poured in, which she, in turn, invested back in her business, spending lavishly to expand, decorate, and furnish Carlisle House until it became a fairy palace of delight. One of the earliest improvements was to build an extension to the already large house, which contained a vast, ornate concert room on the first floor with an apse at one end, huge sash windows, and a rococo ceiling. On the ground floor was a large banqueting room, capable of seating 400 people at one table. Five years later she advertised further improvements, partly to counter the opening of a rival establishment, Almack's. Her expenditure, she said, "will this year alone, amount to little less than 2000l and that, when finished, it will be, by far, the most magnificent place of public entertainment in Europe"[30]. Then she spent an enormous £5000 decorating two rooms in the fashionable Chinese style, and adding a specially designed Chinese bridge to connect two parts of her little empire; this work is said to have been done by Thomas Chippendale, who had his workshops nearby. Such elegant surroundings were a continuing feature of Carlisle House; but from time to time special one-off presentations were made, as on one occasion when the house was transformed for a fete champetre, with pine trees transplanted into the concert room, and Gothic arches hung with "an incredible number of lamps of variegated colours. The Bridge-Room was converted into an elegant garden, the sides were full of shrubs and odiferous flowers, at the extremity was a kind of arbour filled with green house plants and pots of flowers, and in the centre was an elegant pavilion hung with festoons of silk; on the top (to which the company ascended by a temporary staircase), was spread a table for a dozen persons, in the middle of which was a fountain of water, and a reservoir, with gold and silver fish swimming about in it."[31]

The rooms were described by Fanny Burney, after a visit in 1770: "The magnificence of the rooms, spleandour of the illuminations and embellishments, and the brilliant appearance of the company exceeded anything I ever saw before. The apartments were so crowded we scarce had room to move, which was quite disagreeable, nevertheless the flight of apartments both upstairs and on the ground floor seemed endless."[32]

The entertainments put on by Mrs Cornelys included operas, called, for legal reasons, 'harmonic meetings', which were both splendid and charming – so much so that the managers of licenced theatres became alarmed; also concerts, directed by J.C. Bach, and assemblies. But most impressive of all were the masquerade balls that she organised, which came to be known as 'drums' - described as "a riotous assembly of fashionable people of both sexes at a private house; not unaptly styled a

---

[30] *Soho* by Judith Summers. Bloomsbury, 1989. p60
[31] Summers, op cit, p57
[32] Summers, op cit, p56

drum, from the noise and emptiness of the entertainment"[33] Large drums were known as drum-majors, routs, tempests, hurricanes and squeezers.

Accounts of some of these drums have been left to us in diaries, letters, and magazines of the time; one such was held on 26th February 1770. The magazines extravagantly described it as perhaps the most brilliant and characteristic masquerade of any ever known in the kingdom. Among those attending were the Duke of Cumberland as Henry VII; Lord Carlisle as the Running Footman; the Duke of Gloucester in an old English habit, with a star on his cloak; the Earl of Ossory as a Cardinal; the Earl of Mountstuart as the Pope; Lord Edgecumbe as an old woman - Lady Edgecumbe as a nun; Garrick, the great actor, is described as a celebrated doctor, possibly Dr Johnson - his wife as an Italian shepherdess; there was a highlander, a druid, and a political Bedlamite; a double man: half miller/half chimney-sweep. Picked out for special attention were two people in the characters of Tancred and Sigismunda - their dresses were considered to be the most elegant ever seen on such an occasion, and said to have cost twenty thousand pounds. The Countess Dowager of Waldegrave came as Jane Shore; the Countess of Pomfret as a Greek Sultan, and the two Miss Frederics, who accompanied her, as Greek slaves; the Duchess of Bolton, as the Roman goddess Diana, was especially captivating; there was one gentleman in the character of the Devil; another was in a domino entirely made of court cards; several appeared in the characters of conjurors and witches; Captain Watson, of the Guards, who appeared in the character of Adam, had his dress fitted so close, and painted so naturally, that most people, it's reported, started when he approached them, imagining him to be really naked - he was said, though, to have played his character with great propriety and drollery.

What added greatly to the entertainment of the evening was a duet, sung by Mrs. Crewe and Lady Almeria Carpenter, in the characters of ballad-singers, which, the magazine says, so entertained the whole company, that they were encored several times, which they very obligingly acquiesced in. About two o'clock the company began to depart, in effecting which there was great difficulty, and at six in the morning three or four hundred remained in the rooms.[34]

Extravagant and costly as these masquerades were, they were popular enough to be held at frequent intervals: the one described took place on the 26th February 1770, there was another on the 30th March, and yet another on 26th April. The following year was similar: a masqued ball

---

[33] Summers, op cit, p56
[34] Leslie & Taylor, op cit, pp354-5

was given by Joshua Reynolds' Thursday-night club on the 11th February, which cost one thousand guineas. At others, at Carlisle House or the Opera House, in April, were noted among the beautiful women "the inseparable friends Mrs. Crewe and Mrs. Bouverie, dressed as young fellows, the fierce smart cock of their hats much admired."[35]

The crowded nature of the gatherings is captured perfectly in the following description:

"One of the social pleasures of London is a rout. The scene in the street serves as a prelude to that within doors; a long range of carriages fills up every avenue, and some times a party cannot get up to the door for an hour or two. Having, however, accomplished this arduous task, on entering the temple of pleasure, nothing is presented to the view but a vast crowd of elegantly dressed ladies and gentlemen, many of whom are so over-powered by the heat, noise and confusion, as to be in danger of fainting. Everyone complains of the pressure of the company, yet all rejoice at being so divinely squeezed. The company moves from room to room; and the most an individual can do, on meeting a particular friend, is to shake hands as they are hurried past each other. The confusion increases when the supper rooms are thrown open. The tables, it is true, are laid out with Asiatic profusion... but not one fifth part of the guests can be accommodated. Behind each chair, are ladies standing three or four deep; others are enclosed in the doorway, unable to advance or retreat."[36]

Casanova also attended on at least one evening, of which he wrote: "The ball lasted all night without ceasing, as the company ate by relays, and at all times and hours; the waste and prodigality were worthy of a prince's palace. I made the acquaintance of all the nobility, and the Royal Family, for they were all there, with the exception of the king and queen, and the Prince of Wales. Madame Cornelis must have received more than twelve hundred guineas, but the outlay was enormous."[37]

Just as nobility and royalty were attracted to take part in these routs, so were the less fortunate populace of London attracted to hold their own sort of party in the streets outside. Walpole reported: "The mob was beyond all belief: they held flambeaux to the windows of every coach, and demanded to have the masks pulled off and put on at their pleasure, but with extreme good humour and civility. I was with my Lady Hertford and two of her daughters, in their coach: the mob took me for Lord Hertford, and huzzaed and blessed me!"[38] When eating was

[35] Leslie & Taylor, op cit, pp390-2
[36] *The stranger in England* by C.A.G. Goede, 1807; quoted from *Life in the Georgian City* by Dan Cruickshank and
Neil Burton. Viking, 1990. pp46-7
[37] Summers, op cit, p59
[38] Summers, op cit, p61

Sir Ranulphe Crewe, by Henry Weekes

Crewe Hall in the 19th century

Frances Anne Crewe by Daniel Gardner

John Crewe, 1st Baron Crewe of Crewe by Daniel Gardner

Masquerade costume

The Crewe family at Crewe Hall, by Arthur Devis

Master Crewe as Henry VIII
by Sir Joshua Reynolds
i.e. John Crewe, 1772-1825

Sir Ranulphe Crewe, by Henry Weekes

Crewe Hall in the 19th century

Frances Anne Crewe by Daniel Gardner

John Crewe, 1st Baron Crewe of Crewe by Daniel Gardner

finished inside the house, the windows would be flung open and the remains of the food thrown to the many hungry people waiting expectantly below.

Other characters were also attracted to the gatherings. The routs were frequently of a questionable character, with hard drinking, immodest singing, and daring dress; and though the Ton learned how to revel in these circumstances, the exclusivity of the establishment was tarnished by the intrusion of prostitutes. Those members of the moral minority who objected to such revelry, and to such establishments, reported incidents of gross indecency, and "mockery of the most solemn feeling and principles". In February 1771 The Universal Magazine reported the prosecution of "a certain Lady not far from Soho, who does keep and maintain a common disorderly house, and did permit and suffer divers loose, idle, and disorderly persons, as well men as women, to be, and remain, during the whole night, rioting, and otherwise misbehaving themselves".[39] Walpole passed on a bit of scandal, that one of the maids at Soho Square left her job because she could not undergo the fatigue of making the beds so often.

The success of Mrs Cornelys and Carlisle House could not go on forever. From 1760 until 1772 she went from strength to strength, challenged, though never surpassed, only by the opening of Almack's in St. James's in 1765. In 1772, though, a new rival came on the scene, called The Pantheon, located a short distance away, just off Oxford Street. Such was the impact of The Pantheon that within nine months Theresa Cornelys was bankrupt and in jail. Carlisle House struggled on without her, but it failed miserably, and was pulled down in 1791. For her part, after release from prison, she made several efforts to rise to prominence again, but without success. Like Carlisle House she simply became unfashionable: the Ton moved on to new diversions.

The Pantheon was quite unlike any other building of the time. It took £37,000 and two-and-a-half years to build, and when it was completed it looked like something from a fairy-tale. It was magnificent, described by Fanny Burney's father as "the most elegant structure in Europe, if not on the Globe".[40] A foreign nobleman thought it looked like an enchanted palace. It boasted a huge classical rotunda with a coffered dome and colonnades, galleries and statues. The ceilings, even in the passages were of beautiful stucco, and in the ballrooms had panels painted like Raphael's loggias in the Vatican. Edward Gibbon said it was the wonder of the eighteenth century, and of the British Empire. Through one of her characters, Fanny Burney wrote that she was extremely struck with the beauty of the building, which greatly surpassed

[39] Summers, op cit, p62
[40] Summers, op cit, p64

whatever she expected or imagined. She found the main room magnificent, awe-inspiring, and even solemn.[41]

The managers of The Pantheon, like Mrs Cornelys, had determined that their venture should attract the best elements of society, and to this end ruled that no woman of doubtful character would be admitted. Such a description was applied to the beautiful Sophia Baddeley, mistress of Lord Melbourne, and to the mistresses of other aristocrats. On 27th January 1772, the opening night of the Pantheon, Sophia Baddeley was accompanied to the door by a group of young men, armed with swords, determined to gain entrance for her. Constables barred her way with their staves, but the young aristocrats drew their weapons, and forced the constables, at sword-point to give way. The rule, once broken, became redundant, and others followed Sophia Baddeley with reputations far more doubtful than hers.

Not that this discouraged the very best in society from attending. The Pantheon became as popular as Carlisle House had been. Mrs Crewe was there on 30th April 1772, one of about 2000 people. The fourteen rooms were blazing with light and decorations. The suppers and wine were of the best quality, in keeping with the best of the company. On this particular occasion a great many of the ladies chose to adopt male dominoes, and "appeared as masculine as many of the delicate maccaroni things we see everywhere". Not so Lady Villars, who came dressed as a Sultana, ablaze with thirty thousand pounds' worth of diamonds; Oliver Goldsmith was in old English dress, and Joshua Reynolds came as a domino, observing with some satisfaction, no doubt, that he had painted the portraits of so many of the most beautiful women in the room. Mrs Crewe appeared at first as a Spanish nun, and then, with Mrs Bouverie, changed her costume for the two of them to appear as the Merry Wives of Windsor. Through the evening the two of them had great fun plaguing Stephen Fox, who had grown fat in the six years since he courted Frances Anne Greville, so that they insisted on treating him as their Falstaff. Like other masquerades the entertainment continued until dawn, and the revellers made their way home through the London streets just as working people were stirring.[42]

The populace were used to such behaviour from the Ton: there is a story that the Duke of Devonshire regularly arrived home at about 5 o'clock in the morning, always passing a cobbler who had a stall on the corner of Jermyn Street, to whom the Duke bade good night; "Good morning, your Grace," the cobbler would wryly reply.[43]

---

[41] *Evelina* by Fanny Burney. Oxford University Press, 1982. Chapter 23, pp104-5
[42] Leslie & Taylor, op cit, p434
[43] *Georgiana, Duchess of Devonshire* by Brian Masters. Hamish Hamilton, 1981. p40

Mrs Crewe's position in English society has received some attention in this account and to a great extent her status translated across to Paris.

When she arrived in Paris her mother was already there, so this would have helped with introductions to new acquaintances and with information on old friends who were in the city at that time. She had visited Paris with her mother before, in 1773, on that occasion staying with Madame du Deffand, a close friend and correspondent of Horace Walpole. Also in Paris on that earlier occasion were Lady Spencer and her daughter Georgiana, later to become Duchess of Devonshire and a close friend of Mrs Crewe. At that time Madame du Deffand wrote to Horace Walpole that the people of Paris were comparing Mrs Crewe with Georgiana, a strange comparison, perhaps, considering Mrs Crewe was 24 years old and Georgiana Spencer was only 15 when she arrived, and spent her sixteenth birthday there.[44] So, she knew some people from that previous visit, including Madame de Bussy, Madame de Caraman, Madame de Mirepoix and the Marechal Biron who on her previous visit had loaded her with presents; others she had met on this trip at Spa before moving on to Paris. Even more important this time, she had the assistance of Lady Clermont. Frances Fortescue, the Countess Clermont, was a favourite at the French court with her own apartments at Versailles and was in a position not only to introduce Mrs Crewe to the most important figures in French society but also to the royal family itself. Within a fortnight of arrival Lady Clermont took Mrs Crewe and her brother Charles to a ball at Versailles where she was introduced to the King and Queen. The introduction seems to have contained no more than politeness on the part of the royal couple, as Mrs Crewe noted: "[The King and Queen] both talked a good deal to Lady Clermont, and the Queen said a word or two to me about hoping to see my Mother – but She must continue to hope, I fancy, for my Mother has not thought of taking so much trouble"(p99). The impression here is that the Queen and Mrs Greville had already met but Mrs Greville would not go out of her way to repeat the experience. In fact they did meet the following week, at a ball given by the Duchesse de Polignac, where the two talked "a good deal"(p155). It was at such suppers and such balls as these that Mrs Crewe mixed with French aristocracy, including six Ducs, seven Duchesses, four Comtesses and three Marquis. Many of the English people she spent time with were of comparative status: two Viscounts, two Earls, a Duke and a Countess. But there were others, too: a doctor and his wife, young Englishmen making their European grand tour, a secretary at the British Embassy, a Member of Parliament, an historian and the Queen's dressmaker, for example. There were also a number of Frenchmen with military backgrounds – who had, indeed, fought against the British, particularly in

---

[44] *Walpole's correspondence*, op cit, vol 5, pp361-2

America. Suffren had had a long naval career fighting the British; Lafayette had fought against them in America in 1777 and 1779, including the battle for Yorktown; Guines had been a colonel in the Seven Years War; Bouille had been a General and fought mostly in the West Indies; Guibert was a master tactician, producing a standard textbook on the subject, and in 1790 carrying through a fundamental reform of the French army; Castries was the Secretary of War. Castries and Lafayette are particularly mentioned by Mrs Crewe for making reference to the capture in America of her brother Harry, who was a Lieutenant-Colonel in the British army. She recognised the kindnesses that were extended to her brother by the French but was irritated by their continual references to the incident.

Her brother Harry was not with her in Paris but her brother Charles was and appeared to have been travelling with her from Brussels and Spa. At 22 years old he was 14 years her junior. She was also surprised to see another brother, James, turn up who was travelling to "I don't know where"(p139). Her husband John Crewe was with her at the beginning, like Charles having probably been with her in Brussels and Spa; but he returned to London early to attend Parliament. There is no mention of her father Fulke Greville, perhaps because, as Rizzo reports, there was an official separation between her parents in the mid-1780s.[45] Her five-year-old daughter Emma also accompanied Mrs Crewe, though surprisingly she fails to mention this until the 52nd day of the diary. Nor do her three servants get much of a mention: two of them, Dolly and Toby, are named but the second maid remains anonymous throughout.

The mystery of the Friend

The travel diary of Mrs Crewe is very much of its time. The contents first saw light as a series of letters, all sent to one person – an unnamed friend. At a later date the letters were collected together and, she says in her introduction or "Advertisement", blended together with other material and copied to form a "journal"; but she adds "Tho it assumes the Appearance of a Journal, many Allowances are to be made, as it was not originally so"(p73). She then goes on, rather mysteriously "It will be read only by those Friends who have partially called for it, and I am rather intitled to Credit for so dangerous a Compliance with their Request, than answerable for any of its defects"(p73). The danger may lay with inviting curiosity about the identity of the friend to whom the letters were written. At no point is the name of the friend given and since we know that the original letters were at some stage "blended" with other material the opportunity for some kind of editorship at that stage

---

[45] Rizzo, op cit, p249

was clearly available. Nevertheless, a teasing sub-text can be detected throughout the letters, inviting the reader to speculate on the relationship between Mrs Crewe and her friend.

At the beginning she makes a very public statement by addressing the diary to the friend, saying he has encouraged her to write to him and that she is doing so with his permission, implying, perhaps, that this could place him in an embarrassing position. Nevertheless, she says she is flattered and emphasises that she is writing particularly for him. She calls her introduction "a sort of dedication" to him and goes on, in a tone that might well be considered today to be flirtatious, to point out that though it excludes compliments all feelings of kindness and flattery have long been written in her heart. The flirtation is re-inforced, if I'm interpreting it correctly, by the use of a symbol resembling a cross, which was used in the eighteenth century, just as it is today, as a sign of a kiss, either of love or affection; the cross appears regularly throughout the diary. During her time in Paris Mrs Crewe was sending letters to, and receiving them from, not just the "friend" but a number of other people too – none of which would appear to have survived; but at one point, when some time passes without a letter from her friend, she expresses a tetchiness: "I begin to wish to hear from You ~ It is now a long time since I have done so; and till I do I shall not send another Pacquet" (p103). Towards the end of her stay she is missing him: "I certainly wish also to see you and a few more friends in England whom I love"(p131). In this context her love might well be meant in its wider sense, gathering in friends and relatives; but it could also be a screen to hide an amorous love. It's as if a game is going on, the letters being nearly indiscreet but not quite; and if indiscretion is visible then it's made okay by being put into a re-written diary for other people to see. She teases again when she writes: "you were often in my Head when I wrote my Spa and Brussels Journal, but as I knew other People would see them I did not feel quite so secure as I do now"(p189). If she was concerned about security then a reading of the diary does not make it clear exactly what she was concerned about. It might hint at an attraction between Mrs Crewe and her friend but it is not blatant about it. Her concern might make more sense if parts of the letters have been left out when they were "copied fair" and this possibility should not be ignored. Indeed, parts of the diary have been heavily crossed through to obscure what was originally written, so adherence to the original texts was not paramount in the exercise of copying.

The production of her diary to be "read only by those Friends who have partially called for it"(p73) may or may not have been designed to excite some interest in the identity of the recipient of her letters. How successful it was at the time, if, indeed, that was the design, we can't tell; but I think it ill behoves us to deny her the satisfaction, albeit 215 years later. In seeking to identify the friend it's worth noting, first, that Mrs

Crewe makes a number of references to his wisdom and in a manner that suggests widespread acceptance of such:

"I am comforted for that by knowing that this is what you wise people always like"(p87)

"Pray remember, however, that when I make such wise Remarks, it is always with Deference to your Opinion"(p107)

"How pleasant it is to write to you upon all this! and certain I feel that you will explain to me much better what I really think upon this Subject"(p189)

The somewhat unctuous delivery of these lines might jar with the modern reader although they can take on a different hue if said with tongue in cheek, and Mrs Crewe is said to have had that touch of devilry in her character which could turn the same words into provocation and tease. It wouldn't work half as well if the friend did not consider himself to be one of the "wise people".

The first wise person we should examine as candidate for the "friend" is William Windham, mostly because the diary was among his papers when they were acquired by The British Museum in 1909 – they now form part of the collection of The British Library. It's known that Windham and Mrs Crewe were, the period under examination here apart, regular correspondents, many examples being available elsewhere in The British Library's collection. Some are also available in published format in the *Miscellanies of the Philobiblon Society*, published in 1865-6, and in *The Windham Papers*, published in 1913. Windham also kept a diary and recorded dining with the Crewes both before they went to France, in May 1785, and after they returned, in May 1786. This is good evidence they were friends at this time and when, longing to return home, she wrote in the diary "I certainly wish also to see you and a few more friends in England whom I love"(p131), she may have been referring to Windham as much as anybody else. In his introduction to *The Windham Papers* the Earl of Rosebery declared of him "He had, moreover, come under the magic charm of Mrs Crewe. To Mrs Crewe, and Mrs Crewe alone, he confided the secret of his marriage, and he records his agitation at meeting her immediately after the event.[46] Though William Windham may not be remembered today as one of the great figures of British history he was, in his day, considered a major political influence. He served in the House of Commons from 1784 to his death in 1810, including a term of seven years as Secretary for War, which covered the war with France following the French Revolution. During this period of office he had charge of all the assistance given to French royalists; Mrs Crewe was also very active in supporting French émigrés at the same time. By making alliances in turn with Fox, Pitt, Grenville and Grey

---

[46] The Windham papers: the life and correspondence of the Rt. Hon. William Windham 1750-1810. Herbert Jenkins, 2 vols, 1913. vol 1, pxv

Windham was accused of political infidelity, though his defenders would say he was faithful to his principles. At the time of Mrs Crewe's diary Windham was only 35 years old and had most of his achievements before him. Nevertheless, even at this stage of his career he had powerful admirers and supporters and would undoubtedly have been counted by Mrs Crewe as one of the "Wise people".

The second, and in my view more likely, candidate for the "friend" is Sheridan.[47] Gossip of a love affair between Sheridan and Mrs Crewe crops up in numerous contemporary diaries and letters, early evidence of which appears at the time Sheridan wrote *The School for Scandal* in 1777. The play was a phenomenal success and soon after its first production Sheridan wrote and sent to Mrs Crewe four-pages of verse dedicating the play to her:

No state has Amoret; no studied mien;
She frowns no goddess, and she moves no queen.
The softer charm that in her manner lies
Is framed to captivate, yet not surprise;
It justly suits the expression of her face, –
'Tis less than dignity, and more than grace![48]

For the full piece by Sheridan see Appendix 4. The verse was shown around among friends of Sheridan and Mrs Crewe but not published until it appeared in a newspaper nearly thirty years later.[49] Such gallantry

---

[47] Recent biographies include: *A portrait of Sheridan* by Stanley Ayling. Constable, 1985; *Richard Brinsley Sheridan: a life* by Linda Kelly. Sinclair-Stevenson, 1997; and *A traitor's kiss: the life of Richard Brinsley Sheridan* by Fintan O'Toole. Granta, 1997

[48] Amoret was an affectionate title given to Mrs Crewe, probably by either Sheridan or his wife, but also used by Fox and known by the circle of friends amongst whom their verse was distributed. The name comes from the old French, a diminutive of amour or love. It is also a character in Spenser's *Faerie Queene* who is a personification of female loveliness: young, handsome, merry, witty and good; she is as soft as a rose, as sweet as a violet, as chaste as a lily and as gentle as a dove; she loves everybody and is loved by all; an amoret can also mean a love affair – *Brewer's Dictionary of Phrase and Fable*

[49] In 1814 Sheridan wrote the following letter to his 2nd wife: ""Dearest, I enclose you a Letter and a Newspaper professing to publish for the first time some verses of mine to Mrs. (now Lady) Crewe. They are inaccurately printed but on the whole I certainly wrote them but had forgotten them, which is not common with me. From what Quarter they could have been sent to a Newspaper at this late date I cannot surmise – and I certainly have no means of furnishing the remainder of the Poem were I disposed to do it. I hate anything thus surrept[it]iously publish'd to be attributed to me – I never yet own'd or allow'd the printing of anything Play Poems or Speeches but two things to both which I put my name – viz. The Critic and a Political Pamphlet on the affairs of India – I put Pizzarro out of the Question – but this Winter I am determined to give my Friend Rogers full Power to put together and publish all my Scrib[b]lings – and he offers to ensure me four thousand Pounds if done by

was not uncommon, as we've already seen from the verse written about her by Fox. But though Fox and others may have flattered Mrs Crewe there seems little doubt it was Sheridan who developed a sexual relationship with her. There was, indeed, a considerable degree of sexual licence in this society and at this time, and this arose, in part, from the nature of the marriages that were arranged.

It is very likely that Sheridan's wife, Elizabeth, was aware of her husband's infidelity and referred to her doubts about his faithfulness in verses that she wrote to him, replacing his name with that of "Sylvio" and her own with "Laura":-

> "To other scenes doth Sylvio now repair,
> To nobler themes his daring muse aspires;
> Around him throng the gay, the young, the fair,
> His lively wit the listening crowd admires.
>
> And see where radiant Beauty smiling stands
> With gentle voice and soft beseeching eyes,
> To gain the laurel from his willing hands,
> Her every art the fond enchantress tries.
>
> ....
>
> Each anxious doubt shall Laura now forego,
> No more regret those joys so lately known,
> Conscious that though thy breast to all may glow,
> Thy faithful heart shall beat for her alone. "[50]

Despite her suspicions Elizabeth Sheridan often spent time in the company of Mrs Crewe, both in London and at Crewe Hall. In her Paris diary Mrs Crewe lists Mrs Sheridan as one of her correspondents. Ironically it is through one of Elizabeth Sheridan's letters that we can assess with some certainty the continuing relationship between her husband and Mrs Crewe. On 23rd November 1785, just before Mrs Crewe left for Spa, Brussels and Paris, Elizabeth Sheridan wrote to her friend Mrs Canning: "S[heridan] is in Town – and so is Mrs Crewe. I am in the Country and so is Mr Crewe – a very convenient arrangement is it not?"[51] Perhaps Sheridan and Mrs Crewe were saying their farewells before she set off – no doubt they promised to write!

my Authority. When I look at these ver[s]es Oh! how it reminds me what an ardent romantic Blockhead nature made me! They were sent with a M.S. copy of the Play finely bound etc. NB I was not then 25 – by the way She was in truth the Handsomest of the set." (Sheridan's Letters, op cit, vol 3, pp202-3). The newspaper cutting he referred to was dated 12th October 1814 and the letter written 15th October 1814

[50] The Linleys of Bath, by Clementina Black. Martin Secker, 1911. pp139-140
[51] Sheridan's nightingale: the story of Elizabeth Linley, by Alan Chedzoy. Allison & Busby, 1997. p217

The affair between Sheridan and Mrs Crewe lasted through this period but three years later had faded, as reported by Sheridan's sister Betsy in November 1788: "You know that Mrs Crewe among other Lovers (favor'd ones I mean) Has had our Brother in her train. As his fame and consequence in Life have encreased, her charms have diminished, and passion no longer the tie between them, his affection, esteem and attentions return'd to their proper channel".[52]

Many girls married at any early age. Frances Anne Greville was just seventeen when she married John Crewe – Harriot Bouverie, a close friend, was even younger, marrying by special licence at the age of fourteen; Lady Sarah Lennox was wed at seventeen, Lady Melbourne at sixteen, and Georgiana Duchess of Devonshire, was married three days before her seventeenth birthday. It might be said – from a viewpoint of new millennium Western culture, when personal freedom and choice claim great importance in our selection of marriage partners – that these young women were far too young to make rational decisions on their futures. The fact is the choice was rarely left to the couple alone: families became very much involved, looking to protect or improve their status and their wealth: did prospective partners have titles or money, preferably both? Personal attraction between the couple would not be ignored, but it would not be paramount when making a decision. Under those circumstances it is probably not surprising that very often husband and wife did not maintain loving relationships with each other, but rather played at a game of marriage. Marriage was a sort of business alliance, for protecting the family and for producing an heir to continue the business; also for presenting to the world a veneer of respectability. Over and above that, sexual adventures could be pursued as part of life's entertainment, a natural appetite that should be satisfied like any other. Nevertheless, such liaisons had to be discreet, so that personal and family honour could be maintained, at least on the surface. When discretion failed then separation and divorce often followed. The diary of Sarah Lennox is full of fascinating chit-chat that illustrates the marriages and morals of the time.

"Lady Car.[oline Hervey, daughter of the Earl of Bristol] has been married to Vernon the singer & had 20 intrigues with the whole set of actors, not one of which I believe, tho' I believe she is sly enough, but indeed till I have better proof than the reports of this vile town, I never will believe anything"[53]

"I do not find it's true that 17 people are to be parted, as the newspapers said, but there has been as many reports to the full; however I think none is fixed but Ld & Ly Bollingbroke, Mr Finch and Ly

---

[52] Betsy Sheridan's journal: letters from Sheridan's sister 1784-1786 and 1788-1790; edited by William LeFanu. Eyre & Spottiswoode, 1960. p133
[53] Lennox, op cit, p195

Charlotte, & Ld & Ly Fortescue; the 2 latter are because the husbands are stark staring mad, & have attempted to kill their wives & children. The former is because both sides are mad I believe; but seriously speaking I believe Ld B. is much the same as mad when he is drunk, & that he is generally. Ly B.'s reason for parting is that she cannot live with him with safety to her health; Ld B. is very penitent & wants her to come back, but she won't trust him. Her reason is a very good one, but whether she ought to forgive him or not depends on circumstances & tempers, which nobody but themselves can be judge of; he says he is more in love with her than ever, & would marry her now if she was Ly Die Spencer. Everybody that don't love her pities him, but as I heard he had got a woman in the house already I can't say I do."[54]

Though Lady Sarah doesn't mention them in her letters she was probably aware of the liaisons carried on by her brother the Duke of Richmond, who had three daughters by his housekeeper Mrs Bennett, and another by a Miss Le Clerc. The Duke of Devonshire kept a mistress both before and after his marriage, maintained in a handsome villa, and by whom he had a child. The Duchess of Gordon had difficulty marrying off one of her daughters, because of a rumour of madness in the Gordon blood: the marriage went ahead, though, when she assured the suitor that there was, in fact, no Gordon blood at all in her daughter's veins. Lady Melbourne, mentioned above, gave birth to six children, only the first of whom was indisputably fathered by her husband. And so, in just this manner was the whole pattern of sexual liaisons carried on. For the most part known about, but not flaunted - and those that were flaunted were often the cause of separation and divorce. The game had to be played by the rules.

Though it cannot be proven, with the material we currently have to hand, that Sheridan was the "friend" in the diary, he is the most likely person. A third person's candidature should be dismissed without too much thought – in a description of the diary The British Library suggests that it was addressed to "the Honourable Miss Fox" on the basis that it is bound with another diary, written by Mrs Crewe in 1795, describing a visit to Wales, and the Welsh diary has a clear inscription addressing it to Miss Fox. I suggest it is only by chance the two were bound together and that the tone of the Paris letters are more likely to suggest the friend is a man than a woman.

The family, then and now

Mrs Greville was fortunate enough to have three of her children with her in Paris, an indication that, though she didn't get on with her

---

[54] Lennox, op.cit., pp183-4

husband she was still close to her children. Apart from Frances Anne – Mrs Crewe – all her children were boys, the first-born of whom, Algernon, had died at the age of six under tragic circumstances. He had been inoculated against smallpox, from which he was recovering when he accidentally took or was given a draft of medicine intended for his father. He suffered convulsions before dying 24 hours later. There were four other boys, three of whom made military careers, of sorts, and the fourth of whom went into the Church. James was born in Lorraine, France in 1753, attended Harrow School before going on to university at Cambridge and then to become a Deacon at Durham in 1777, Rector of Stockton on Tees from 1780-1782, Rector of Whickham in Durham from 1782-1816 and finally Rector of Peasemore in Buckinghamshire from 1816. Mrs Crewe seems surprised when he turns up in Paris – "He is going to travel I don't know where, and means to spend a few days at Paris in his Way"(p139). Charles Greville, on the other hand, was already in Paris with his mother when Mrs Crewe arrived. The youngest of the children – 23 at the time – his sister expresses a great deal of affection for him, though others were not so kind. Sir Gilbert Eliot described him as "a very disagreeable coxcomb, with very little merit to recommend him excepting his face".[55] Mrs Crewe represents him full of energy and eagerness to savour the delights of Paris, yet giving great consideration to the needs of his mother and his sister. At one stage he says that life in Paris is little suited to his taste but before long goes continually to the balls at Versailles, dines regularly at the home of the controversial Madame de Coigny with other young men of fashion, and goes his own way in the evenings. When he starts to make plans to return home his sister is a little disappointed, hoping he would stay a little longer with their mother, "but indeed he is so willing to Accommodate himself to us both in all Respects and has done it in so many Instances already that it would be cruel to Interfere with any of his Plans at Present"(p191). Though he would rather "go like the wind night and day"(p195) on his journey home he settles instead for travelling with his sister, a decision for which she is thankful when they meet with an accident and their coach is overturned.

At the time of the diary Charles was a half-pay Captain with the 45th Foot Regiment. His son said at a later date that Greville's education had been neglected, though he did attend Westminster School for two years before joining the army at the age of 16. The facts of his career seem to indicate it was an unsettled and probably not very successful one: ensign 39th Foot 1778, Lieutenant 90th Foot 1779, 48th Foot 1781, Captain 45th Foot 1783, half-pay 1783-9, Captain 58th Foot 1795, retired 1796. There

[55] *The House of Commons, 1790-1820*, by R. G. Thomas. Secker and Warburg, 1986

is an undated letter in The British Library from Mrs Crewe to Sheridan[56] in which she says she is in agony about her brother Charles being turned out of his position in the army and urging Sheridan to intervene. In 1792 he was travelling in Italy where he was described as "a specimen of the London fine gentleman, but one who appears to have been designed by nature for something better. Even fashion and affectation had not quite spoiled him".[57] His uncertain army career was transformed when, at the age of 30 he married into the powerful Whig family of the Duke of Portland, taking for his wife the eldest daughter Charlotte. His father-in-law then secured a seat for him in Parliament, representing Petersfield in Hampshire, and a minor post as under-secretary at the Home Office. But he made no impact either in Parliament or at the Home Office and gave up both positions after a short time. Two letters from one of his friends, Granville Leveson Gower, give an insight to his life-style and manner at about this time: "Charles Greville is here, and very pleasant. I always think him much more so in the Country than in London. He and I and Culling Smith do nothing but ride and play at chess and sing from morning till night, and almost from night till morning"[58]; in the second letter he expresses irritation at Greville's "incessant chattering".[59] His departure from the Home Office in 1798 was followed by a patchwork of sinecure places which indicate a lack of focus in his life and a dependence on the influence of his wife's family: Comptroller of Cash in the Excise Office, Receiver-General of Taxes in Nottinghamshire, Naval Officer to Demerara and Essequibo, Secretary, Registrar and Clerk of Council of the Island of Tobago. Lord Glenbervie wrote in 1818 that he had a love of imparting "accurate and confidential information (as he thinks he convinces you by the authorities he hints at or, with direct qualification and caution against being cited, actually names) in all matters of foreign and home politics and ministerial and court news and intrigues".[60] He died in 1832. Charles Greville may not have made much of a mark in public life but he had three sons who did, all earning a place for themselves in the *Dictionary of National Biography*: Algernon Frederick served as the Duke of Wellington's aide de camp and ensign at the Battle of Waterloo and went on to become his Private Secretary; Henry William became Attaché at the Paris Embassy and known as a diarist; and Charles became an intimate friend of both Wellington and Palmerston,

[56] British Library ref: 35118,f.193
[57] *A dictionary of British and Irish travellers in Italy 1701-1800*; compiled from the Brinsley Ford Archive by John Ingamells. Yale University Press, 1997
[58] *Private correspondence of Lord Granville Leveson Gower (First Lord Granville) 1782-1821*; edited by his daughter-in-law Castalia Countess Granville. John Murray, 2 vols, 1916. vol 2, p224
[59] Leveson Gower, op cit, vol1, p106
[60] Thomas, op cit

accounts of whom he left in his often published *Greville Memoirs* (see bibliography).

We meet in the Paris diary another brother of Mrs Crewe, Henry Francis Greville, known as Harry, who also joined the army but, his capture by Indians in America apart, had a more impressive cv. He too attended Westminster School but when he left chose the Coldstream Guards rather than a foot regiment. He saw action in the American War of Independence and rose eventually to the rank of Lieutenant-Colonel in the 4th Royal Irish Dragoon Guards, retiring in 1793. He died in Mauritius in 1816. Like his brother he had sons who went into the armed forces, George Greville becoming a Major in the army and Henry Francis rising to the dizzy ranks of Vice-Admiral in the Navy.

The Navy was also represented at the earlier generation. Mrs Crewe's fourth brother, William Fulke Greville, was a Captain in the Royal Navy, serving also for a short time as Member of Parliament for the Irish seat of Granard in 1798. He was next in age to his sister but outlived all his siblings, dying in 1837 at the age of 86. It was William who was painted with his sister by Reynolds and had his portion of the picture cut out by an irate father. William receives no mention in the Paris diary.

Nor do the siblings of John Crewe receive any attention in the diary. He had four sisters – Frances, Sarah, Emma and Elizabeth – and a younger brother, Richard. This brother, like his wife's brothers, set his sights on the army as a meaningful career, spending some time in America during the war of independence, and some time in Kingston, Jamaica where he married a young lady with the impressive name of Milborough Alpress. He rose to the rank of Major-General before leading a civilian life as precarious as that of soldier, supporting himself at the gambling tables. He was described in 1795 as "a clever sagacious Man of the World, a professed Gambler, living by his Profession… knowing all things and everybody, a Man of Parts, well practiced in Life, prompt, intrepid and gentlemanly".[61] Such a precarious way of life had its downs as well as its ups, and brother Richard had to be supported substantially by John Crewe. The head of the family gave a helping hand also to one of his sisters, introducing his sister Elizabeth to her future husband, his old tutor from the Grand Tour, John Hinchliffe.

Much more importance, in the diary, is attached to two of the Crewe children, Emma – who, at the age of five or six, travelled with her mother – and John, aged 13, left back in England, clearly missed by Mrs Crewe and the object of her purpose as soon as she returned across the Channel. The little girl, Emma – though christened Elizabeth Emma – was, in fact, the second daughter of the Crewes, an earlier child, Frances, having died three years earlier, when she was about eight years of age.

---

[61] *The Journal of the Rev. William Bagshaw Stevens*, edited by G.Galbraith. Oxford, 1985. pp 285, 300

This earlier child was the subject of a wonderful painting by Reynolds, one of a pair with a painting of her brother John, aged about 4 and dressed as Henry VIII (see p24).

Little Emma Crewe, then aged about 6, can make no impression on the reader of the diary, so little is she mentioned. With the means at their disposal it may be assumed that the Crewes could quite easily have left their daughter back in England, so credit must be given for taking her with them. Mrs Crewe may well have remembered with pleasure her own childhood trips to the continent with her parents and decided it was a pattern worth following. There is a charming portrait of Emma, aged about eight by Gainsborough (see p169). The Crewes would appear to have been successful in bringing up their child, if Fanny Burney's description, written six years later, is accurate: "My Father & I were then taken to Hampstead by Miss Crewe, in Mrs. Crewe's Carriage. She is a very sweet Girl, about 14 years of age, I fancy, extremely well bred, sensible, attentive, & intelligent."[62] At that time she was, in fact, only 12 years of age, so clearly gave an impression of maturity and confidence, although in later life she reflected that her upbringing had been handicapped by the beauty and brilliance of her mother.[63] Nevertheless her wit was said to surpass her mother's and she became equally accomplished as an hostess. She developed a talent for singing, in particular songs with pathos and emotion in them, that brought tears to the eyes of her audiences. In 1809 she married Foster Cunliffe and together they built a new house on the estate at Madeley, which had come to the Crewe family through the Offleys, but where the old manor house had deteriorated through lack of use. In the early years of the marriage, though, much time was spent looking after her mother whose health was failing in the years leading to her death in 1818. Her father lived on to the age of 87 and she similarly devoted time to caring for him. Such behaviour was in sharp contrast to that of her brother John who had behaved so badly he was banished to live abroad. In consequence Emma became the major beneficiary in the will of her father, enjoying an income from the estates that exceeded £10,000. It was a condition of the will, though, that she and her husband change their name to Cunliffe-Offley to continue the family's link to the past. Elizabeth Emma Cunliffe-Offley never had the same impact on society as her mother, yet she managed the family property well, maintained a fashionable life in London, and was instrumental in bringing up her brother John's two daughters, Henrietta and Annabel. She died in 1850 without having children of her own.

---

[62] *The journals and letters of Fanny Burney*, op cit, vol 1, p193
[63] *Monckton Milnes: the years of promise 1809-1851*, by James Pope-Hennessy. Constable, 1949. p310

If Mrs Crewe's diary was a reflection of life then it was little Emma who received scant attention and her brother John who was their mother's darling; yet life has a nasty way of turning things on their head, and so it was in this case. It was John the son who grew to be a high-spirited young man and sought adventurous times in the army, who travelled as a member of staff with his distant cousin Earl Macartney to China, who fought in the Napoleonic wars where he lost an eye, and who eventually rose to the rank of General. But while Emma had good sense, intelligence and responsibility towards her family, John gambled very heavily, lost very heavily, gave away the money his father raised to pay his debts, married and lost his wife's fortune, contracted a sham marriage (using a billiard-marker as the supposed parson!), and subsequently had an illegitimate daughter.[64] His marriage, not surprisingly, was unhappy and when his wife died at the age of 48 his children were made wards of court. All in all a great disappointment to his mother and a discredit to his father who, in the end, cut him out from his will and encouraged him to live abroad, near Liege in Belgium where he died in 1835. He had two daughters, Henrietta and Annabel, both of whom were brought up at Crewe Hall when their father went abroad, but when they came of age Henrietta sided with her father and went to live with him in Belgium. Many years after Henrietta told her nephew, the Marquess of Crewe, that her father had calculated his liabilities, at their worst, at £80,000[65] – at 2006 prices an enormous £3.4 million calculated from 1800, or £5.18 million calculated from 1835. Annabel, on the other hand, chose to stay on at Crewe Hall and as a consequence her father never again spoke to her: she it was who much later remembered being told stories there by the housekeeper, the grandmother of Charles Dickens, a snippet of information that opened a chink of light on Dickens' family background that the author himself had sought to extinguish.

The 2nd Lord Crewe's only son was Hungerford, a name bestowed from his mother's side of the family. If the father sought a dangerous, profligate and scandalous life then the son pursued one of peace, sound financial management and religious conviction. Hungerford, 3rd Lord Crewe was intellectually limited, shy, tall and rather awkward. His great niece, Lady Cynthia Colville, who spent much of her childhood at Crewe Hall, described him as strange and eccentric, "doubtless… a psychological case".[66] She recounts many of his eccentricities but recollects her childhood as a happy one and remembers her great-uncle with affection. Such awkwardness meant he never found a wife and, though he maintained a London house, didn't participate in debate at the

---

[64] *Crowded life*, by Lady Cynthia Colville. Evans, 1963. p18
[65] *A history of Crewe Hall*, by Ray Gladden (ms)
[66] Colville, op cit, p18

House of Lords. It should come as no surprise that such a character developed from such a dysfunctional family: his mother died when he was just eight years old, after which he was placed with his 78 year-old grandfather; his own father was disgraced and living abroad; and any equanimity he sought to hold onto during his schooldays at Eton was shattered when one of the masters committed suicide while Crewe was in the room. The title and property at Crewe came to him when he was a young man of 23 and thereafter he devoted much of his life to the house and farms that became his responsibility. He improved cottages and estate buildings, erected a new church and school, and between 1837 and 1842 alone spent £30,000 on improvements to Crewe Hall and its stables, £1.72 million at 2006 prices. Disaster struck in 1866 when a major fire all but destroyed the interior of the building. It then became the major purpose of Hungerford Crewe's life not only to rebuild and restore the hall to its former glory but also to improve and extend it. Employing Edward M. Barry – son of Sir Charles Barry, architect of London's new Houses of Parliament – he devoted the next 13 years and £150,000 to rebuilding Crewe Hall[67], more than £8 million at 2006 prices. Crewe enjoyed his investment for a further 15 years, dying in 1894 at the age of 81.

Because the 3rd Lord Crewe died without having married, and without children, and since his sister Henrietta did likewise, the position of his other sister Annabel became pivotal to the family history. Annabel had married, in July 1851, the writer and politician Richard Monckton Milnes, who was created first Baron Houghton in 1853. Although Hungerford Crewe outlived both his sister and her husband they had three children, Robert, Florence and Amicia and it was Robert who, at the age of 36, inherited Crewe Hall, the Crewe estates, the family paintings and the family history, as well as property of a more modest kind in Yorkshire from the Milnes side of the family.[68] Robert Offley Ashburton Milnes was born in 1858 and educated at Harrow and Cambridge. At the age of 25 he took up employment as an Assistant Private Secretary at the Foreign Office but within two years his father died and he moved from the Civil Service to the House of Lords, supporting the Liberal Party. Before that year was out there was a General Election in which Gladstone was returned and in the new administration Milnes was given a role as one of the Whips in the Lords. Milnes had married young, at the age of 22, his wife Sybil Graham being just six months older. They had four children in quick succession,

[67] information on work carried out at Crewe Hall comes from Ray Gladden's manuscript *A history of Crewe Hall*
[68] James Pope-Hennesy wrote biographies of both father and son: *Monckton Milnes*, published by Constable in two volumes 1949-51, and *Lord Crewe: the likeness of a Liberal*, also published by Constable, in 1955.

Annabel in 1881, Richard in 1882 and the twins Cynthia and Cecilia in 1884, and were said to make an attractive and popular couple. It came as a particular shock when, during a visit to Crewe Hall with the children, his wife contracted scarlet fever and died within a few days, aged just 30. Just two-and-a-half years later his only son Richard, known as Dicky, died at the age of 7, struck down with intestinal bovine tuberculosis after drinking bad milk. At a time when Irish home rule was tearing apart the Liberal Party Milnes took responsibility as Viceroy of Ireland and it was during his three year tenure of this post that his uncle Hungerford died, leaving him the Crewe empire. Though he was unable to inherit the title of 4th Lord Crewe of Crewe – not being a direct descendent through the male line – he was offered an Earldom the following year and chose Crewe as his title, thus becoming the first Earl of Crewe. He remained a widower for eleven years but at the age of 41, much to the surprise of friends and family, married again, taking for his bride the 18-year-old Margaret Primrose, youngest daughter of Lord Rosebery, and the same age as his own daughter Annabel. Crewe went on to become a major figure in the Liberal Party, as Lord President of the Council, lord privy seal, leader of the House of Lords, Secretary of State for India, British Ambassador in Paris, and Secretary of State for War. He also served a term as chairman of the London County Council and was chancellor of Sheffield University from 1918-1944. As a life-long friend of King George V Crewe often stayed at Windsor and Balmoral, and on one occasion the King and Queen Mary stayed for several days at Crewe Hall. It was against this background that the King decided to raise Crewe's title from Earl to Marquess in his coronation honours list. There might have been optimism for continuation of the family line when another son was born in 1911, named Richard again, like the son who had died more than 20 years earlier, but known in the family as Jack. Unfortunately he lived only to the age of 11. This Richard had a sister, Mary Evelyn Hungerford, born 1915, who eventually married the 9th Duke of Roxburghe.

The Marquess of Crewe lived through to 1945, in his 88th year the most distinguished of all the Crewes. Long-life has echoed down the centuries – Uncle Hungerford had been 81, the 1st Baron Crewe 86, and Sir Ranulphe Crewe 87; Nathaniel Crewe, Bishop of Durham lived to 88, the Marquess's sisters Cynthia and Cecilia to 82 and 100 respectively. At the time of writing his half-sister Mary, Duchess of Roxburghe is 90. Something that lasted even longer, but died out in 1945, was the presence of a Crewe in the Houses of Parliament, which started in 1597 with Sir Ranulphe and continued at every generation through to the last Lord Crewe, a total of 348 years!

With only daughters to succeed him the Crewe property was distributed between them. His wife lived through to 1967. His eldest daughter, Annabel, married twice, firstly into the ancient Irish family of

O'Neill, where one son, Shane, became the 3rd Baron O'Neill, and another, Terence, became the Prime Minister of Northern Ireland and was created Baron O'Neill of The Maine. Annabel's first husband was killed in the First World War and she married secondly James Dodds, with whom she had two sons James Colin and Quentin. The family changed their name from Dodds to Crewe in 1945 and Quentin Crewe went on to become a well-known author and journalist.[69]

Crewe Hall still stands today but was sold to the Duchy of Lancaster in 1936. In 1947 it was leased to a chemical manufacturing company called Calmic, who were taken over in 1966 by the Wellcome Foundation. Wellcome made Crewe Hall their UK headquarters, took out a new 99 year lease in 1970 and spent a considerable sum of money renovating the building and the grounds. However, following a merger between Wellcome and Glaxo a change of company policy resulted in them moving out in 1994. The house was eventually sold and turned into a high quality hotel by the Marston Hotel group, and the grounds were sold as Crewe Hall Enterprise Park to Edinburgh Properties.

The French political scene in 1786

International relations between France and Britain had been turbulent since the middle of the century. From 1756-63 the Seven Years War drew into conflict Britain, Prussia and Hanover on one side, France, Spain, Sweden, Austria, and Russia on the other, with fighting not only in Europe but spread across the globe in Canada, the West Indies and India. The resulting Treaty of Paris saw France cede to a victorious Britain French Canada and all the territory France had claimed to the east of the Mississippi, some West Indian islands, including St Vincent and Tobago, and some of the foothold it had in India. Not surprisingly, it was with some satisfaction that the French watched the subsequent difficulties that Britain had in governing its North American colonies. The British Parliament's introduction of a Stamp Act in 1765, to gather revenue in America, led to fierce opposition there, culminating in the so-called Boston Tea Party in 1773. More rebellious outbreaks developed and Britain sent troops to enforce Britain's rule. The first battle between British troops and American rebels was at Bunker Hill just outside Boston, which resulted in the death or injury of 400 Americans and a thousand British. On 4th July 1776 the Americans issued their Declaration of Independence and prosecuted a war that was to last through to British capitulation in 1782. At the beginning of the conflict

---

[69] Quentin Crewe's autobiography was published by Heinemann in 1991 with the title *Well, I forget the rest*. He died in 1998. One of his daughters is the journalist and novelist Candida Crewe

the Americans sent Benjamin Franklin to France to seek support for their cause, resulting in financial contributions and active participation by a number of French individuals. Many French politicians, though, sought government intervention in the rebellion, believing there was an opportunity to win back some of the losses from the Seven Years War. Official support came in February 1778 when a treaty of commerce and friendship was signed between the French and the Americans. As a result the British began attacking French merchant ships carrying supplies to America with the inevitable result of war between Britain and France. Substantial French troops and naval forces were sent to fight with the Americans in 1778 and 1780, though the French were as much interested in defeating the British in the West Indies as on the American mainland. In 1779 the French also attacked and captured the poorly defended British trading posts in Senegal and, more audaciously, planned, together with the Spanish, to invade England. A turning point in the war came in October 1781 when the appearance of a French fleet in Chesapeake Bay, with three thousand troops aboard, was enough to persuade the southern British army, already surrounded in Yorktown by the Americans, to throw down its arms. It was a crucial defeat, for which King George blamed the French. Britain abandoned the conflict with the Americans in November 1782 but not before inflicting a serious naval defeat on the French in the Caribbean in the Battle of the Saintes. In 1785 the first American Minister to the Court of St James was received by the King in London; and in 1785 Mrs Crewe arrived in Paris.

All of this was very close to Mrs Crewe: her husband had been part of the Parliament making decisions about the war with America; her brother Harry had been fighting in America; and her close friends Charles James Fox and Edmund Burke were prominent opponents of the British Government's American policies. Not surprisingly recent events in America were a topic the French loved to raise with Mrs Crewe. With unconcealed irritation she writes in the diary: "...the French People never abandon a subject till it is quite Threadbare, and my Brother Harry's having been taken prisoner in America, and having received Kindnesses from very distinguished French Officers .... have made our Family of Importance, and, I do assure you, I am tired to Death with the same sort of Stuff which they will bestow upon you, in large Quantities, and upon every occasion; with very bad Taste, I think, for after all, my Brother was not the only Brother taken Prisoner in America"(p93); and then again, later: "[Monsieur de la Fayette] talked to me very much about my Brother Harry's Captivity in America. – a theme they all hold forth upon, because it is certain that several French Officers had an Opportunity of displaying much gallant Generosity to a fallen Enemy. The Duc de Castries never sees me that he does not allude to his Services upon that Occasion, and he certainly did Cloathe him when he was naked, and go so far as to lend him two hundred pounds: but this puts me in Mind of the Epigram

> To John I owed great Obligation
> [But John, unhappily, thought fit
> To publish it to all the nation:
> Sure John and I are more than quit]."(p99)

At one point in the diary Mrs Crewe wrote that she could not be presented at the French Court, although the opportunity had been offered to her brother Charles. Since one member of the family was eligible to be presented it seems likely to have been reluctance on Mrs Crewe's part rather than lack of opportunity, and such reluctance may well have arisen from the American conflict.

Her views on the French Court are valuable, coming, as they do just a few years before the French Revolution. Most of the comments she makes about the King and Queen are of a personal nature: about their appearance and social behaviour, though such criteria were not insignificant in defining the attitudes of the French people, particularly towards Marie Antoinette – and that told heavily against her both before and during the revolution. Comments on the King are generally favourable, with him striking Mrs Crewe as good humoured and unaffected – she reports people saying he was a good Prince but had a "want of grace and bow", and then in French "it's not that he doesn't have goodness on his face but that he has a shortage of it"(p157). She writes less kindly of the Queen and since her contact was not extensive her impressions are formed mostly from the people she meets and to whom she talks. She did meet her enough, though, to make a judgement on her appearance, which was not complimentary: "…her Face …. is not what one can call handsome and yet has something in it which, for a Queen at least, is very good – Her Figure was fine formerly, but it is become clumsy to a great Degree and, tho She is under Thirty, She has on this Account been obliged to give up Dancing"(p155). Other comments are far from flattering: "ever since this Queen came to the Throne People's Minds have been dissipated"(p127); "I am inclined to feel quite tired and Disgusted with the Noise She is always making about nothing at All"(p147); "I have heard several old Persons complain terribly of the height to which Frivolité is carried, merely because her Majesty is much prouder of the Title of petite Maistresse than of Queen of France"(p147); "I conclude there is not much Solidity in her Composition"(p155); "The Duc de Nivernois talked a great deal about the Cardinal de Rohan's Affairs Yesterday – He seems to think the Queen has behaved with too much Severity upon the whole, but that She does not deserve the Abuse that is heaped on her by many People. La Marechalle de Mirpoix was more Unreserved, and spoke indeed with very great Violence against her the other Day, accusing her of wanting Common Humanity"(p193).

Richard Brinsley Sheridan by Sir Joshua Reynolds

William Windham by Sir Joshua Reynolds

Fulke Greville by Ozias Humphry

Hungerford Crewe, 3rd Baron Crewe of Crewe
By Spy (Lesley Ward)

The Marquess of Crewe
By Arthur Ambrose McEvoy

Crewe Hall 1992
From a photograph by Michael Allen

Marie Antoinette was not a popular Queen with the people of France: considered extravagant at a time of economic difficulty and interfering when it came to matters of State, her Austrian nationality didn't help. Though she tried to develop an image of simplicity and financial restraint, partly demonstrated through the dresses designed and made by Rose Bertin, and the paintings of Vigée le Brun, she failed to win the affection of the French people. A defining crisis of this unpopularity was acted out in 1785-6, around the time of Mrs Crewe's visit, and has become known since as the Affair of the Diamond Necklace. The figure at the centre of the affair, born Jeanne de la Rémy, was the daughter of a serving maid and an impoverished nobleman, the latter of whom could claim descent, albeit illegitimate, from the last Valois King of France. Left to fend for herself through begging she attracted the attention of a sympathetic woman, the Marquise de Boulainvillers, who not only looked after Jeanne and a younger sister, but had her line of descent confirmed by the Judge-at-Arms of the French nobility, which resulted in a small state pension. At the age of twenty-two she married Nicholas de la Motte, an army officer, and set upon a campaign to use her link to a royal past to gain a better, and wealthier, position in society. She began calling herself the Comtesse de la Motte, developed this to Comtesse de la Motte-Valois, and finally Comtesse de Valois, and moved to rented rooms in the town of Versailles where she hoped to attract the attention of the Court. Though this met with only limited success it did give her the idea of claiming to have become a close friend of the Queen, a claim supported by a series of letters addressed to her by Marie Antoinette. The letters were, in fact, forgeries produced by a friend, Rétaux de Villette, but they convinced some people that the Comtesse de Valois was a favourite at court. The seeds of a scheme were sown when Jeanne met the Cardinal de Rohan and an Italian charlatan he was sheltering called Cagliostro. The Cardinal, though from one of France's most important families, and entitled to call himself Prince, was unpopular with Marie Antoinette, yet was desperate to win back her favour, and this information was passed to Jeanne by Cagliostro which she soon turned to her financial advantage. She told de Rohan that she had spoken to the Queen on his behalf and as a result Her Majesty was becoming more favourably inclined towards him; over a period of time she carried letters to the Cardinal purported to have been written by the Queen, each friendlier than the last until Jeanne considered it time for the sting and a letter from the Queen asked the Cardinal for a loan of sixty thousand francs for a charity donation, to be handed to their go-between, which he supplied. The sting was re-played three months later. But now the Cardinal wanted some greater assurance of the Queen's favour. Using a prostitute called Nicole Le Guay, whom Jeanne had taken up and given the name Baronne d'Oliva, they arranged a clandestine meeting with de Rohan one dark evening in the gardens at

Versailles. Nicole le Guay looked remarkably like the Queen – in fact had been selected for that very reason – and was to play a part in a swift, shadowy meeting: the "Queen" handing to de Rohan another letter and a rose and whispering the words "You know what this means". Though she forgot to pass the letter the ruse worked and the Cardinal was satisfied for a while. But then came a plan of mind-boggling extravagance. It involved a diamond necklace created some years before by the court jewellers Bohmer and Bassenge, and made for Louis XV to buy to give to his mistress Madame du Barry. Made up from 647 brilliants and 2800 carats it was valued at 1.6 million francs and represented a huge investment for the jewellers. Unfortunately Louis XV died before he could buy it. Left with it on their hands the jewellers tried to sell it to Marie Antoinette who, in one of those spells when she didn't wish to appear extravagant, declined the offer, even though Bohmer made a scene in Court, sobbing that he would be ruined and threatening to take his life. Bohmer later heard that the Comtesse de Valois was a relative and close confidante of the Queen and he begged her to seek a change of mind from Marie Antoinette. Valois, her husband and their friend Villette saw a golden opportunity and hatched their plot. More forged letters were sent to de Rohan, commissioning him to buy the necklace on behalf of the Queen, pointing out the difficulty for her of buying it directly. Repayment of the money was to be made to de Rohan in 6-monthly instalments. On the 1st February 1785 the necklace was handed to de Rohan who handed it on to Jeanne de la Motte who handed it immediately to Villette. It didn't take long to break up what the jewellers had so carefully put together and take the stones to London to sell. Over the following six months the Cardinal became concerned when the Queen failed to wear her new purchase in public and deeply worried when the first of his 6-monthly repayments didn't materialise. Eventually the jewellers took the matter to the Queen and on 15th August 1785 the Cardinal de Rohan was called before the King, admitted he had been taken in and was thrown into the Bastille, together with the Comtesse de Valois, the prostitute Le Guay and Cagliostro (also, for some reason, Cagliostro's wife).

The affair was still the scandal of Paris when Mrs Crewe arrived and would not be resolved until a trial was held the following May. In the meantime there was confusion about what had really happened. The King and Queen were furious that they had been dragged into a scandal not of their making, that forged letters from the Queen had been written, and that the conspirators had made the Queen appear, once again, acquisitive and profligate. The problem for them was that too many people believed she really was involved, that this was typical of her behaviour and that she was trying to throw the blame on innocent people. The French people's dislike and distrust of Marie Antoinette was carried to new depths as they argued about whom to believe. As an example Mrs Crewe reported an epigram that had been produced about the Queen and the prostitute Le Guay:

"Vile species bold, you well
play the role of a Queen."
"Why not, my Sovereign,
you often play at mine."(p148)

In the diary the Duc de Nivernais talked to Mrs Crewe a great deal about the affair, expressing his view that, though the Queen had behaved with too much severity towards the Cardinal, she did not deserve the abuse heaped upon her by many people. On the other hand La Marechalle de Mirepoix was more critical of the Queen "and spoke indeed with very great Violence against her the other Day, accusing her of wanting Common Humanity in keeping him in the Bastile 'till his Trial"(p193). No matter that reality was softer than rumour: "While de Rohan was to be colorfully depicted by his lawyer Target as languishing in 'irons' in the Bastille, he actually moved into a specially furnished apartment outside the prison towers where he spent nine months entertaining an unending stream of distinguished visitors. Oysters and champagne were laid on as a collation for guests, and the Cardinal had choice works from his library and a retinue of servants to help him overcome the hardships of incarceration."[70]

Cagliostro may not have fared so well as de Rohan, and certainly attracted the sympathy of Mrs Crewe: "Every Body is now reading Cagliostro's Memoirs, written in the Bastile where he is now confined on Account of this Affair of the Cardinal De Rohan's – People had done talking of that Prelate when we arrived here, but these Memoirs have awakened the public Attention to him. This Cagliostro had a Strange Suspicious Character till he put out the Account of his Life, which is so Interesting and Melancholy that every one seems Shocked at his having been placed in the Bastile so Precipitately. – His poor Wife, who can no way have been complicated in all this, is likewise in some other Corner of the Prison. The very Name of the Bastile always struck me with Horror, and since the other Morning that I drove round The Dreary Dyke and walls that Chill the Blood, I have found the mention of it still more terrible!"(p189)

The trial did not take place till May 1786, after Mrs Crewe had left, but no doubt she followed the outcome from London. De Rohan was acquitted of all charges and was celebrated by the people of Paris as the victor against the Queen. Cagliostro was similarly cleared. Jeanne de la Motte represented herself as a dispossessed orphan from an older, more worthy royal line, falsely accused by a modern avaricious Queen. She claimed Marie Antoinette really did want the diamond necklace and really had written letters to the Cardinal. The letters had been hurriedly

---

[70] *Citizens*, by Simon Schama. Viking, 1989. p208

burned by de Rohan, which should have helped her case, but the court didn't accept her story and sentenced her to a public flogging, branding and indefinite imprisonment. Nevertheless the accusations against the Queen and her reaction to events had reinforced public prejudice against Marie Antoinette who came out of the affair as a spendthrift and a vindictive slut who would stop at nothing to satisfy her appetites. When la Motte, with help, escaped from prison a year later and fled to the safety of London, she poured out from there a non-stop flow of vitriolic and pornographic pamphlets, letters and memoirs, all directed against Marie Antoinette.

Though the Queen may have been a focal point for the anger of Parisians there was a much broader target for the disgust of ordinary people, frustrated with the extravagance of the Court and with the whole range of aristocratic society. Such anger and frustration was, as we know, to boil over into revolution and though Mrs Crewe was moving in those very same circles that were despised she had the insight to see that all was not well. On 1st March she reported there had been a carnival lasting through three days, during which there had been much singing and shouting, drunkenness, fighting and deaths. She goes on to say: "But you are to know there is a little Policy working at such Times at the Carnival, and it is actually a Measure of Government, not merely to Wink at Excesses, but even to furnish the poorer Sort with Money to produce them; for the more Debauched Men are, the more Abject and the more Contented under their Slavery they become, and, deluded by the false Glare of riot and Intemperance the less likely are they to form Reflections which in the End might be Dangerous to their Tyrant! I know it is the Fashion to say that the lower Classes of People in France are happy and Contented – I own I have my doubts about it – There is a Sort of Rivalship in Gaiety, and much of their Happiness is only External, and probably the Effect of Habit; but they have many actual Wants, and tho' they Sing away their Cares, it is like the moaning Song, perhaps, of a poor Weak Child, who puts himself to Sleep that way" (p195). It's not certain if these were her own observations or if she was simply re-iterating what she had heard from others; perhaps the former since her thoughts were contrary to what she said was the fashionable view, i.e. that "the lower classes of people in France were happy and contented". It seems unlikely she would have learned anything from talking to ordinary people – such a past-time features nowhere in her itinerary – but she may have been sharp enough to watch people in the streets, the parks and the shops and form an opinion that way. Wherever it came from it echoed the predictions of contemporaries Rétif de la Bretonne and Louis Sébastien Mercier, the former seeing a disastrous revolution born out of the lower classes' growing spirit of insubordination, and the latter drawing attention to an air of melancholy constraint which indicated a painful and hard struggle for life.

It's clear from Mrs Crewe's diary that Paris was a popular destination for English travellers, which might seem surprising considering the recent hostilities between the two countries. Nevertheless, the English were eager to go there and the French were pleased to receive them, so why was this? With an abundance of self-confidence the French believed Paris to be supreme among the capital cities of Europe, a city they liked to show off. Unlike many other European cities it was not seasonal – there was no tradition of the leaders of society leaving their homes in the capital at specified seasons and travelling to country estates. Paris operated all year round. It was a centre for theatre, for literary and artistic activity, for a growing interest in science; it had attractive buildings, especially the homes, or hotels as they were termed, of the rich and aristocratic; it had three royal palaces: the Tuileries, the Louvre and the Palais Royal; and it had a royal court at nearby Versailles which, though it may not have matched the heady days of Louis XIV, was still bold, colourful, extravagant and remarkably open to view. The French liked to flaunt their capital and if the English found fault then maybe that had as much to do with national rivalry as it did with French failures. Throughout her diary Mrs Crewe constantly makes comparison between British and French behaviour and practice, nearly always to the detriment of the French, though impartiality does not shine through as one of her virtues. The attraction of Paris was its busy-ness: there was so much to do, so many people to see, so many supper parties, balls and even breakfast parties to attend; there were so many wealthy people claiming to run the best salons; there was fashion and theatre and culture to keep up with; there was also gambling and sexual adventure. Paris was described in the 1780s as a whirlpool of dissipation, pleasure and indulgence. Some, though not all, of this comes across in the diary.

One of the first places Mrs Crewe visited was the Palais Royal, which had undergone a transformation since her previous visit in 1773. The Palais Royal had been turned into the most spectacular spot for pleasure and politics in Europe by the Duc de Chartres (who became the Duc d'Orleans in 1785). Royal palace in law as well as in name it bordered the capital's other two royal palaces, the Louvre and the Tuileries, and had once formed the gardens of Cardinal Richelieu. The combination of the Duc de Chartres' profligate life-style and his entrepreneurial instinct led to an extravagant plan to turn what had been gardens into an arcaded resort, combining shops, cafes, theatres, and places of more doubtful recreation. The plans were expensive and it was not until 1784, six years after it was first mooted and just two years before Mrs Crewe's visit, that it began to resemble its original vision. In the meantime a wooden gallery had been erected running along the Palais; this was known as the *camp des tartares* and rapidly became notorious as a haunt of prostitutes and pickpockets. Inside, for a few sous visitors gazed at the huge girth of the four-hundred-pound German Paul Butterbrodt, and (for a few sous more) examined the credentials of a naked (wax) "belle Zulima" allegedly dead for two hundred years and in a marvelous state of preservation. In 1785 the old Duc d'Orleans died, and left his son with enough money to complete the work. By then the Palais Royal had succeeded in bringing a raw and Rabelaisian popular culture right into the heart of royal and aristocratic Paris. As the private property of the Duc d'Orleans it was almost entirely safe from the police, which gave it the freedom to develop unshackled by controls. Theatre formed a major part of the enterprise. The Theatre Beaujolais opened with three-foot-tall marionettes and continued with child actors; and at the Varietes Amusantes, the farces and melodramas of the boulevards moved in alongside, both playing to packed houses. Inside the confined spaces of the boulevard theatre it was almost impossible to maintain any kind of formal distinctions of rank. Nicolet's theatre held four hundred people crammed into a space not much more than forty feet by thirty-six. The tallow candles barely gave enough light to allow for much in the way of social display and Nicolet's dirt-cheap prices meant that people of drastically different social worlds were pressed together like sardines. All sorts of cafes flourished, from the more staid Foy to the risqué Grotte Flamande. .There were all kinds of shops: grocers, bookshops, jewellers, haberdashers, silk merchants, fan makers, tobacconists. Visitors could visit wig makers and lace makers; sip lemonade from the stalls; play chess or checkers at the Café Chartres (which still exists in 1999 as the restaurant Le Grand Véfour); listen to a strolling guitar-playing abbé (presumably defrocked) who specialized in bawdy songs; peruse the often vicious political satires, written and distributed by a team of hacks working for the Duc; ogle the magic-lantern or shadow-light shows; play billiards or gather round the miniature cannon that went off precisely at noon when struck by the rays of the sun. The cafes became meeting places for disaffected *philosophes* and political clubs were established in what became a centre of opposition to the court at Versailles. Large crowds filled the avenues and arcades, where promenading (not to say soliciting), gazing and inspecting were a major pastime. All classes of people were jumbled together and in the melee it was easy to mistake a flashily dressed courtesan sporting imitation brilliants for a countess decorated with the real thing. Young soldiers dressed to impress girls with their uniforms on which insignia of rank were either unmarked or indeterminate. In their black robes noble magistrates from the Parlement were dressed in much the same fashion as humble barristers and clerks. And it is evident that contemporaries relished this social potpourri. Louis-Sebastien Mercier adored the Palais Royal, where he witnessed "the confusion of estates, the mixture, the throng"; he said "this enchanted little spot is in itself a little town of luxury.... it is the very temple of pleasure, where vice is so bright that the very shadow of shame is chased away".[71] And Mayeur de Saint-Paul, who wrote even more lyrically, insisted "all the orders of citizens are joined together, from the lady of rank to the dissolute, from the soldier of distinction to the humblest official in the Farms."[72] Respectable women, like Mrs Crewe and her mother, were safe in the Palais Royal only between 11am and 5pm – outside of those hours they were likely to be accosted or assaulted. At 11pm all the lights were extinguished and daytime indecency gave way to outright debauchery.[73] Mrs Crewe first visited in the company of her husband and her brother and was much taken with the place: "The Scene there is the busiest and most entertaining I ever saw – There are Shops of every kind, and in short, it is full of Shews and Sights which give it the Appearance of a large Fair – One may go up Stairs and down Stairs, or under the Piazzas, or into the Gardens: All is a Scene of Gaiety and Business, and Chearfullness!" (p77) Not for her a description of its sordid side. Nor did it put her off going again two days later with her mother, though she doesn't say whether or not a man accompanied them on that occasion.

Besides the Palais Royal Mrs Crewe might have visited the other two Parisian palaces, the Tuileries – to which she makes no reference – and the Louvre. The latter she did visit but only, it would seem, to attend a meeting of the Académie Francaise – it's strange she doesn't refer to the King's art collection housed there, particularly since she and her husband had some very fine paintings of their own at Crewe Hall, collected over many generations.

She gives considerably more space to another of Paris's main attractions, the theatre. In all she made nine visits, seeing comedy, drama, and opera (which also included dance). In the 1780s Paris boasted three new theatres: the Opéra was rebuilt after burning down in 1781, the Théatre Francais, home of the Comédie Francais, opened on the Left Bank in 1782 and the Comédie Italienne opened in 1783. Mrs Crewe was faint in her praise of the new buildings: "The Theatre is new and has a very pleasant Appearance; tho, I believe it is abused on Account of its Size, which they say is too large considering the many others there are in this Town"(p97). If it was, indeed, Sheridan she was writing to then maybe she was being tactful since another visitor, Arthur Young, writing in 1787 wrote despairingly "after the circular theatres of France how can one relish our ill-contrived oblong holes of London?"[74]

---

[71] *Before the deluge*, by Evelyn Farr. Peter Owen, 1994. pp31-32
[72] Schama, op cit, p136
[73] good descriptions of the Palais Royal are given in Schama's *Citizens* and Farr's *Before the deluge*, from which much of this information is taken
[74] Farr, op cit, p79

She was more balanced, though, in her views of what was enacted on the stage. Moliere's *Monsieur de Pourceaugnac* came in for heavy criticism, Mrs Crewe finding it "so much more indelicate than any thing that ever was represented at Sadler's Wells, or our lowest Theatres, that it quite astonished me to see a Paris Audience submit to it – One slurs over many things in Reading Moliere; but really as they acted this, it was impossible to avoid Disgust"(p97). The indelicacies must have come, as she hints, in the acting rather than in Moliere's words which, certainly in the editions I've seen, would not bring a blush to a young ladies' cheek. Greater offence might have come from her visit to one of the small theatres at the Foire St Germain where plays attracted people of all ranks, from the highest to the lowest, and could be crude, indecent and earthy, which may be the reason she says nothing at all about what she saw. They were also very popular and she only managed to get "baddish places"; as if to make up for this she goes on "however we scraped up an acquaintance with some odd people that sat near us". If she didn't like the older Moliere play then a new comedy pleased her even less; it was "so entirely devoid of Intrigue, Wit, humour or Merit of any kind, that I hardly thought the Actors would be allowed to get through with it" (p145). In fact none of the plays received much praise from her, a point that might be assigned to some difficulty in understanding the nuances of the language. Though Madame du Deffand said in 1773 that Mrs Crewe knew the French language well, she does express difficulties from time to time: "There is great comfort, I think, in being now and then released from the Labor of expressing one's self in a Foreign Language, which, by the Way, is often not only Fatiguing, but Embarrassing likewise"(p143); and then, after a visit to the theatre: "it has several Allusions in it to the Court of Louis the fifteenth – but they are lost upon me, so that I may well be forgiven for not admiring it as I otherwise ought to do"(p173). Where there was music to accompany the words Mrs Crewe found much more to praise: "It was a very fine spectacle" she said of one opera; "this is an amusement perfect in its kind" of a smaller musical piece at the Italian Theatre; then, of *Richard Couer de Lion*, "I saw a more beautifull, and splendid Opera at the smallest Theatre, than ever was presented in England"(p105); she was likewise pleased with the opera, Dardanus: "it is impossible not to be often delighted with the great Opera at Paris"(p113).

When it comes to individual performers she hands out praise to the dancers: "The Dancing is very fine, and Gardelle, Mademoiselle Gamaise, with two or three other famous Performers capital indeed!" (p96); but when it comes to the actors is unimpressed with Mademoiselle Raucourt, one of the French favourites: "She excells in The Violent Stile… The Eye is pleased with Madame Rocourt but the Heart is untouched"(p189). She had comments, too, on the audiences, recognising their appreciation of Dardanus: "Here indeed the Audience, even to the lowest of them, by the Shouts which they frequently send forth, and the many inconveniences which they contentedly suffer on crouded Nights, sufficiently prove how capable they are of tasting this Species of Entertainment"(p115); but she was not quite so pleased when she attracted the attention of the whole pit of the theatre by inadvertently hanging her cloak over the edge of the box, a major *faux pas* it seemed.

There was a pattern to life for the bon ton in Paris in the 1780s. The theatres, for example, were best visited on certain days of the week: the Opera on Tuesdays and Fridays, the Comédie Francaise on Wednesdays and Saturdays and the Comédie Italienne on Mondays and Thursdays – on Sundays all the theatres were full. On these nights the best performers were on display and the best society attended. For the most part Mrs Crewe conformed to this ritual.

There were two other types of theatre in its broader sense that she attended: firstly the Académie Francaise, a body formed as early as 1635 which had, by the second half of the eighteenth century, become the leader of literary opinion in France; and secondly the Lycée, a newly founded institution giving lectures on literature, history, mathematics and a range of sciences. She gives a detailed description of the meeting of the Académie: "About one we Sallied forth with Lord Downe and three French Ladies to the Louvre where the Academy is – Their Room, they tell me, is as large as our House of Commons, but I confess it did not appear to be so to my Eye. We found Crouds of Carriages making up to the great Gate of the Palace, with some Difficulty arrived there, and with more Difficulty got tolerable Places afterwards. Having waited upwards of two Hours for them an universal Buzz announced the arrival of the Forty Members some of whom are such Favourites that they received loud Applauses as they passed by"(p159). She then goes on to describe the participants and the style of their oratory.

The other institution, the Lycée, was only founded in 1786 and her visit must have been to one of the very earliest lectures – indeed she describes the topic as Monsieur de la Harpe's first lecture. La Harpe lectured on a range of literary topics, collecting them together and publishing them between 1799 and 1805 as *Lycée, ou cours de littérature ancienne et moderne*. He began, she said, with a dissertation on languages: "He read with very great simplicity and good Taste, and several Rules which he laid down, and Opinions which he advanced had great Force" (p165). But she thought she had come across his ideas in other writers on the subject. She observed that the audience clapped at various points of the lecture, a fashion new to her and which she disliked. She disliked also an apparent attack on the English language: "I did not like to hear him abuse our Language without Mercy, and say that it was a Combination of Sounds scarcely human! and that it might be compared to the Hissing Noise of Animals more than any other. I never heard before that it was so dissonant to the Ears of Foreigners"(p167). These comments from La Harpe brought some laughter from the audience and a focus of attention on Mrs Crewe and her English friends. Perhaps it was light-heartedness from the lecturer; but ever bold in her defence of anything English, especially against the French, she counter-attacked (in the diary, not in the lecture-hall) with: "I am sure we might with some truth retort that the French Language has a constant nasal Sound which our Ears are as little delighted with"(p173). She reports that several Frenchmen came up to the English party at the end of the lecture and protested at the injustice done to the English language. Mrs Crewe, though, still bristling with indignity, dismissed these attempts at pacification as insincere French politeness. It seems she was no more taken with Monsieur de la Harpe's ideas than she was with the "violent stile" of Madame Raucourt.

She was intrigued, though, by the idea of the Lycée "it is an Institution Paris is very proud of, tho some People think it is too lazy and Confused a way of getting at Knowledge; that the wise People will not become wiser by it, because the Lectures are not deep, and that other's will only change their Ignorance for Superficialneſs"(p167). She thought the lectures on history and literature were fine for women – "but what, for God's Sake, have we poor Women to do with Chimistry or Anatomy?"(p167) Or, she says, for other sciences.

It's worth pointing out that eighteenth century society was fascinated by the influence on life of "science" and that Mrs Crewe was as aware of developments as most. References to science echo through her diary. She writes of the science of French medical practitioners being behind that of the English; of the workshop of the dressmaker Mademoiselle Bertin having on it "the stamp of science"(p117); she says of French people "if they say they know any thing – it is often Science, and not savoir, which they have"(p107). Much space is given to the craze for mesmerism or "animal magnetism" as it was also known, to which Mrs Crewe refers often as a science; but in introducing the subject she makes reference to three other recent developments, each of which is worth some expansion here. She writes: "Is it not too, extraordinary that such a Capital as Paris, with Men of real Science to Appeal to, should yet be found to tolerate such incoherent Stuff? Yet surely after what one has seen and heard of within these twenty Years concerning Electricity, Balloons, Diving Bells &c. it may be permitted us to follow those Philosophers a little way with "Modesty enough"(p83).

As far as ballooning was concerned Mrs Crewe had thrown herself into the phenomenon as much as most other people at the time. Balloon flights had taken Britain and France by storm in the 1780s. In 1783 the Montgolfier brothers had raised a 60-foot balloon to a height of 6000 feet in front of the King and Queen at Versailles. Later that same year came the first manned flight. In September 1784 Vincenzo Lunardi and Jean-Pierre Blanchard launched the first balloon in Britain at the Artillery Ground in London – the Duchess of Devonshire cut the rope and Mrs Crewe sent up one of her gloves in the car[75]; the balloon stayed in the air for 24 miles[76]. The Duchess of Devonshire feted Lunardi and Blanchard and on 1st December 1784 she organised another ascent for them from Grosvenor Square, attended by the Prince of Wales and a hundred Whigs and their ladies – there can be little doubt that Mrs Crewe would have been one of them. All the surrounding streets were blocked with spectators, some standing on carriages. The following month, January 1785, Blanchard and Jefferies became the first men to cross the Channel by balloon. Ballooning became a craze, with all manner of people keen to take part. On 5th May 1785 Mrs Crewe's friend William Windham became an early aeronaut, taking off from Molesey, near Hampton Court and descending nearly 40 miles away at Rochester in Kent, a journey taking about seven-and-a-half hours. Notes made at the time by Windham are preserved in the British Library.[77] The craze eased off after Pilatre du Rozier was killed in another attempt to cross the Channel in June 1785, his balloon exploding in violet flame. Her awareness of electricity was probably not so intimate. It was in 1745 that Musschenbroek invented the first device – later known as the Leyden Jar - that could store large amounts of electric charge. Within a year after the appearance of Musschenbroek's device, William Watson, an English physician and scientist, constructed a more sophisticated version and transmitted an electric spark from his device through a wire strung across the River Thames at Westminster Bridge in 1747. The Leyden jar revolutionized the study of electrostatics. Soon "electricians" were earning their living all over Europe demonstrating electricity with Leyden jars. Typically, they killed birds and animals with electric shock or sent charges through wires over rivers and lakes. In 1746 a Leyden jar was discharged in front of King Louis XV by sending current through a chain of 180 Royal Guards. In another demonstration, Nollet used wire made of iron to connect a row of Carthusian monks more than a kilometre long; when a Leyden jar was discharged, the white-robed monks reportedly leapt simultaneously into the air. In the United States, Benjamin Franklin sold his printing house, newspaper, and almanac to spend his time conducting electricity experiments. In 1752 Franklin proved that lightning was an example of electric conduction. Joseph Priestley, an English physicist, summarised all available data on electricity in his book *History and Present State of Electricity* (1767).

---

[75] Leslie and Taylor, op cit, p451
[76] *Georgiana Duchess of Devonshire* by Amanda Foreman. HarperCollins, 1998. p173
[77] British Library ref no. Add. 37925, volume LXXXIV of The Windham Papers

Mrs Crewe's reference to diving bells probably arose from the invention by John Smeaton (1724-1792) of an air pump for use in the bell, which gave their feasibility a great leap forward. Smeaton was also remembered for building the 3rd Eddystone Lighthouse, made of dovetailed blocks of Portland stone.

Each of these was a genuine scientific development, but neither Mrs Crewe nor a great many of her acquaintances, could be sure if "animal magnetism" was the discovery of a scientist or a charlatan. Franz Anton Mesmer, 1734-1815, was a German physician whose system of therapeutics, known as mesmerism, was the forerunner of the modern practice of hypnotism. Mesmer's dissertation at the University of Vienna in 1766 suggested that the gravitational attraction of the planets affected human health by affecting an invisible fluid found in the human body. In 1775 Mesmer revised his theory of animal gravitation to one of Animal magnetism wherein the invisible fluid in the body acted according to the laws of magnetism. According to Mesmer, animal magnetism could be activated by any magnetized object and manipulated by any trained person. He surmised that disease was the result of obstacles in the fluid's flow through the body, and these obstacles could be broken by crises or trance states, which often ended in delirium or convulsions, in order to restore the harmony of personal fluid flow. Mesmer devised various therapeutic treatments to achieve harmonious fluid flow, and in many of these treatments he was a forceful and rather dramatic personal participant. Accused by Viennese physicians of fraud, Mesmer left Austria and settled in Paris in 1778. He established a curious clinic at Place Vendome, to which the sick came by the thousands for expensive cures. His consulting rooms were dimly lighted and hung with mirrors. The sick sat mesmerized around a vat of chemicals, iron filings, and crushed glass, holding hands or joined by a cord, maintaining an unbroken circuit. Dressed as a magician, Mesmer glided among them to the sound of soft music, making mysterious passes. There were more convulsions than cures, but enough cures for the French government to offer Mesmer a yearly sum for his secret. It proved to be a highly lucrative practice but not surprisingly attracted the antagonism of the medical profession, and in 1784 Louis XVI appointed a commission of scientists and physicians to investigate Mesmer's methods, with Franklin, Guillotin, and Lavoisier among its members. Since Franklin was too indisposed to travel to Paris, the committee came to him in Passy and held one of its most important experiments in his garden. Mesmer's assistant, Dr. Deslon, who was also first physician to the Comte d'Artois, had magnetized an apricot tree, announcing that it would profoundly affect anyone touching it. He stood at a distance as a twelve-year-old boy was led blindfolded toward four trees, none of them magnetized or anywhere near the apricot tree. At the first tree, the boy perspired and coughed. At the second he felt a pain and stupor. At the third he complained of an increasing headache and said he was getting closer to the magnetic tree, though he was further from it than ever. At the fourth tree he fainted. "Imagination," said the report, with Franklin first among its signers, "is the principle. . . . Persons who thought they were magnetized felt pain, warmth and great heat, when they were not touched, and when no sign had been used. With some subjects, of very excitable nervous temperament, we produced convulsions, and what are known as crises." A second report stated that animal magnetic fluid was non-existent. Women, said a secret report, were especially susceptible to men such as Mesmer; in their case, the sensations experienced were at least in part erotic, and therefore his methods objectionable. Denounced as a fraud, Mesmer eventually left France, taking his fortune with him. Whatever may be said about his therapeutic system, Mesmer did often achieve a close rapport with his patients and seems to have actually alleviated certain nervous disorders in them. More importantly, further investigation of the trance state by his followers eventually led to the development of legitimate applications of hypnotism.

By the time Mrs Crewe arrived in Paris Mesmer had moved on – she reports in her diary that he was now in London – but had left behind supporters and practitioners of his ideas, one of whom, the Marquis de Puységur, she met. Puységur had published in 1784 *Mémoires pour servir à l'histoire et à l'establissement du magnètisme animal* and a copy of this was passed to her by the Duc de Guines. Like many people Mrs Crewe was curious about the new phenomenon but at the same time deeply sceptical. "This Book has to a common Mind, at least to mine, all the Appearance of being written by a Bedlamite"(p83), she wrote; and then "he mentioned two or three such proofs of its Effects, as would have made my Hair stand on End, if I could have admitted them"(p79). She calls Puységur eccentric and his book incoherent, but still tries to use her brand of common sense to explain the effects of mesmerism: "I am induced to think it only a Species of Electricity which operating upon a heated Imagination, has at times great Influence over the human Frame... I verily believe these People have made some Discovery that Respects Nerves and the finer Organs of the human Frame"(p105).

Mrs Crewe's brush with mesmerism might have ended in Paris but we know she visited a Doctor Mainauduc in London in October 1788 in the company of Mrs Sheridan. Her companion was "thrown into a state which She described as very distressing. It was a kind of fainting without absolute insensibility. She could hear and feel but had no power to speak or move".[78]

---

[78] *Betsy Sheridan's journal,* op cit, p123

Social life in Paris

One of the greatest attractions for visitors to Paris was the social round: visiting friends and acquaintances, taking breakfast, dinner or "English tea" with them, exchanging views, playing cards, attending balls, routs and fetes, all of which Mrs Crewe explored, described, criticised and praised. Society kept consistent hours, as she describes: dinner at 2.30, visiting from 5pm followed by the theatre, and supper at about 10pm. Supper might be followed by a ball, a rout or just a group of people gathered to talk and play cards; few gatherings broke up before twelve or one in the morning. At first she found it difficult to adjust to this pattern but before long was praising her new way of life: "If you ask me what I seriously think of the Life at Paris, I will tell you fairly that, were I a French Woman I verily believe I should prefer it to that of London for many Reasons, but more particularly on the important Account of <u>Hours</u>, which are here regular and wholesome ones"(p131). The mornings, though, were not as convenient: "I cannot reconcile myself to Paris Mornings – they are by much too short for Comfort, and certainly for Correspondence"(p145), and "in point of Morning one is sadly bilked of it"(p131). As time wore on, though, the novelty wore off. By the third week of February she was writing: "You can't think how comfortable we all are when we English People meet at Night to talk over what we have seen in the Day, to Discard all Candour, and Unanimously to determine that <u>our own Country </u>is the only one to live in!"(p185)

If there is one thing she is consistently critical of throughout the diary it is the formality of visiting and meeting people. It was old-fashioned, she believed, just as it had been in England thirty or forty years before: stiff, dull, and heavy. She found the French excessively polite, with an abundance of ceremony and civility. Visits followed a certain format: "Image to yourself a Ceremony of five minutes upon the first coming in; the Curtsy begins at the Door, then the Lady of the House is to be addressed with Compliments and Speeches about nothing at all, then two or three more things are to be said for the good of the whole Circle, then little Jokes may be aimed at from one Side to the other of the Chimney Piece" (p88); "The women sit regularly in a Circle, and rise at the arrival of every Mortal; so the Bows, Curtsies, and Speeches on setting off are so much more numerous than with us"(p125). It wasn't long before Mrs Crewe tired of visiting. "I hate the Ceremony of formal visits", she wrote; and ""a pure cold and heavy Duty it was"(p97). She described them as "a heavy Tax upon the Time of a Stranger"(p107), and said it was "an Exertion to keep up regular Conversation"(p111). Back in England she was a great hostess herself, inviting the great and the good into her home, so probably felt able to comment on and judge the French way of doing things. She felt the French did not understand the management of such gatherings, claiming they had not been long used to conducting them. An important difference in France, she felt, was the lack of card tables, which would have helped break down large circles of people into smaller groups all of which would have their own flows of conversation. As it was, in a large circle conversation was limited to one person at a time, which meant that most people couldn't participate as much and the timid probably not at all. Although she made a great many visits during her stay, and received a number of people into her own apartments, it's very clear her preference was to mix and talk with her own group of English people at supper time.

But if Mrs Crewe found comparatively small social gatherings tedious she had a different attitude towards larger gatherings. She first attended a rout, staged by Mrs Hobart on 2nd January. Somewhat similar to balls, routs tended to be more riotous though the diary, perhaps diplomatically, gives no indication of the extent of the riotousness on this occasion. Indeed, Mrs Crewe skips over what actually happened at this rout, other than reporting some conversations. Whatever it was she says that people did exactly as they chose and she liked it very well, as did everybody else. Just a few days later she was attending a more formal ball at Versailles, attended by the King and Queen, where again she greatly enjoyed herself: "You cannot conceive any thing more gay and brilliant than this Ball Room. It is ornamented with every thing that is festive, and illuminated in the best Manner. The Young Men and Women Dance in Quadrilles, and are Dressed in whatever is the most recherche"(p99). Two weeks later she was at Mrs Hobart's again, attending what she described this time as a really delightful fete. Once again she fails to give any description of the evening other than comparing it favourably with the formality of French gatherings. It would appear that comments had been made at some stage about her unwillingness to attend small groups whilst large gatherings attracted her: "many People wonder that I, who decline so, some small Parties, should yet rush into Crouds and not complain of Fatigue. but you are to know that I think the being jumbled with a number of other People is not half so harrassing as an Exertion to keep up regular Conversation with Strangers"(p111). The following week she was attending a ball at the home of the Comte de Caraman and on this occasion gives a little more detail. After arriving late and finding the company at supper she is rather graciously invited to join the meal at the table of the mistress of the house. Following a lengthy supper the gathering retired to the ballroom where she says she was vastly well entertained with the dancing: "Monsieur de Noailles shewed off very much in his Dance, and acquitted himself very well. He seems to be a leading Figure in the great World of Paris; but his Manners are so Coxcomical… The Dresses in general struck me as very like those I have seen at the Prince of Wales's Ball – and in point of Dancing, I could discover no Difference from our Cotillions, except that the Men keep on their Hats, and have upon the whole a much better Air than our Macaronies"(p135). She was not pleased, though, to be shown to a seat which she was expected to keep to all evening: "I could not help thinking the whole time that I liked a good honest English Ball much better. In the first place, every body with us has more Liberty than is permitted here"(p135). Dancing, she infers, is left to the young people, meaning those aged under 30, so she could only sit and watch. At the next large gathering she attended, in the Duchesse de Polignac's apartments at Versailles, she makes no reference to dancing, but describes a gathering of 80-100 people first of all taking supper and then milling about talking. Marie Antoinette's attendance at this party gave rise to a cutting remark from Mrs Crewe with regard to the Queen's dancing: "Her Figure was fine formerly, but it is become clumsy to a great Degree and, tho She is under Thirty, She has on this Account been obliged to give up Dancing, which She was very fond of"(p155). This was, perhaps, a little unfair of Mrs Crewe since she would have known that Marie Antoinette had given birth to her third child less than a year earlier; however, she would probably not have known the Queen was 4-5 months pregnant with her fourth child. The Duchesse de Polignac's was the last large party she attended though she was invited to two more: firstly to a ball given by Madame de Coigny, which would have started with dancing for the children to which she would have taken her five year old daughter Emma, and secondly to a ball given by the Duc and Duchesse de Castries. Unfortunately she was suffering from a feverish cold on the night of Madame de Coigny's ball so couldn't attend – unfortunate, too, for little Emma, who doesn't seem to have done much at all on this adventure with her mother and then misses out on the one big occasion when she might participate.

Mealtimes register as a major element of social intercourse throughout the diary – dinners, suppers and breakfasts tumble into each other day by day, a succession of invitations out and comfortable evenings at home. Breakfast would not have been taken until late morning since people didn't usually go to bed till the early hours. Dinner was always at 2.30 and supper from 10pm, often taken in a large gathering as a preliminary to a ball, a party or similar get-together. Supper parties were considered at this time to be the acme of good living. There was a particular craze among Parisians in the 1780s to adopt English fashions and this is touched on in several places. Mrs Crewe attended two breakfasts "a l'Angloise" and whilst it might be thought that this would have pleased her national pride, it didn't. For the first Lady Clermont had assembled some of the "very fine Folks of this Place" who were good humoured and willing to please, yet Mrs Crewe found that it was "not crouded enough to afford Amusement to a looker on"(p81). The second was at the Chevalier Jerningham's and consisted of twelve or fourteen people, which Mrs Crewe rather perversely – or as she might say "in a spirit of contradiction" – found too mixed and too crowded. At times there was no pleasing her! She also reports in several places on taking tea, already in the 1780s deemed to be an English tradition. "Last night Madame D'Andelot….. gave the English a Tea drinking at her House – For, you must know, they think here that we are never quite happy unless when we meet round a Table for that Purpose"(p129). On this occasion she found the arrangements old fashioned, as if copied from Samuel Richardson's novels *Pamela* and *Clarissa*, published forty years earlier. She also recounts an incident at Versailles where Lady Clermont had been invited to take tea with the King and Queen: "…the King then followed her, undertook the Management of part of the Tea Equipage, particularly that of the Lamp and Tea Kettle, which in the hurry Occasioned by his Civilities he threw Down; Spilling the Water upon her Gown, and the Oil upon the Floor" (p193). It's an interesting insight to know that tea was made at the table rather than fetched in ready-made by servants, and that a particular "tea kettle" was used, heated over a flame fuelled by oil. Such details can be of interest to us today, yet Mrs Crewe fails to give us much information on the food she ate or the drink she took. She refers to eating boiled chicken quietly at home one evening and of taking some cold meat at Versailles; there is a reference to a supper where "I sat for an hour or two very well satisfied with looking at what presented itself before my Eyes in the Shape of Cookery or Desert"(p155); but this apart we don't know how well catered for she was in relation to food. Nor is she any more forthcoming on drink. It's interesting to note that besides tea the French also drank coffee, taken, it would seem, after dinner(p107). She makes no complaint on the quality of food or drink but does draw attention to the water: "Apropos – the Water here disagrees with many People, and, if ever you come to Paris, pray remember that Circumstance and put Lemon peel into it"(p87). Alcoholic drinks are referred to only in passing, when she asserts the possession of good wines as a stamp of a man of elegance, and that drunkenness amongst Parisians is caused by "Spirituous Liquors which do not Deaden their Anger so much as our thick Porter would"(p195). Of the many meals she attended two are worth a brief mention. Firstly, a small dinner party for five or six people she was invited to at the home of an English couple, Doctor Lee and his wife – there is a nice touch when she writes of trying to find out what she might take as a present, much the same as people often take small gifts when they go out to dinner today. The second dinner was in sharp contrast at the home of the young Duc and Duchesse de Castries – Mrs Crewe reports that he kept a public table and people poured in very fast "and the Sort of Scramble which they all seemed to make for Place's reminded me very much of a common Ordinary at a Race"(p157), a common ordinary being a meal prepared at a fixed rate for all comers.

Another topic that occupied Mrs Crewe a great deal during her stay was how to dress fashionably. From the beginning she was concerned to be safe from ridicule: "What a puzzling Matter Dress is become within these two or three years: All the old Laws belonging to it are repealed, so that many a poor Body, who has not much Judgement or Taste, Sins more innocently, and is laughed at for an Affectation of her own, tho her appearing so uncouthly proceeds merely from Ignorance, or Indolence and letting the Milliner decide"(p95). Her saviour was Lady Clermont who advised not only what to wear but who to buy from: designer labels were as important in the 18th century as they are in the 21st! Lady Clermont's advice was good but never ending: "I have a great respect for her, and think highly of her Virtues, but all the long Lessons and Lectures She gives me about Dress do, I must own, wear one to a Mummy!"(p89). The tradespeople tested her patience as well with tiresome explanations about breadths of lace and shapes of sleeves. One of the leading fashion icons of Paris was Mademoiselle Bertin, much favoured by the Queen and subsequently used by many fashionable leaders of society. Mrs Crewe is taken to the workshop of Mademoiselle Bertin, of which she gives a humorous description though doesn't say if she purchased anything. She injects a sense of the ridiculous into Mademoiselle Bertin's pomposity and follows this up at a later date when attending a ball at the Caraman's – also attending this ball was the Baroness de Stael, daughter of Jacques Necker, who appeared wearing a dress made by Mademoiselle Bertin. The dress was greatly talked about since Bertin asserted it expressed the genius of her father and the virtue of her mother; Mrs Crewe would have none of it, declaring that if it did so then it expressed itself in a language that she, for one, didn't understand. Constant analysis of fashion irritated her: "I by no means desire or think that it is necessary to talk on very wise or learned Subjects – I only mean to say, that almost all Subjects are tiresome, if discussed every day and for Hours together, and that that of Dress in particular is surely a very barren One after a few things have been said upon it." (p149). Nor was it just women's fashion that upset her – she felt that men's pre-occupation with their dress led to a loss of dignity and she aimed a particular salvo at the fashion in buttons, which made her "quite Sick!" It would seem that men's buttons each carried a letter of the alphabet: "You must puzzle for two Hours sometimes about the Name of one of their Common Women. The Anagram is spread all round him, and, look which way you will, this Name or sane Motto /which perhaps, When Descyphered, is not fit to be read/ you are to talk of Afterwards" (p149). Yet for all her criticisms she clearly valued the clothes she bought and couldn't wait to get back to England with them: "I long to Feel at home – to make Enquiries after old Crewe Hall – to Prepare for the Journey thither in Summer, when I shall Shew off with my Paris Fashions"(p183).

The diary provides some interesting insights into the modes and difficulties of transport in 1786. Adverse comment is made on the narrowness of Parisian streets, which frequently caused coaches to back up and scrape wheels with each other. She refers to a traffic jam of carriages that built up as she made her way to the Louvre, where she arrived with some difficulty, and an another occasion, at Versailles, she grew frightened to drive through the streets alone since they were so full of people. The narrowness of the streets flurried Mrs Crewe, as did the driving of young men who dashed about in their one-horse cabriolets like "Chariotteers", making awkward and dangerous imitations, according to Mrs Crewe, of the English skill in coachmanship. She found the French coaches she had to travel in to be "odious", even if she conceded the coachmen drove safely enough. As the weather continued "sloppy" for some time, though, she came to appreciate she was always under cover when alighting from a coach. This was in contrast with the customary use of sedan chairs in London – a mode of travel not taken up in Paris – from which people were "obliged to Wade through Part of a Street or up a Flight of Steps"(p193), which could be damaging to silk shoes and long dresses. There was something similar to a sedan chair in Paris but she couldn't quite find a name for it: "I am carried in an odd Sort of Vehicle across the Court"(p193). If Mrs Crewe was not enthusiastic about her means of transport in France then she gives us good evidence to explain why. On no fewer than three occasions she was involved in accidents, each of which shook her nerves. The first occurred little more than a week after arrival when, travelling at speed in a post chaise, one of her horses tumbled down, throwing off the postillion and bringing the coach to a sudden stop, which left the passengers too frightened to open the door and get out. Three weeks later another horse fell down, just as they were crossing the Bridge of Sèvres, leaving her stuck with her maid on the bridge for three quarters of an hour: "both terrified to Death, because we were on so narrow a part of it that every Carriage which came by gave us a Shock, as if it meant to tip us over into the Seine"(p139). But the worst accident occurred on her way home, travelling the route from Paris to Calais. Mrs Crewe reported the roads to be good but her carriage was very heavy, pulled by horses driving three abreast, and the weight put a great deal of pressure on the horses as they drove downhill. One horse sought to escape the weight pushing from behind by heading for the side of the road and in so doing overturned the coach into a pit. Mrs Crewe and her brother Charles were thrown across the carriage, her brother contriving not to land on top of her. Rescue from their overturned carriage came from their servants, travelling behind, and some local farm workers helped persuade the carriage into an upright position once more. The accident left Mrs Crewe badly shaken but determined to overcome the fears it induced: "for several Stages after our Accident I hardly could bear the Appearance of a Hill, or the Sensation which the Chaise gave me when I inclined at all on one Side. But Heaven be praised! a good Night's Rest and a little Exertion of Mind have restored me again to the State I was in"(p207). Nevertheless, she was uneasy for the remainder of the journey, and back in England travelled behind the heavy carriage in a lighter chaise.

Conclusion

In this introduction I have described Mrs Crewe's family and social background, and highlighted some of the events and customs that were important to her and are of interest to us today. But there is much more to find in her diary: her descriptions and opinions of doctors, customs house officials, the weather, gardens, shopping and so on. Mrs Crewe was a lively observer, opinionated, patriotic and, though it doesn't come out in the diary, still beautiful enough to be courted by men from both sides of the channel. The result is a unique document that can be enjoyed at least as much today as it was in the eighteenth century.

THE DIARY

OF

FRANCES ANNE CREWE

Frances Anne Crewe
By John Downman

A Journal

kept at Paris from

December 24ᵗʰ 1785 to March 15ᵗʰ 1786[1]

by

F.A.C.

Je n'enseigne point, je raconte.[2]
                    Montaigne

1 the original front page says the the diary runs from December 24th 1785 to March 10th 1786, when in fact it starts on December 26th and ends on March 15th.

2 Je n'enseigne point, je raconte: I do not teach, I recount – Michel Eyquem de Montaigne, 1533-92, French essayist who laid the foundation for the English essay, as developed by Bacon, Cowley and Dryden.

3 she had travelled to Spa and Brussels first, before moving on to Paris.

4 From Shakespeare's Hamlet, Act 3 Scene 4, lines 116-118:
> *"Alas! how is't with you,*
> *That you do bend your eye on vacancy*
> *And with th' incorporal air do hold discourse?"*

5 tournure – shape, form.

6 The Rue Universite, on the south bank of the Seine, running parallel with the river.

7 Her mother was Frances Greville, born Frances Macartney in the 1720s. She died in 1789. See The Introduction pp.10-13

8 Mrs Crewe's brother, he was 24 years old at this time and a Captain in the army. Born 2nd November 1762, he married 31st March 1793 Lady Charlotte Bentinck, daughter of the 3rd Duke of Portland. He died 26th August 1832. For further information see the Introduction pp31-32.

9 Frances Fortescue, Countess Clermont, 1734-1820, the eldest daughter and co-heiress of Colonel John Murray, M.P., married in 1752 William Henry Fortescue, first Baron and Earl of Clermont, 1722-1806. She was a great friend of Mrs Crewe and Georgina Duchess of Devonshire. Masters writes of them together at Tunbridge Wells in 1778: "The vileness of Tunbridge Wells was however alleviated by the company of Lady Clermont, Mrs Crewe, and the seven-months pregnant Lady Melbourne, and they managed to pass the time in games of whist and a frolic called 'laugh and lay down, which is in great vogue amongst us'. At one of these parties, Mrs Greville, it seems, added to the fun by setting her head on fire. It was the ladies' condition which attracted most attention, for they were either with child or doing their best to become so, the Tunbridge waters being expected to aid pregnancy once established, or to prevent it if threatened. Georgiana reported on 26 October that Lady Clermont had miscarried, adding the delicious gossip, "To tell you the truth as it is pretty certain Mr Marsden the apothecary was the Father, I fear some wicked method was made use of to procure abortion, and this is more likely as Mr Marsden might bring the drogue from his own shop. You will allow that her toothache was very symptomatical, tho she carryd the affair off with her usual art." (Masters) In November 1775 she was writing to the Duchess of Devonshire from Paris: "I am quite a court lady, receive civilitys from everybody, and particularly the Queen. She

Advertisement. ~

The following Journal was written in letters to a Friend, and blended with other Matter; but, upon being told that it would be easy to separate and make it unite with what had been before written at Spa, and Bruſsells,[3] I have had it copied fair, and mean that it should be considered as a Sequel to the others. Tho it aſsumes the Appearance of a Journal, many Allowances are to be made, as it was not originally so. For apparent Inconsistences, and for Faults which arose from the Indulgence I felt certain to receive – But I know not why I apologise – It will be read only by those Friends who have partially called for it, and I am rather intitled to Credit for so dangerous a Compliance with their Request, than answerable for any of its Defects.

To a Friend

Paris December 26th 1786

You are very good to approve of the Nonsense I have already written at Spa and Bruſsells in the Journal way, and I am much flattered by your desiring me to continue it for You – To say the Truth I begin to tire of Journalising in the Manner I have done, and wish no longer –
  "To bend my Mind on Vacancy
  "And with th' incorporal Air to hold Discourse[4]
and therefore, since I have your Permiſsion to addreſs myself to You, I will in future write what occurs to me in regular Epistles, which I shall send to you in Pacquets just as I feel inclined. Before I left England I promised to write as I have hitherto done for them all, but in doing so I have forever wondered at my own Impertinence, since it has very frequently happened that I have been forced to relate such minute Events as can hardly even be interesting to any one dear Friend! All this I must desire you to take as a Sort of Dedication – It is one of the very few from which Compliments are excluded – however, as I am at Paris, you shall have a French tournure[5] instead, for I will aſsure you with great truth that all I feel that is kind or flattering, has been long written in my Heart.

*sent me a coach the other day to go a hunting; when she got off her horse she came up
to the coach, made me get out and carry'd me to see the wild Bore and the King, who
by the way is not so wild as I thought he was." "You would laugh if you were to see
me here, I am ashamed when any English are present, it is not to be described, the
rought the King and Queen made about me, and of course all the courtiers".
(Devonshire, pp28-9). The Chevalier de Boufflers described her in 1786 as fat
(Webster, p211).*

*10 Richard Colley Wellesley, 2nd Earl of Mornington (1760-1842) of Dungan
Castle, County Meath, the eldest son of Lady Mornington; educated at Eton and
Oxford, he succeeded as the 2nd Earl of Mornington in 1781. He played an active
and ambitious part in Irish politics, entering Parliament in 1784 but disappointing
his friends by his failure to speak through nervousness. In Paris with his mother at
the time of Mrs Crewe's visit he returned early to London for the new Parliament and
took part in the debate on Richmond's fortifications plans on 27th February, voting
with the Administration. Pitt, who was favourably disposed towards him, appointed
him to the Treasury Board in September 1786. He sat in Parliament for Beeralston
in 1787, Windsor in 1790 and Old Sarum in 1796; he was appointed governor-
general in India in 1797; he was created the Marquis of Wellesley in 1799. He was
made ambassador to Spain in 1809, Foreign Secretary from 1809-1812 and Lord
Lieutenant of Ireland 1821-28 and 1833-34. His book Dispatches, about his time
in India, was published in 1836-7. At the time of the diary he was 26 years old,
and it may well have been on this trip he first met his future wife, Hyacinthe
Gabrielle Roland. She was a girl of modest means, frequently seen promenading in
the Palais Royal and said to be free with her favours to men. Vigée Le Brun painted
her in 1791. The two were not married until 1794 but by that time had produced
three children. As an interesting footnote, the couple were the great-great-great
grandparents of Britain's Queen Elizabeth II (Goodden, pp57-8).*

*11 Mr Wellesley was probably William Wellesley-Pole, 1763-1851, the second son
of Lady Mornington; he succeeded his brother Richard as 3rd Earl Mornington and
2nd Viscount Wellesley in 1842; he was educated at Eton and became a naval officer,
taking the additional name of Pole in 1778 when he succeeded to a cousin's estates; he
sat as an MP from 1790-94 and 1801-21; he was Secretary to the Admiralty in
1807 and Chief Secretary for Ireland from 1809-1812; he was Master of the Mint,
with a seat in the Cabinet from 1814-23, and Postmaster-general 1834-35. He
married in 1784, and since there is no mention of his wife in Paris, it is possible that
the Mr Wellesley referred to could be his brother Arthur who would have been only
17 or his brother Gerald who was only 16.*

*12 she visited Paris with her mother in 1773, staying with Madame du
Deffand, a friend of Horace Walpole. Letters sent from Madame du Deffand
to Walpole at this earlier time are given in Appendix Six.*

Paris

Monday Even:ʒ ~ Hotel du Rome - Rue Universite [6]

Monday 26th December 1785

We arrived here the day before Yesterday, and found my Mother[7] and Brother Charles[8] in this Hotel, which is large enough to contain us all. They have spacious Apartments with Drawing Rooms and Antichambers up Stairs; and we have some below that are really magnificent, and furnished in a very clean commodious Manner – Dinner was served up just as we arrived, and Lady Clermont[9] came in five minutes after to give us welcome. – Yesterday morning was paſsed in receiving Meſsages of Civility and settling Engagements for the Week. In the Evening Lady Mornington, and Lady Ann Wellsley, Mr. Richd. Burke, Miſs Payne, and Mr. Labord were admitted. Lord Mornington,[10] Mr. Wellsley,[11] and our Family Party, which is now pretty large, all supped very comfortably together. and Now, if I dared hazard an opinion on the Subject so soon after my Arrival, I should certainly say that the Pleasantest Life one can lead in Paris is the devoting the Mornings to the seeing of Sights, and at Night meeting with our English Acquaintance to talk them all over in this Manner – I mean if one does not intend to reside so long as to become acquainted with the Inhabitants – But it is a Life which I fear, it will be impoſsible for me to lead, as I was here thirteen years ago,[12] and my Mother has a numerous Acquaintance from whom I must receive Civilities.

Tuesday Evening

Tuesday 27th December 1785

Mr. Crewe, my Brother Charles and I, walked some time this Morning in the Palais Royalle Gardens – The Scene there is the busiest and most entertaining I ever saw – There are Shops of every kind, and in short, it

13 Mrs Crewe describes the innocent side of the Palais Royal but doesn't see, or more likely chooses not to refer to, its more libidinous aspect. See the Introduction, pp45-47.

14 Armand Charles Augustin, Duc de Castries, 1756-1842. His father, the Marquis, was Secretary of War, and his father-in-law the Duc de Guines. During the revolution he attracted attention because of a duel with Charles de Lameth following an argument about the political situation and soon after left for England. Here he raised a corps of émigrés which, in 1795 was despatched to Portugal. He returned to France in 1814 following the restoration of the monarchy.

15 Marie Louise Philippine, Duchesse de Castries, sister to Madame de Juigné and daughter to the Duc de Guines, married 1778. She visited Strawberry Hill, with her father and her sister, in 1783, when Walpole described them as extremely natural, agreeable and civil. She died in 1796.

16 From Shakespeare's <u>Hamlet</u>, Act 5 scene 1, line 226.

17 Louis Jules Mancini, Duc de Nivernais, 1716-1797 – Nivernois to Mrs Crewe. He had served as Ambassador to London, Rome and Berlin, was popular, well cultured and attractive. Vigée Le Brun wrote: "The Duc de Nivernais who is always quoted as the model of a cultured, refined sensibility, was also dignified and gentle in his manner without being in the least bit affected. He was especially noted for the respect he showed to women, of whatever age.... [he] was a small, thin man. Although very advanced in years when I made his acquaintance he was still extremely vivacious."(Memoirs, p63) Lord Chesterfield urged his son to spend time with the Duc: "I do not know a better model for you to form yourself upon... He will show you what manners and graces are" (Webster, p123). He acted, painted, composed music and verses, played the violin very well, yet still had time to acquit himself well in the Army. Though married when only fourteen for the greater part of his life he maintained a relationship with Madame de Rochefort. His wife died in 1782. His house in Paris was in the Rue de Tournon, which ran from the Seine to the Luxembourg Gardens. He had also a country house at Saint Ouen, 5 miles north of Paris, which is indulgently described by Webster: "Nothing more enchanting can be imagined than this country-house ...on the banks of the Seine ...Birds were the particular passion of the duke, and he loved them so much that he could not bear to shut them up in cages, so he hit upon an original device for keeping them near him. Close to the chateau was a little wood through which a stream wandered, and over the whole of this the duke had almost invisible wire netting stretched, covering the treetops and so transforming the wood into an immense aviary... the duke's writing-table and bookcase were arranged at the foot of a tree in the middle, and quantities of birds were turned loose inside the netting. Here the dear old man sat peacefully at work every morning." (Webster, p.185) When the revolution came he stayed out of trouble until 1794 when he was thrown into prison and had his estates seized. He was due to be guillotined but the page containing his name was torn from the register and he survived long enough to see the end of the terror and eventual release. He died three years later.

is full of Shews and Sights which give it the Appearance of a large Fair –
One may go up Stairs and down Stairs, or under the Piazzas, or into the
Gardens: All is a Scene of Gaiety and Busineſs, and Chearfullneſs![13] –
Mr. Labord came and dined with us to day: and since he went I have had
here the Duc,[14] and Ducheſse de Castries,[15] two young People whom I
knew in England, and, who seem from the obliging Offers and fine
Speeches, which they have just been making, to have resolved upon
being very civil to us.   I have poſitively determined however on not
making my public Entry, till I have rested myself a few Days; for my
Head turns round with all that I have heard and seen already about the
Paris World, and the Etiquettes which are to be observed concerning
Dreſs &c. – Lady Clermont gives herself great trouble about Trades
people whom I must use, and fashions which I must follow – I am, you
may be sure very glad of this, as it saves me from it all. I have begged of
her however to let me be safe from Ridicule in the Article of Dreſs, but
she tells me, that there is much leſs risque of that here than in London,
where more latitude is allowed with Respect to Age – Apropos to this,
Mrs. Hobart called on my Mother yesterday Morning, and by what I saw,
and the Oddities I have been told of her, She seems to be performing
the same Ridiculous Part on this Stage which She has so long appeared
in on the London one, and with as much Perseverance too as ever. Poor
Woman! Such sort of People, who seem born to divert the World, and
yet live upon it's Indulgence make one at Moments feel quite
melancholy! "but it were considering too curiously to consider so."[16] –

near 10 O'Clock – same evening

Just as I had written thus far in walked Lady Clermont and my Mother,
who had been paying some Visits – And in five minutes after them, the
Duc de Nivernois,[17] and then Madame de Castries' Sister Madame de
Juine[18]. The Duc de Nivernois made a Million of fine Speeches about
my dining at his House on Thursday next: but I told him, I had said I
should not go out this Week after two O'Clock, and that I was besides
under the Neceſsity of receiving my Friends. Mr. Crewe, my Mother, and
Brother Charles will go, and that, I think, may satisfy him. Oh how I
hate grand Entertainments: – Lady Clermont has been teizing me the
whole Evening about going to Versailles, and God knows where with
her, All this must be done, She says – and, as food for Curiosity, I shall
like it well enough in a few Days – At present it by no means accords
with my Ideas of Amusement. No. No. and my head has ach'd too much
to enjoy any thing long.~

18 Marie Louise, wife of the Comte de Juigné; married 1782, died 1792.

*19 Marie Anne Gabrielle Josephe Francoise Xaviere de Caraman, sister to
Madame de Cambis - she had married the Comte de Caraman in 1750.*

*20 Gabrielle Francoise Charlotte Cambis, 1729-1809, sister to Madame de
Caraman and niece to Madame de Mirepoix; married in 1755 the Vicomte de
Cambis. She had been the mistress of the Duc de Lauzun, a Parisian Casanova,
who had also been a lover of Madame de Genlis. Cambis went on to become mistress
of the Duke of Richmond. In the 1760s she was part of a gambling frenzy and had
joined with Madame de Boufflers and Madame de Boisgelin to form an inseparable
trio. By 1786 she would appear to have left her wild ways behind. It was said she
had a particularly subtle wit. In October 1789 she emigrated to England, taking a
house on Richmond Green in 1791, where she died in 1809.*

*21 Louisa Clarges, 1760-1809. Born out of wedlock to a pensioned-off mistress
Louisa Skrine had a poor start to life. Her mother died before she was six years old
and her stepfather had spent a large fortune. Nevertheless she became noted for her
musical abilities, adept at the harpsichord and with an exquisitely trained soprano
voice; she was also delicately beautiful, sprightly, and playful. With such attractions
she captured the heart of 26-year-old Sir Thomas Clarges who, five years earlier had
been rejected by another beautiful singer, Elizabeth Linley, who went on to marry
Sheridan. During the years of her marriage she is described as a laughing, giddy girl,
beautiful, heedless and silly, but good-natured and dedicated to her music; but it was a
brief marriage, lasting only five years, Sir Thomas dying in 1782, leaving behind him
not only his wife but also four children. He also left her very rich. Within three
months of his death she set off for the continent, accompanied by Mary Carter, where
they travelled for nearly three years, during which they met Mrs Crewe in Paris. Mrs
Crewe had met her in London two years earlier and though her description of Lady
Clarges as "very amiable and interesting" is not enthusiastic she nevertheless appears
comfortable with her and is pleased to be able to leave her mother in her company. On
her return from abroad Louisa Clarges set up home in Mayfair's South Street and
Molly Carter in the nearby Hill Street. Lady Clarges never re-married but continued
to devote her life to her children and continued throughout her life with her passion for
music. She died at the age of 49 and was buried in Petersham, Surrey. The best
account of her life is given in Betty Rizzo's Companions without vows.*

*22 Susannah Goulburn, eldest daughter of William, 4ᵗʰ Viscount Chetwynd,
married Munbee Goulburn, 1782. Though the marriage lasted only 8 years, ending
with his death in 1790, they had three children: Edward, Henry and Frederick.
Henry was the most successful, an MP 1808-56, serving as Chancellor of the
Exchequer in 1828-30 and 1841-46, and Home Secretary 1834-5. She lived to
1818. Her husband's family, originally from Cheshire, had settled in Jamaica in the
17ᵗʰ century. Munbee Goulburn was sent from Amity Hall in Jamaica to be educated
at Eton and Oxford and afterwards resided in London at Portland Place.*

Thursday Morn.⁸

Thursday 29ᵗʰ December 1785

Soon after Breakfast Yesterday my Mother and I walked a great while about the Palais Royal, We then called at Madame de Caraman's[19] and at Madame de Cambise's.[20] They are Sisters, whose Society I remember to have been very fond of when I was last at Paris. The House of the former is large and Spacious indeed: and so it ought to be, for it contains a Family that sit down fourteen to Dinner every Day. By the Way, this Custom at Paris is much more like what one meets with in Dublin than London, when an Elder son Marries, he brings his Wife to live at the Paternal House; and it frequently happens that there are four of five Families living together in one Hotel. Madame de Cambise is a Sensible and agreeable Woman, much liked by some of my Friends in England. ~

My Aſsembly last Night consisted of Lady Clarges, Miſs Carter (who is with her) Mʳˢ. Goldburne, Mʳ. Hales (Secretary of the Embaſsy) and the Duc de Guines: I felt very happy on seeing Lady Clarges[21] – We had not met for two Years, and there is something in her, I think, very amiable and interesting – Mʳˢ. Goldburne[22] is a beautifull Woman, about two and twenty, who has been some time I find, on the Continent – She is a Daughter of Lord Chetwynd's, and is Married to a strange West Indian, they say, who makes her Life unhappy. I never saw her before, and was last Night really Struck with her Beauty, which seems to be of the Right Sort in the great Points of Features, Countenance, and Figure. They may say what they please but a handsome English Woman is a thousand times superior to a handsome Foreigner – I have seen nothing like Mʳˢ· Goldburne since I left England – Mʳ. Hailes was likewis a perfect stranger to me till last Night – all I could make out of him was, that he seemed to be a civil good sort of Softly Character. Miſs Carter my other new Acquaintance: and who lives with Lady Clarges, is certainly one of the most independant People I ever saw, but good humoured singular and sensible. The Duc de Guines (our old Ambaſsador) staid with me some time after they were all gone. He spoke in most flattering Terms of our poor Country, and we afterwards talked about the Rage here for Animal Magnetism; and he mentioned two or three such proofs of its Effects, as would have made my Hair stand on End, if I could have admitted them – He confeſsed that like all other Systems, it had bewildered the Imagination and produced much absurd Doctrine and many Lies, "but says he, without

79

23 Franz Anton Mesmer, 1734-1815, a German physician whose system of therapeutics, known as mesmerism, was the forerunner of hypnotism. Mesmer suggested in 1766 that the gravitational attraction of the planets affected human health by affecting an invisible fluid in the human body. In 1775 he revised his theory of Animal Gravitation to one of Animal Magnetism where the invisible fluid in the body reacted to magnetism. According to Mesmer, Animal Magnetism could be activated by any magnetized object and manipulated by any trained person. Disease, he believed, was the result of obstacles in the fluid's flow through the body, and these obstacles could be broken by trance states, which often ending in delirium or convulsions. This would restore the harmony of personal fluid flow. Mesmer devised various therapeutic treatments to achieve harmonious fluid flow, and in many of these treatments he was a forceful and dramatic personal participant. However, the nature of his treatments attracted disbelief and criticism. His consulting rooms in Paris were dimly lighted and hung with mirrors. The sick sat "mesmerized" around a vat of chemicals, iron filings, and crushed glass, holding hands or joined by a cord, maintaining an unbroken circuit. Dressed as a magician, Mesmer glided among them to the sound of soft music, making mysterious passes. There were more convulsions than cures, but enough cures for the French government to offer Mesmer a yearly sum for his "secret.". Curious and desperate Parisians ensured a highly lucrative practice but his methods continued to attract the antagonism of the medical profession, and in 1784 Louis XVI appointed a commission of scientists, with Franklin, Guillotin, and Lavoisier among its members, to investigate Mesmer's methods. A report stated: "Decisive experiments have demonstrated that imagination apart from magnetism produces convulsions, and that magnetism without imagination produces nothing. . . . The animal magnetic fluid . . . is non-existent." Women, said a secret report, were especially susceptible to men such as Mesmer; and in their case the sensations experienced were at least in part erotic, making his methods objectionable. Denounced as a fraud, Mesmer eventually left France, taking his fortune with him. Whatever may be said about his system, Mesmer did often achieve a close rapport with his patients and seems to have alleviated certain nervous disorders. More importantly, the further investigation of the trance state by those who followed after him eventually led to the development of legitimate applications of hypnotism.

24 An acquaintance from her visit to Spa. Like her he moved on to Paris, but after a very short time there found himself in trouble. On February 8th 1786 the Duke of Dorset wrote from Versailles to the Duchess of Devonshire "Roger Damas, brother to Charles Damas, fought a duel the other day with the young Comte de Broglie, the latter was very much wounded par deux bons coups d'épée, but is out of danger. They quarrelled about a flower which fell from M^{de} de Coigny's nosegay, and which poor flower Roger Damas picked up and insisted upon throwing the dice upon. They were playing at Hazard, chez la Duchesse de Lorgnes." (Bessborough, p106).

being an Enthusiast I must believe it has great Powers" – –   He added that Mesmer[23] had made a dangerous Use of his Science, but that a Man of Consequence, (whose Title and name I forget) had studied it so as to be usefull to his Fellow Creatures, and that, as he was a Friend of his, he would ask him some Day before I left Paris, to exhibit before me some of its Effects. – The Duc de Guines aſured me he had often seen "People put into the Sort of Sleep which the Somnambules have, – that he had seen them write Letters in that State, – and in Short appear at the time just as Lady Macbeth is represented to be on our Stage. ~ But all this, he tells me I shall see myself, if he can prevail upon his old Friend to invite me to his Bacquet – which is a Tub, which they sit round, and from which Iron Tubes are directed to the Body. ~ My Mother supped last Night at Madame la Marechalle de Mirpoix's but I declined going, and indeed I wish to escape from Suppers, if poſsible. This morning I am going to a Breakfast Lady Clermont Says she has made for us. I will tell you all about it when I return.~

The same Evening

My Mother, Mr. Crewe, and Charles, are gone to dine with the Duc de Nivernois. I have eat my boiled Chicken quietly at home; for my Cold continues very bad, and I am not able to bear much Fatigue. after we had got some Air in the Morning we went to Lady Clermont's Breakfast a L'angloise, which I thought a bad busineſs enough, because I knew hardly any body there, and it was not crouded enough to afford Amusement to a looker on. She had aſsembled some of the very fine Folks of this Place, who all seemed good humoured and willing to be pleased. I thought Monsieur Damas,[24] my Spa Acquaintance, was there – He and I mustered up several little Jokes about poor old D'Adhemar,[25] which kept us going for some time: and in short, we all behaved vastly well, taking "Abundance of Pains, (as the woman in the Farce says,) <u>to be easy</u>".[26] The only Englishmen I perceived were Lord Downe and Mr. Byng. They are both young Men upon their travels I believe, but I don't know. The Ducheſse de Castries told me her Father the Duc de Guines beg'd we would dine with him next week, and Intended sending a regular Invitation – And the Duc de Castries desired we would dine at the Marechall his Father's when we went to see Versailles. All this and much more, I fancy, must be done during our stay at Paris. I fear it; and yet there is something ungratefull in not feeling pleased with Civilities of this Sort; I might almost say, brutal; but the Truth is, I have so unfortunate an Indolence of Disposition that I confeſs I should much prefer a Sight of Paris and It's Neighbourhood in a more quiet Way. ✗ [27]

25 Jean Balthazar, Comte d'Adhemar was the French Ambassador to London from 1783, said by Nathaniel Wraxall to be far inferior to his counterpart in Paris, Lord Dorset (Wraxall, p.620), perhaps because he was not a professional diplomat but a placement for one of the factions at work in Versailles. He was said to be fashionable at one time, one of his attributes being the ability to sing and play the harp at the same time. He was also comical and wrote delightful verses. The Duchess of Devonshire was amused by him and reported in a letter to her mother (October 1785) "...D'Adhémar was forbid Lord Parker's house for having put his leg on L^y P's lap. When it was once there, as he had the palsey in it, he c^d not get it back again, and when she was in a passion about it he s^d: c'est que je voulez m'allonger..." [I wanted to stretch it] (Bessborough,p101). Politically d'Adhemar was favoured by the Polignac family but he was opposed by the Queen.

26 this probably comes from The widow bewitched(1730) a comedy by John Motley, though the line only reads "abundance of pains" without the reference to being easy.

27 For the first time a symbol resembling a cross appears at the end of the entry, which was used in the eighteenth century, just as it is today, as a sign of a kiss, either of love or affection. From this point on it appears regularly.

28 She is referring to Armand-Marie-Jacques de Chastenet, Marquis de Puységur, who published his book Mémoires pour servir à l'histoire et à l'establissement du magnètisme animal in 1784.

29 James Burnett, Lord Monboddo, published The origin and progress of language in 6 volumes between 1773 and 1792. Considered a learned but eccentric work it nevertheless anticipated Darwin's theory regarding an affinity between humans and monkeys.

30 from Shakespeare's Macbeth, Act 5, Scene 1, line 79
'Foul whisperings are abroad. Unnatural deeds
Do breed unnatural troubles; infected minds
To their deaf pillows will discharge their secrets.
More needs she the divine than the physician."

31 From Shakespeare's Hamlet, Act 5 scene 1, line 228.

32 Count Alessandro di Cagliostro, 1743-95, an Italian charlatan, born into a poor background, his real name was Giuseppe Balsamo. When thirteen years old he ran away from school, and was afterwards sent to the monastery of Caltagirone, where, a novice among apothecary monks, he picked up his scanty knowledge of chemistry and medicine. He soon made the monastery too hot for him, and in 1769 he set out to seek his fortune. In company with the Greek sage Althotas, he is vaguely represented as travelling in parts of Greece, Egypt, and Asia. At Rome he married a very pretty woman, Lorenza Feliciani, who became a skilful accomplice in his schemes, and in

Friday Morning

Friday 30th December 1785

The Duc de Guines sent his Friends the Marquis de Puisagenes' Book upon Animal Magnetism[28] Yesterday, and as I dined alone, I amused myself with dipping into it the early part of the Evening. He treats first of Mesmer and his Discoveries, and after paying great Compliments to his vast Genius and Capacity as the Father of such a Science he relates the several Cures which he himself had affected at his own Country House. This Book has to a common Mind, at least to mine, all the Appearance of being written by a Bedlamite! Lord Monbboddo's on the origin of Language[29] does not strike me as more extravagant than this excentric Writer, in the Instances he gives of Cures which he has performed by Magnetism on the human <u>Mind</u> as well as the Body! He not only makes People sleep like Lady Macbeth but discovers all their Secrets, like her, to whosoever happens to be in the Room. This must sometimes breed strange Work, I should think, especially if any of them should "need more the Divine than the Physician"[30] – But this, I am told, is not all – he gives them the Gift of <u>Prophecy</u> – however I have not gone so far in this Book yet. Is it not too, extraordinary that such a Capital as Paris, with Men of real Science to Appeal to, should yet be found to tolerate such incoherent Stuff? Yet surely after what one has seen and heard of within these twenty Years concerning Electricity, Balloons, Diving Bells &c. it may be permitted us to follow those Philosophers a <u>little</u> way with "Modesty enough"[31] – beyond this they become Vexatious! – M^r. Richard Burke called in Yesterday Evening, and we both read together part of this Book, which we were as much amazed at as if it had been a Fairy Tale. He tells me that many of the fine People here used to go to Cagliostro,[32] a Man who has lately made much Noise in the Cardinal de Rohan's Affair[33] – He gave himself out as Two Thousand Years old, and I laughed heartily at a Conceit of his Servant who upon being questioned by the People at the Door as to his Master's real Age, said he could not pretend to ascertain it, for that he had only lived with him three hundred Years. His Master, it seems, played off his Part to the full as well, and frequently talked with the most unembarraſsed Familiarity of Heroes and other extraordinary Persons of Antiquity, with whom he formerly lived. – One Story I must tell you – it has diverted me extremely every time I have thought of it – "I happened to be in Judea, says he, exactly at the time that Christ flourished – We were both of us fond of the same Philosophial Pursuits, and above all attached from the Similarity between our great Objects, each of us striving to do all the Service he could to Mankind. – We often met in a Walk which led towards Mount Sion, and remember, perfectly well I said

1771 the pair set out on their wanderings, visiting Germany, London, Paris, Spain, Warsaw, and other European centres. Successful alike as physician, philosopher, alchemist, and necromancer, he carried on a lively business in his 'elixir of immortal youth', founded lodges of 'Egyptian freemasons', and at Paris in 1785 played a part in the affair of the Diamond Necklace, which lodged him for a while in the Bastille. In May 1789 he revisited Rome; on December 20, the Inquisition detected him founding 'some feeble ghost of an Egyptian lodge'. He was imprisoned, and condemned to death for freemasonry. His sentence was commuted to life imprisonment in the fortress of San Leone, near Urbino, where he died. Such is the usual account, made familiar by Carlyle's Miscellanies, *but his early history is somewhat obscure.*

33 this refers to the Affair of the Diamond Necklace – for an explanation see the Introduction, pages 41-44.

34 Mrs Crewe refers here to James Graham, 1745-94, a quack doctor. He studied medicine at Edinburgh, without qualifying, and spent some time in America. On returning to this country he began to advertise wonderful cures, first at Bristol and Bath and later in London. In London he established a 'temple of health and hymen' at The Adelphi, using electricity, milk baths and friction techniques to encourage fertility in women and to cure impotency in men. Queues of desperate women attended his establishment, some couples paying an exorbitant £50 to have sex in his 'celestial chamber, on his 'electromagnetic bed', while an orchestra played outside the room and a pressure-cylinder pumped in 'magnetic fire'. Patients were also expected to drink his patented elixir at a guinea a bottle. His establishments were supported by lectures that he gave and 20 publications he produced. Although denounced in the press as a charlatan he became fashionable, treating such eminent people – and friends of Mrs Crewe – as the Prince of Wales and the Duchess of Devonshire. He was imprisoned on several occasions for misdemeanours and in the end developed a fervour for religion, styling himself 'the servant of the Lord O.W.L' (Oh Wonderful Love). Though it isn't mentioned by Mrs Crewe he was in Paris in 1786 giving lectures.

35 Cocklane ghosts became a general phrase used to denote imagined terrors, arising from a scam set up in London's Cock Lane near Smithfield in 1762. William Parsons, the owner of number 33, claimed he heard knockings from the ghost of his sister in law Fanny Kent, who had recently died of smallpox. Initially he intended to blackmail her husband with a suggestion of murder but the story of a ghost caught the imagination of Londoners. The ghost became known as scratching Fanny and was said to have possessed the 11-year-old daughter of Parsons. Londoners became agog at this phenomenon and, headed by royalty and the nobility, attended the premises in their thousands, being allowed into the little girl's bedroom fifty at a time. Eventually a committee of eminent People, inluding Samuel Johnson, investigated the phenomenon and found that the knockings of the ghost derived from nothing more than a board that the child had secreted in her bed. Parsons was put in the pillory at the end of Cock Lane where the local people "treated him with compassion".

one Day to Jesus, faith you may say what you will my Friend, You certainly carry your Disinterestedneſs too far – Don't you see they will not believe you? Pray mark that Tree there! – well, depend upon it, all you will get by your fine Conduct will be to die upon that. – He would not believe me, but you all know it turned out just as I said it would! – Another Story leſs known is still more diverting I think: tho I protest I find some Difficulty mentioning it even here – it is that talking one Day in this same Style, he made the old observations concerning Genius in early Youth "– I known several said he who promised fair but disappointed all their Friends. and I have known the reverse, for I was at School with J,C – t and at that time "He was reckoned a very dull Boy indeed." – That there should be Refinements upon D^r. Graham[34] and Cocklane Ghosts[35] in this Place, where the Imagination runs riot upon every Subject, does not surprize me, but that there shoud be People of Consequence to <u>mix</u> in such Society, and in Short, that any thing should engage <u>general Attention</u> which seems to strike at the Root of <u>Common Sense</u>, is what one feels unwilling to credit. The Marechall de Mirpoix, Lady Clermont, and Madame de Cambise came also last Night. Madame de Cambise is a very agreeable pleasant Woman – She has a sort of independant Manner which I like very well, for with that She is very civil and good humoured. ✗

Saturday Morning

Saturday 31ˢᵗ December 1785

People dropped in as usual Yesterday in the Evening, for I am not yet well enough to undertake to do Violent things this miserable Weather – indeed I am not sorry to avail myself of so good an Excuse as a Weak State of Health for not going to several Parties which I have been invited to, and which I should think sadly tiresome. My Mother, my Brother Charles, and M^r. Crewe, all go their different Ways in an Evening – I receive whoever comes and we all meet at Supper to talk our Adventures over – By what we have hitherto related to each other I confeſs I can discover nothing very delightfull or curious in a Paris Life. The Mornings, which with us are looked upon as of great Importance to one's Comfort, last a very Short time in every House here; for the Hour of dining is half past two, and, few Societies break before twelve or one

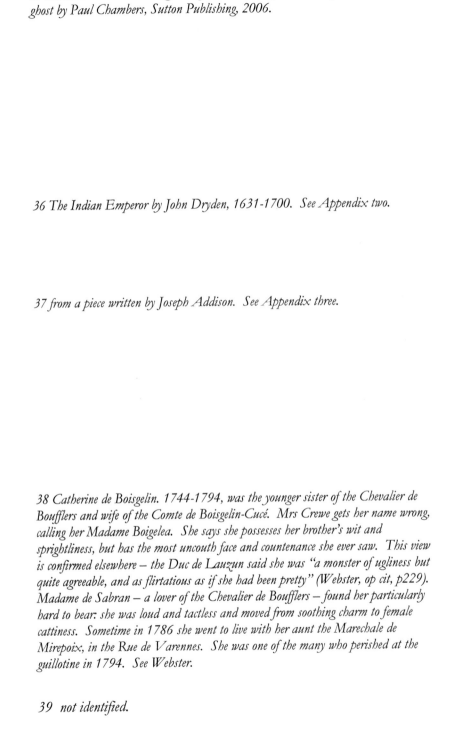

35 continued   As this book goes to press I note the publication of The Cock Lane ghost by Paul Chambers, Sutton Publishing, 2006.

36 The Indian Emperor by John Dryden, 1631-1700. See Appendix two.

37 from a piece written by Joseph Addison. See Appendix three.

38 Catherine de Boisgelin. 1744-1794, was the younger sister of the Chevalier de Boufflers and wife of the Comte de Boisgelin-Cucé. Mrs Crewe gets her name wrong, calling her Madame Boigelea. She says she possesses her brother's wit and sprightliness, but has the most uncouth face and countenance she ever saw. This view is confirmed elsewhere – the Duc de Lauzun said she was "a monster of ugliness but quite agreeable, and as flirtatious as if she had been pretty" (Webster, op cit, p229). Madame de Sabran – a lover of the Chevalier de Boufflers – found her particularly hard to bear: she was loud and tactless and moved from soothing charm to female cattiness. Sometime in 1786 she went to live with her aunt the Marechale de Mirepoix, in the Rue de Varennes. She was one of the many who perished at the guillotine in 1794. See Webster.

39 not identified.

O'Clock in the Morning. I don't see how it is poſsible that there should be much comfortable Intercourse before Dinner. At five in the Afternoon every body drives about to visit every body, and therefore those who are indolent, or sick or sorry, get many Visitors – After this Time, the Operas and Plays are resorted to: which in point of Convenience I am told, do not approach to ours; the Boxes, except a very few, being little scanty Seats, and it being with great Difficulty that People get away again. But all this I shall be better able to inform you of, when I shall have seen them myself   – And indeed I am determined to put down my Thoughts concerning every thing without fear or shame – I am aware I shall often write a great deal of Nonsense; but I am comforted for that by knowing that this is what You <u>wise</u> People always like, and I feel that it must be pleasant, to observe the Effect which great things have upon ignorant and <u>weak Minds</u>. – The great Effect of the Savage's Description of a Ship in a Play of Dryden's[36] is one proof of this, and there are many more equally strong, such as Moliere's old Woman, and the Bantam Ambaſsador in The Spectator.[37] Lady Clarges Miſs Carter, M[r]. W. Conway Lord Downe, Monsieur Damas, Madame Boigelea[38], and Miſs Payne[39] called Yesterday Evening. Lord Downe seems to be a very sensible pleasant Young Man, and I hear him well spoken of by every Body. Madame de Boiglea is Sister to the famous Chevalier Bouflers[38], and, I am told, poſseſses a great deal of his Wit and Sprightlineſs. – She ought to poſseſs something poor Woman! for to be sure a more uncouth Face and Countenance I never Saw. Lady Mornington sent here in the middle of the Evening to enquire who was the best Physician to apply too here, as Lady Ann has just been taken very ill. She is apt to be alarmed however, and I hope I shall hear to Day that her pretty Daughter is recovered. Apropos – the Water here disagrees with many People, and, if ever you come to Paris, pray remember that Circumstance and put Lemon peel into it. I have not seen the Duke of Dorset yet, but I hear a melancholy Account of him; Is it not very remarkable that both French and English Ambaſsadors should, nearly at the same time, fall ill of the same uncommon Disorder? They are very full here of a bon Mot they have made du Roi d'Angleterre. I have been asked fifty times, if it is true that His Majesty said, qu'il y Avoit <u>bon</u> <u>Intelligence</u> entre les deux Ambaſsadeurs

40 etrennes – new year's gifts.

41 Henry IV of France, 1553-1610.

42 L'Académie francaise, formed in 1635 and installed in The Louvre in 1672. The Académie's initial purpose was to perfect the French language and to this end they began the compilation of a dictionary, first published in 1694. In the latter half of the 18th century the Académie became the leader of literary opinion until interrupted by the revolution. It was suppressed in 1793, partially restored by Napoleon and restored with its original title in 1816.

43 Antoine Leonard Thomas, 1732-85, an impoverished and delicate poet who specialised in the eulogy. He was said to be particularly melancholy, often sitting through the dinners to which he was invited silent but for the occasional groan to himself. He wrote to one of his patrons, Suzanne Necker "When you have nothing better to do write and scold me. The subject is a good one, and you will find plenty of material." (Cronin, p143) Cronin says that posterity has unanimously scolded Thomas for turning out reams of versified drivel (p144). Nevertheless, Mrs Crewe was interested in "poor Monsieur Thomas, for I recollect liking every thing I have met with of his".

Monday - January 2ⁿᵈ.

Monday 2ⁿᵈ January 1786

Yesterday and the Day before several People called here in the Evening – It is pure tiresome to receive Company in this formal Way: but I hope my Plan of Life will soon change, and that I shall be able to get out a little; tho the Weather is so much colder than ever I felt it anywhere, then the Mounting up great Stone Stair Cases, and parading through all the cold Antichambers which belong to this Town, will be a severe Busineſs at first. Every one who came here last Night talked of <u>Ettrennes,</u>[40] that is of the Presents which People had made to each other on Account of it's being <u>New Year's Day</u>; for this Custom is so general that they all complain of it's being abolished; and indeed I should think It must occasion a vast deal of mutual Trouble. ~ The Duc de Nivernois when he came in <u>fell a</u> kiſsing a fine Comteſse in the Circle two or three times on each side of her Cheeks, and I could not imagine what it all meant till they informed me that her Husband had been presented with the <u>Cordon blue</u> at Versailles in the Morning. This is their first Order, and so far Answers to our blue Ribband, but it is not near so fine a thing, because it is more common. There are a hundred Knights of the Cordon blue and I think only twenty five of the Garter: We were offered Tickets for their Installment, and I should like to see it, but I fear it will not happen during my stay in Paris. – The six men who were Knighted Yesterday by the King are to appear, it seems, in the exact Dreſs of Henry the fourth of France,[41] many old Customs of Chivalry will be observed on the Occasion. My Mother has been offered a Ticket for the Royall Academy,[42] on the Day that Monsieur Guibert, Author of the Tactique, is to make his funeral Oration upon Monsieur Thomas,[43] and if I can poſsibly get one I will, for every Mortal says it will be a fine Piece of Eloquence. I feel much interested besides about this poor Monsieur Thomas, for I recollect liking every thing I have met with of his. Lady Clermont dined with us Yesterday, and stayed part of the Evening. I have a great respect for her, and think highly of her Virtues, but all the long Leſsons and Lectures She gives me about Dreſs do, I must own, wear one to a Mummy! for tho I wish to have every thing made well, and to appear to the best Advantage, without aiming at the <u>Pink</u> of <u>Taste</u> and magnificence, I cannot stand tiresome Conversations, all my Mornings with Tradespeople she sends to me, and hearing as tiresome Explanations afterwards about different Breadths of Lace, and different Shapes of Sleeves, &c. Mʳˢ. Hobart too came in last Night armed at all Points; but their Disquisitions respecting Dreſs and Mademoiselle Bertin were quite a Comedy to me. ✗

44   Mary Carter, 1730-1812, known to her friends as Molly.   Rizzo writes that Molly Carter came from a comfortably off Welsh family, though a brief description of her family attached to her letters (see below) says she was the daughter of Thomas Carter of Rathnally, County Meath.   Rizzo suggests that her family was sufficiently large not to be able to set her up in society.   Her father died, she says, when she was only 14 and it's likely that for some years she lived with, and looked after, her eldest brother Thomas, for some of the year in London, where he sat as a Member of Parliament, and at other times in Wales.   When her brother died in 1767 she was unmarried and had only a small capital to live on and at that stage she had to carve out a niche for herself.   The role she developed was as companion, guide and teacher, which on several occasions involved lengthy trips on the continent.   It's likely that she travelled to Florence with the family of Sir Charles Gore in 1773.   From about 1777, at the age of 47, she became companion and guide to 17 years old Louisa Skrine, who in that same year married Sir Thomas Clarges.   When her husband died in 1782 Louisa Clarges, now a wealthy woman, set off with Molly Carter for a tour of the continent, taking in Paris, Italy, Switzerland and then back to Paris again, on the return visit meeting Mrs Crewe, as reported in the diary.   Her singularity is noted by Mrs Crewe and others and in her book Companions without vows Betty Rizzo makes the case that Molly Carter was a lesbian, though she is uncertain of a sexual relationship between Carter and Clarges.   Lady Clarges and Miss Carter returned to London towards the end of 1786, having been abroad for more than three years, Clarges to a house she took in Mayfair's South Street and Carter to her own house just around the corner in Hill Street.   In 1792 she travelled again, this time for two years with Lord and Lady Palmerston, visiting France, Italy, Switzerland, Germany and Holland.   Letters written during this trip, with a few others, were printed, a rare copy of which is held at The British Library (Mrs Mary Carter's letters).   George Canning met her on at least five occasions in 1795, mistakenly thinking her the sister of Mrs Elizabeth Carter (author and daughter of a Kent clergyman), on each of these occasions at the home of Charles Ellis, Member of Parliament and later created Lord Seaford.   Canning wrote: "[Miss Carter] is a very pleasant, clever, entertaining and good-natured elderly lady…. a valuable addition to society.   I wonder how it happens that I have never met her before", and then later: "…and Miss Carter too improves every day upon acquaintance".   In later life she continued to mix foreign travel with a life in London but began to falter in her seventies.   She died at the age of 82.   The best account of her life is given in Rizzo's Companion without vows from which the following description is taken: "She also had a remarkable character.   Good humoured and strong-minded, she was not inclined to direct the lives of others, in which, however, she took a great friendly interest, always willing to do what she could to oblige or assist.   She never displayed malice and was high-spirited with a great sense of fun.   She was well informed and had excellent common sense and judgement.   Her empathetic nature gave her genuine sensibility, and she had a 'masculine intelligence', a combination that made her a mature altruist with a perfectly developed capacity for self-preservation.   She had no faith in limitations set on women and was independent in thought and action." (Rizzo, p268).

Tuesday

Tuesday 3ʳᵈ January 1786

Yesterday Morning I went to the famous Hotel de Jabac where all sorts of Toys are to be sold, and I there saw the new fashioned Buckles, Boxes, and Trinkets which will be worn this year both in Paris and London. I purchased a few things and then went to the famous China Shop here where I was likewise tempted to spend a little Money. There is it is certain, no kind of Comparison between the most common sort of China in France and the best our country ever produces; and one pays a fourth part only here for what is at least four times as beautifull. The great Objection, however, against buying French China is the Duty laid upon it in England, and which actually comes to as much as the Purchase, however the Master of the Shop told us he had lately sent a great Quantity to Ireland, from whence one might get it, I should think, easily enough – After Dinner Madame de Roncherolle was let in. She is a very good sort of agreeable Woman, but I hate the Ceremony of formal Visits, and am quite certain, if the most intimate Friends in London were all resolved to visit each other in the Stiff Way they do at Paris, there would very soon be no such thing as Friendship, it would be all form and nothing more. Image to yourself a Ceremony of five minutes upon the first coming in; the Curtsy begins at the Door, then the Lady of the House is to be addreſsed with Compliments and Speeches about nothing at all, then two or three more things are to be said for the good of the whole Circle, then little Jokes may be aimed at from one Side to the other of the Chimney Piece – but I defy any great succeſs from them, when the want of a Fire Skreen, or the dropping of a Muff is to disturb the Situation of all the Company. Miſs Carter⁴⁴ says the Visiting here is exactly what it was in England thirty or Forty Years ago, and I believe so, I recollect too that several of the old fashioned Speeches of Civility made by our People of the last Age had the same turn of Expreſsion that the French give to their Compliments; and the youngest of them on first Meeting are to the full as ceremonious as our old Folks on a Sunday Evening. they are, however much more at their Ease than we are, and much pleasanter, I think, for common chitchat in a tête a tête. We went to Mʳˢ. Hobarts Rout, which I liked very well, and indeed so did every bodyₓ The Rooms were not crouded, and the People did exactly as they chose to do – There were all the English here, and many French People besides – Some of the latter were so extremely civil and so full of fine Speeches, with their <u>Desespoir</u>⁴⁵ and <u>Enchantment</u> that my "Blank Verse was obliged to halt"⁴⁶ for me ~ But, lest you should suppose that I am giving myself more Airs than I have a

45 Desespoir – despair; despondency.

46 from Shakespeare's Hamlet:
"…and the lady shall say her mind freely, or the blank verse shall halt for 't." Act 2, scene 2, lines 339-340.

47 Henry Francis Greville, 1760-1816, brother to Mrs Crewe, he was a Lieutentant-Colonel in the British Army. See the Introduction, page 33.

48 Asgill was an 18-year old Captain in the British army, serving in America. He was captured at the surrender of Yorktown in 1781 and condemned to be hanged in reprisal for the execution of an American soldier. However, Asgill's parents appealed to the French Foreign Minister Vergennes, who in turn brought the situation to the attention of the French King and Queen. Antoinette pressed for his release, which the Americans granted, and 2 years later Asgill travelled to Versailles to thank her. The story became a minor phenomenon, inspiring a novel, poems and a play.

49 should be encomiums or encomia: praise.

50 Mrs Greville had a reputation as a poet. Her best known piece was Ode for indifference, first published in 1759, and is probably the one referred to here; see Appendix One.

51 fete and consu and recherche – entertained, consulted and studied.

52 Marie Henriette de Polastron, who married Francois Léonor, Comte d'Andlau in 1736. Mis-spelt d'Andelot by Mrs Crewe, a mistake also made by Horace Walpole (see his Correspondence). She was known for her wit and together with the Comtesse Diane de Polignac they were said to constitute the only intellectual element at the court of Marie Antoinette – the others were mostly "butterflies" (Webster, pp111-2). Madame d'Andlau was the paternal aunt of the Duchesse de Polignac and a close friend of Eléonore de Sabran, with whom she travelled through Holland and Belgium in 1783, taking in Spa. Madame d'Andlau died in 1792 or 1793.

Right to, and that I take things as Compliments which are merely forms, I will inform you that it is my Fate to be here in very great Request, not on my own Account, but because the French People never abandon a subject till it is quite Threadbare, and my Brother Harry's[47] having been taken prisoner in America, and having received Kindneſses from very distinguished French Officers, – the Letter he wrote to my Mother upon Asgill's Busineſs (which the Duc de Nivernois, Madame de Cambise, and others have translated)[48] all these Circumstances have made our Family of Importance, – and, I do aſsure you, I am tired to Death with the same sort of Stuff which they will bestow upon you, in large Quantities, and upon every occasion; with very bad Taste, I think, for after all, my Brother was not the only Brother taken Prisoner in America, nor can a well written Letter deserve such laboured Encomius.[49] I am much more, indeed I am highly flattered by the Reception my Mother's Ode has met with,[50] and I ought certainly to have mentioned that as the great Source of our Paris Popularity – The Duc de Nivernois has put this too into French Verse, and it is read all over Paris – so that you may perceive from all this, even if Mr. Crewe, my Brother and myself had not the least Merit of our own (which I won't allow) we should still be fete and consu and recherche[51] and God knows what; at a great Rate while we are here. The Viscomte de Noailles was at Mrs. Hobart's last Night, and I thought he never would have finished his Offers of Civility about Boxes at the King's Theatre. Dinners at Versailles &c Madame de Andelot[52] (who means I find to be our Ambaſsadreſs) came up too, with about fifteen Offers saying, it would be impoſsible for her to do half that had been done for her on the Score of Civility, when She was in England. But I told them both, I was under Lady Clermont's Directions, who had made me promise not to Stir a Step without her at first, and I did not at all know what was to happen yet about Balls and other Entertainments. – The Poor Duke of Dorset looks sadly indeed, and seems to be much dejected, which is by no means to be wondered at. Monsieur de Noailles was introduced to my Mother, and displayed a great Quantity of eloquent small Talk – All that would go to the House of Commons with us is here sprinkled over private Discourse – this may sometimes, perhaps, give a Poignancy to what one hears, but it might often be much better Suppreſsed, because it does not blend well or naturally, I think, with the ordinary chit chat of Life. It strikes me as like paying a Morning Visit in a Court Dreſs – This Viscomte de Noailles however is one of the cleverest young French Men I have seen, and I recollect his beginning to appear so at the Age of Nineteen. There is one Custom which People had at Bruſsells, and which they have here too, that I by no means like, and it is, if a Dramatic Piece, or any other new Publication is talked of, they send it immediately to you, and expect that you shall be ready to discuſs it with them the next time you meet – Now you are to know that

53 a tippet was a woman's fur cape for the shoulders, often consisting of the whole fur of a fox, marten, etc.

53a possibly for their butler William Dickens, grandfather of Charles Dickens, who died in October 1785. I can trace no death of a member of the family.

54 Richard Burke, 1758-94, son of the influential statesman, and great friend of Mrs Crewe, Edmund Burke – in Edmund Burke's published correspondence he is referred to as Richard Burke Jr., to differentiate him from an uncle with the same name. In a letter to his father, dated December 25th 1785 Richard Burke described his first meeting in Paris with Mrs Crewe. "I have just been at Mrs Crews who came the night before last. She has been ill at Brussels but is quite recover'd. Mr Greville is with them. They laught at me exceedingly for my ignorance of every thing that has been going on in England for this three months. They say Lord Cork will be marryed to Miss Moncton. How is he to get rid of Lady Cork? Why she has been dead these two months &c &c. Ever since I have been here, I have lived in a happy Sequestration from English newspapers of which I find I am insensibly adopting my Uncle Richard's notions. I write this just going to bed, which I am very glad to do having been up most part of last night at Mad[am]e de Polignac's reveillon, which is a given after the three Christmas midnight masses. Adieu. Adieu." (a note in Burke's letters suggests that the Mr Greville referred to in this letter is Mrs Crewe's father but, considering she makes no mention of him in her diary, and that her mother and father were separated at about this time, it seems much more likely that Richard Burke is talking about her brother Charles Greville). Some years later Lord Holland wrote of Richard Burke that he was "sincerely attached to his father. It was his only virtue. He had every quality that could render him disagreeable to other persons, and no great talents to counterbalance them. Hence he was disliked and neglected by the members of opposition. But the affection of a child naturally blinds a parent to his failings, and Burke saw none in his son". In 1794 he died of TB, aged only 36, and only 2 weeks after winning his seat in Parliament.

55 pelisse: a high-waisted loose coat, usually fur-trimmed; or a fur-trimmed cloak.

56 La Comédie-Francaise was the first state theatre of France, built around a company established by Moliere in 1658. In 1782 it moved into a theatre specially built for it near the Palais du Luxembourg.

57 Monsieur de Pourceaugnac, a light farcical work written by Moliere in 1669. The plot revolves around an arranged marriage between a young Parisian girl and a provincial lawyer, neither having seen the other. The girl's lover seeks to destroy the arrangement with claims that the lawyer is already married, is in debt and is mad. Similarly the lawyer is led to believe the girl is promiscuous. In the end the lawyer is driven off and the two lovers are united. It's difficult to see what Mrs Crewe found disgusting about the play unless, as she said, it was the way in which it was acted.

what I like is merely to be told of what is good, then to get it myself, and take my own time over it. - Monsieur de Noailles is to send me two Books to day, and a Spirit of Contradiction has already seized me about both – But I must confeß a Spirit of Contradiction has travelled with me, and I often and often have panted after poor old England! -

Thursday Morn.ᵍ

Thursday 5ᵗʰ January 1786

I am in the Agony of Preparation for the Ball at Versailles to Night. Lady Clermont is sending Meßages every two Hours about Caps, Tippets[53] and Etiquetts of every Sort. Thank God! we are in Mourning,[53a] for that will cover a Multitude of Sins. What a puzzling Matter Dreß is become within these two or three years: All the old Laws belonging to it are repealed, so that many a poor Body, who has not much Judgment or Taste, Sins more innocently, and is laughed at for an Affectation of her own, tho her appearing so uncouthly proceeds merely from Ignorance, or Indolence and letting the Milliner decide. – However in Paris, I find, the Women leave off wearing Flowers and Feathers on their Heads at the Age of Thirty. This is so good and safe a Rule that it is a pity we have not adopted it. – it would save many an unfortunate Woman from being set down as ridiculous for the rest of her Life! – But the Dreß with us inclines all to Arcadian. And surely last Spring in London every Woman seemed more like a Shepherdeß out of her Element than any other thing – Recollect the Straw Hat placed on one Side, The Apron pinned up in a Nymphish Stile, with a thousand little Adjustments after the rustic Manner that, to my Eye, are perfectly unfit for an universal Fashion, which is to include Young and Old, fat and lean in short, Women of the most opposite Descriptions. And Pray why is People's Dreß to be always poetical any more than their Language? – should not what occurs every day bear an even tenor – and not keep either the Mind or the Eye for ever on the Stretch? – My Brother Charles and Mʳ. Burke[54] are to be of the Party to Versailles, and, it seems, we must set off at about half past five O'Clock. It is much colder than I ever felt it in England in my Life, but it is a fine clear Frost, so that with Peliße's[55] and Furrs of different Sorts we shall, I dare say, do very well. – Last Night my Mother and I went to the French Comedy[56], and saw two bad Pieces enough. – By the bye, the Monsieur de Pourceannac of Moliere[57] is so much more indelicate than any thing that ever was represented at

57a   *should be Madame de Guiche*

58   *Louis Antoine de Gontaut, duc de Biron, 1700-88, marechal de France in 1751.   He was described by Madame de la Tour de la Pin as the last great gentleman of the period of Louis XV, or at least, the last to preserve the traditions of that day.   In her Memoirs she wrote: "He was eighty-five when I was only fifteen.   One day he told me that from his earliest youth he had given much thought to the various difficulties of old age in society and that having himself when he was my age been extremely bored and badgered by certain of his elders, he had resolved if he should himself live to a great age to avoid inflicting the same suffering.   He advised me to do the same...The Marechal de Biron was Colonel of the Gardes Francaises and they adored him.   There was nothing military about them except their uniforms.   I had seen him when I was a child, parading before the King at the head of his men in the review held every year on the little plain of Sablons near the bridge at Neuilly.   He owned a magnificent and very beautiful house in Paris (now the Musee Rodin), set in a splendid garden of three or four acres, with hot-houses filled with rarest plants.   The Marechal lived in magnificent style and did the honours of Paris in the grand manner. He owned boxes in all the principal theatres and although he never went himself, his boxes were always occupied by foreigners of distinction, particularly the English, whom he preferred above all the others, and among whom he selected the most notable.   It was a much-coveted honour to be received at his house.   He never gave balls, but there would be a concert at his house whenever some foreign singer or great musician visited Paris.   He gathered about him everyone of distinction, always with the greatest courtesy and in the grand manner, but with unsurpassable ease amid all the spleandour, for that was his natural setting...   His wife, from whom he had been living separately for fifty years on account of some misdemeanour of which I know nothing, survived him and died on the scaffold with her niece, the Duchesse de Biron. The Marechal de Biron died in 1787 or 1788, and his funeral was the last spleandour of the monarchy.   Never had there been anything so magnificent." (La Tour du Pin, pp51-53)   Mrs Crewe was clearly honoured by Biron, who not only offered her his boxes at the theatre but also invited her to his home (though she couldn't find anything there worth mentioning).*

59   *Born Mademoiselle de Messey, she married in 1765.   Mrs Crewe indicates that Madame de Bussy had recently become widowed; her husband was Charles-Joseph Patissier, Marquis de Bussy-Castelnau, 1718-1785, a cousin of the Caramans and friend of the Beauveau family.   He spent most of his life fighting for the French in India and was at one time a prisoner in England.*

60   *ganses: braid, gimp, piping, loop; a tape-like trimming of silk, wool or cotton, often stiffened with wire.*

96

Sadler's Wells, or our <u>lowest</u> Theatres, that it quite astonished me to see a Paris Audience submit to it ✗ – One slurs over many things in Reading Moliere; but really as they acted <u>this</u>, it was impoſſible to avoid Disgust. The Theatre is new and has a very pleasant Appearance; tho, I believe it is abused on Account of its Size, which they say is too large considering the many others there are in this Town. – We called afterwards on Lady Hampden, where we found a Party of English People, and where we paſſed our Time comfortably enough till we returned to Supper. There is a very decent Sett of English here at present, but they are of course much more dispersed than they were at Bruſſells. My Mother and I dedicated last Wednesday to the returning of Visits, and a pure cold and heavy Duty it was – however we agreed that it was better to get them chiefly over – We were admitted at the Ducheſſe de la Valiere's, at a Madame de Buſſy's, at Madame de Guirche's,[57a] and at the Marechal Biron's[58] – at Madame de Buſſy's[59] the Room was hung with Black, and you are to know it is the Custom here for Widows to furnish their Apartments with entire mourning for the first Year, and a more Gloomy Appearance I never saw than this poor Woman's, without even a looking Glaſs or the smallest Symptoms of Luxury about her. ~
The Marechal offered me his Boxes at all the Theatres during my stay – He is a poor good old Soldier who is always remarkably kind to the English ~ When I was here Thirteen years ago, he loaded me with Presents and attended my Mother and me with his Drums and Guards to several Places – and he is all Civility now. – It really made me quite melancholy to see the good old man so much more enfeebled and weak than he was! –

Friday Morning

Friday 6ᵗʰ January 1786

It was near three O'Clock this morning when Charles and I returned from Versailles and you shall now hear how it all was. ~ Lady Clermont arrived here soon after two in the Afternoon to make a Recapitulation of what She had before said on the Score of Dreſs, and at about six She set off to prepare some Tea for us in her Apartment at the Palace of Versailles. – My Head was then ornamented, and, as it had been determined that I must not go twelve Miles in the Ganses,[60] I was to wear, I took the Liberty of covering myself with Peliſſes and great Coats

61 at full speed, rapidly.

62 hair blown all over the place.

63 the rider of the leading near horse in a team pulling a coach, guiding the team.

64 a square dance of five or more figures for four or more couples.

65 in great demand.

66 Marie Joseph, Marquis de Lafayette: a major figure in revolutionary France, Lafayette lived from 1757 to 1834. He fought against the British in America in 1777 and 1779, taking part in the battle of Yorktown. In 1784 he visited for a 3rd time when he received an enthusiastic reception from the Americans. In 1787 Lafayette was called to the Assembly of Notables and sat in the Estates General and in 1789 sat in the National Assembly. He tabled a declaration of rights based on the American Declaration of Independence. The French National Guard was formed by him and he struggled to maintain order but the Jacobins were against him and he was forced to flee to Liege. Napoleon had him liberated in 1797 and he went on to sit in the Chamber of Deputies from 1818-1830.

67 a quote from Matthew Prior, 1664-1721:
> *"To John I owed great obligation;*
> *But John, unhappily, thought fit*
> *To publish it to all the nation:*
> *Sure John and I are more than quit."*

68 Adrien Louis Bonnieres, Duc de Guines: Guines was a good musician, playing the flute, often accompanied by his daughter on the harp, and had the distinction of commissioning Mozart's flute and harp concerto K 299. This love of music coupled with his good humour had made him a friend of Marie Antoinette. He was good-humoured but over-weight and there is a story he wore tight-fitting breeches, to make him look slimmer, the tightest of which he would wear only on those occasions when he stood – a looser pair would be employed if he had to sit. Guines served first as a colonel in the Seven Years' war before being appointed ambassador in London. In 1775 he became the target of an attack by France's Controller General of Finances, Turgot. Turgot sent three abbés to England on a secret mission to encourage wealthy Huguenot industrialists to return to France to help build up the French economy but neglected to tell Guines. When the abbés made a nuisance of themselves Guines sent them back to France, displeasing Turgot who complained to the King. Turgot accused Guines of passing information to the English regarding the situation in America and had the ambassador recalled to France. An investigation was held which concluded that Guines was innocent of the charge and that his name had been besmirched. In recompense the King turned Guines from a Comte to a Duc. At the time Mrs Crewe met him he would have been 51 years old.

in quantities, for bitter Cold it was! – Lord Downe and M[r]. W. Conway called just as we were setting off, and we all laughed heartily at the Figures both my Brother and I were forced to make of ourselves, and the Trouble it was necefsary to take previous to this Amusement. At six we set off in a Post Chaise, away we went tantivy[61] with our Chevaux enragès[62] for about two Miles, then – and what happened then? Why one of the Horses tumbled down, our Postilion[63] was thrown off, and there we were stopped Short, and so frightened as to open the Door and get out. The poor Man however was saved by his Jack Boots, and as there was no fear of such Horses running away, in case the same Accident happened again, we made our Minds pretty easy about it, and pursued our Journey very safely to the Palace. Lady Clermont had got her Tea ready for us, and after that Ceremony was over, away we went in an odd sort of Sedan Chair acrofs large Courts to that part of the Palace where the Dancing was, and where the Queen had ordered a Box to be kept for Lady Clermont's Use. You cannot conceive any thing more gay and brilliant than this Ball Room. – It is ornamented with every thing that is festive, and illuminated in the best Manner. – The Young Men and Women Dance in Quadrilles,[64] and are Drefsed in whatever is the most recherché.[65] – The King, Queen, and all the Royal Family walk about and sit down just as the Spirit happens to move them. They both talked a good deal to Lady Clermont, and the Queen said a word or two to me about hoping to see my Mother – but She must continue to hope, I fancy, for my Mother has not thought of taking so much trouble, and I think She is perfectly in the right about it. – Monsieur de la Fayette[66] came, and asked after several People in England. He has a much greater Simplicity in his Manner than any Frenchman I have yet seen, and he speaks English almost as well as an Englishman. He talked to me very much about my Brother Harry's Captivity in America. ~ a Theme they all hold forth upon, because it is certain that several French Officers had an Opportunity of displaying much gallant Generosity to a fallen Enemy. The Duc de Castries never sees me that he does not allude to his Services upon that Occasion, and he certainly did Cloathe him when he was naked, and go so far as to lend him two hundred pounds: but this puts me in Mind of the Epigram
    "To John I owed great Obligation[67] ✗
The Duc de Guines[68] told me he hoped to procure the Company of the Marquis de Puisagenes to meet us at Dinner next Tuesday, and that he had already asked him to give us some Proofs of his Skill in the Science of Magnetism – But do you know I feel ashamed to reapeat what they say upon this Subject here: and, as I hear you have Mesmer now with you in England, I refer you to him for further Instructions, at least for further Investigations which I am not equal to. When the Court went to Supper, we returned to Lady Clermont's Apartment where we got some

69 Wife of Aymar Joseph, Comte de Roquefeuil, 1714-82. Mrs Crewe says she became well acquainted with her at Spa and describes her as a pleasing little woman who she is bound in gratitude to like, since she was full of obliging civilities towards her. At one point during the stay Madame de Roquefeuil was ill in bed and after receiving little help from her doctor Mrs Crewe felt great sympathy for her, describing her as "quite at the mercy of her miserable French physician". Her husband had been a Vice Admiral and in 1744 had commanded the French Brest fleet that was commanded to support an invasion of England – at that time there were fears of the French carrying across the Young Pretender to the British throne.

70 Christoph Willibald von Gluck, Austro-German composer, 1714-1787. The Queen brought Gluck to Paris in the 1770s, where his new ideas on opera influenced fundamental change on both writing and production. He attacked the stiff formality of French opera and introduced a freer, more natural presentation. There developed in Paris an opera war between the new style, represented by Gluck, and the old style, represented by Piccini. Gluck's great successes in Paris were Iphigenie en Aulide, Orphee, and Iphigenie en Tauride.

71 Niccola Piccini, Italian composer, 1728-1800, writing about 140 operas. His early career was spent in Italy before being invited to Paris in 1776 where he was drawn into competition with Gluck. Piccini became the representative of an older, formal style of music whereas Gluck was challenging the old style with freer, more natural productions. He produced Roland in 1778 and Atys in 1780. An attempt was made to compare Piccini with Gluck by commissioning each of them to produce an opera on the subject of Iphigenie and Tauride, which Gluck produced in 1779 and Piccini 2 years later. But Piccini was an unwilling contestant, being an admirer of his opponent and he did nothing to encourage his supporters. His most popular French opera was Didon, first produced in 1783. He left Paris at the time of the revolution but returned in 1798 and died there two years later.

72 Maximilien Gardel, 1741-1787, who should not be confused with his brother Pierre, also a dancer. He was a French dancer and choreographer at the Paris Opera from 1781-87, and the first to dispense with the customary mask (1773) which he refused to wear in order to show that it was he who was dancing and not his fellow dancer Gaetano Vestris.

73 Mlle Gaimaise: not traced. It's possible that Mrs Crewe has mis-spelt the name as she has with others. My judgement is that she is referring to somebody from the family Gamas, of whom there were a number active in French theatre at this time.

74 the Italian Theatre: up until 1780 this had been known as the Comédie italienne, at which date it changed to Opéra Comique. The theatre staged dramas set to music which differed from grand opera in that the music appeared only as passages between a spoken dialogue. It delivered a programme primarily of comedy and farce. In 1783 it moved to a site in the Salle Favart, where it still exists today.

cold meat before we set out again. You must know, I could not be presented at this Court, or, of course, partake of the Supper. – and my Brother Charles, tho he had that Privilege, chose rather to come away with us. I am glad I have seen all this, for it really is a very pretty Sight. ~

Sunday

Sunday 8ᵗʰ January 1786

On Friday last my Spa Friend Madame de Roquefuelle[69] sent to offer me a Place in the Marechall Biron's Box at the great Opera, and I accepted of it. It was a very fine Spectacle. Gluck[70] and Piccini[71] are now the favourite Composers here. Their Taste in Music is, I think, much improved within these ten or twelve Years, and their Theatres on that Account much worth going to. ~ I still think, however, one may trace a great deal of the abominable French Stile of Composition: but this is more, perhaps, in the manner of Expreſsion than in the Composition itself. The Dancing is very fine, and Gardelle[72], Mademoiselle Gaimaise,[73] with two or three other famous Performers capital indeed! Yesterday my Mother and I went to what is called the Italian Theatre,[74] which is that Theatre where smaller Musical Pieces are performed. We were very much gratified, for this an Amusement perfect in its Kind, and I find that, which is most frequented now ~ I confeſs I wish the regular French one was upon a better footing than it is at this time, for there is nothing I like better than seeing some of their Pieces in five Acts both in Tragedy and Comedy – What we call <u>genteel Comedy</u> is what they excell in more perhaps, than we do, for they have Studied the <u>nicer</u> Parts of civil Life with more minute Accuracy. Indeed Manners seem to be their Fort, as well as the light Surfaces of Affectation, and the little nameleſs Distreſses which arise, in the Society of a Capital, amongst Courtiers, and others, who may be considered as of the same Claſs, and Subject to similar Embarraſsments and Pleasures. ✗

75   John Christopher Burton Dawnay, 5th Viscount Downe, of Cowick Hall in Yorkshire, 1764-1832. He was 21 years old at the time the diary was written, had been educated at Eton and succeeded to his title on the death of his father in 1780. When Mrs Crewe met him in Paris he had already completed his tour of Italy, accompanied by his tutor Mr Pidow, and was on his way back to England. He is described by Mrs Crewe as a very sensible, pleasant young man who is well spoken of by everybody, an opinion echoed by the Blackett's in Italy ("A very good kind of young man" – Ingamells).

76   Wellesley, Lady Anne Wellesley was the daughter of Lady Mornington – I don't have her date of birth but she married in 1790 and died in 1844.

77   Anne, Countess of Mornington, eldest daughter of Viscount Dungannon, married Garret Wesley, 1st Earl of Mornington and Viscount Wellesley in 1759. Her husband had died in 1781. She had four sons, one of whom was Arthur Wellesley, at the time this diary was written only 17 years old, but later to be created first Duke of Wellington. Mrs Crewe calls her Lady Mornington though she was the Countess of Mornington – she lived from 1742-1831 (Burkes Peerage, pp.2672, 2784-6), so at the time of the diary she would have been 44 years old. Her eldest son, Richard, and her daughter, Lady Anne Wellesley, were with her on this visit.

Monday Morning

Monday 9ᵗʰ January 1786

Last Night we supped very comfortably at this Hotel, for we brought Mʳ. W Conway and Lord Downe[75] home with us from Lady Clarge's, and we found Mʳ. Labord already here. I believe I have before observed that there is nothing I like so well as winding up the Day with a few People with whom I may feel quite at my ease; and the looking forward to the Supper Hour has frequently consoled me for many of the formal Duties that belong to the preceding part of the Day. – People may say what they please of the Ease of a French Life, I must still presume to think that one's time here is much leſs at one's own Disposal than in London. In the first place, <u>we</u>, very seldom pay Visits of mere respect in an Evening – here every Mortal is visited in this manner – and, in short, the <u>Mechanical</u> or <u>technical</u> Part of Politeneſs , (if I may be allowed to use either of those Words) is much leſs attended to in London than in Paris. ~ The Duc de Nivernois was here Yesterday Morning, and he made us fix upon a Day for another fine Dinner at his House, which is to be on Friday next. He is a man my Mother has long known, and She speaks highly of him. From the little I have seen of him, I think he poſseſses much Elegance and Taste. To day Madame de Roquefuelle, is to dine with us – This I cannot object to, for we got pretty well acquainted at Spa, and She is besides a pleasing little Woman, Whom I am bound in gratitude to like, for She is full of obliging Civilities to me. Poor Lady Ann Wellsley[76] has been confined to her House several Days – I call upon her Mother[77] when I can, for she is in sad Distreſs about her, tho I hope there is nothing at all alarming in her Illneſs now. Miſs Payne too is at Home and in Bed, which is very hard upon her, but indeed the Weather is so suddenly changed from Extreme Cold to Extreme Heat, that it is not Wonderfull People should suffer. I begin to wish to hear from You ~ It is now a long time since I have done so; and till I do I shall not send another Pacquet.

Wednesday

Wednesday 11ᵗʰ January 1786

We had Yesterday a great Dinner at the Duc de Guines.   I never saw a more beautiful and agreeable House than his in any Town.   It has an

78 *Armand Marie Jacques de Chastenet, Marquis de Puységur, 1752-?* An ardent disciple of Mesmer, Puységur published in 1784 *Mémoires pour servir à l'histoire et à l'establissement du magnètisme animal*, and this is presumably the book he gave to Mrs Crewe. Puységur carried out experiments on his estate at Busancy and in front of Parisian society, deriving a religious-like belief in himself. He wrote: "I continue to make use of the happy power for which I am indebted to M. Mesmer. Every day I bless his name; for I am very useful, and produce many salutary effects on all the sick poor in the neighbourhood... I have only one regret - it is, that I cannot touch all who come... I own to you that my head turns round with pleasure to think of the good I do. Madame de Puysegur, the friends she has with her, my servants, and, in fact, all who are near me, feel an amazement, mingled with admiration, which cannot be described; but they do not experience the half of my sensations."(Mackay) .

79 *she is referring to her son John – see the Introduction, page 35.*

80 *Richard Couer de Lion, written by Andre-Ernest-Modeste Gretry, 1741-1813.*

Advantage too which hardly any other House in this Place has to recommend it, that of Cleanlineſs, which he says he learnt in England. We saw and conversed at this Dinner with the famous Marquis de Puisagur,[78] who was very communicative on the Subject of Magnetism. But I will send you the Book itself, and you may read in it all and much more indeed than he told us, provided you have Patience to wade through it – for my own part, a very few Instances were enough for me. The Duc de Guines seems to be a <u>Believer</u>, but most other People of common Sense are not. By what I can gather concerning this Science, I am induced to think it only a Species of Electricity which operating upon a heated Imagination, has at times great Influence over the human Frame. This Marquis de Puisagur is an Enthusiast himself however, and told us <u>seriously </u>that he had a patient at present under his Care who appeared to every other Person to be at the last Extremity – neverthelefs he <u>knew</u> She would recover the Twenty fourth of this Month, because <u>She had</u> herself told <u>him so in her State of Sleep walking</u>. ✗ It is it seems, in this State the Patient is supposed to foretell his own Fate, not from a Gift of Prophecy, but from a conscious Sensation not unlike, perhaps, that which some People have previous to the return of their Insanity. ✗ You are to know I verily believe these People have made <u>some</u> Discovery that Respects <u>Nerves </u>and the finer Organs of the human Frame – And after all, it is no more than I recollect Lord Bacon in his Eſsays says ought to be done before Physic can be said to be perfected. But they are not this Man's wild Stories, nor many other Stories I have been told in Paris, which lead me to this Opinion; It is the effect which has been produced upon Lord Downe and Mr. W Conway and many others. And yet I confefs there are many People easily imposed upon by grofs Ignorance. I was so fatigued after the fine Dinner Yesterday that I excused myself to the Duchefse de Castries, and after paying a Visit to Madame de Rocherolle, came home very quietly to write to John.[79] The Night before last, I saw a more beautifull, and splendid Opera at the smallest Theatre, than ever was presented in England, I believe. It is called Richard Couer de Lion,[80] and is composed upon the old Plot which Blondel lays to release him from Captivity. It is managed with a degree of ingenuity that quite charmed me, for, as I heard a French man say on the Stair Case, "there is a <u>Gradation</u> of <u>Interest</u> from the beginning to the End of it" They abound in such Phrases here, and nothing would surprise you more than those which they use in common Discourse. Some of them are vastly exprefsive; and to be sure the French Language may, from its light and flexible Nature, be much more easily played with than our's, or I fancy any other living one. Besides this: I incline to think the very frequent Visiting here and almost <u>necefsity</u> which there seems to be for eternal <u>talking</u>, has given and constantly cherishes among them, a nicer Power of

81 she is pointing out the affectation of using "one", often associated in Britain today with upper-class pretensions; "one always finds this; one normally thinks that".

82 Bouille, Francois Claude Amour, Marquis de   mis-spelt Boulie by Mrs Crewe. A cousin of Lafayette, Bouille was a French general. Born 1739 he entered the army at the age of 14 and spent much time in the West Indies. In 1787-88 the King nominated him a member of the Assembly of Notables and in 1790 he was made commander-in-chief of the army of the Meuse, Saar and Moselle. In this position he dealt harshly with a mutiny at the Nancy garrison in 1790, breaking one soldier on the wheel, hanging a further 20 and sentencing 41 to life imprisonment on the galleys. He was involved with the attempted escape of Louis XVI in 1791 and had to flee France. After fighting for other armies in Europe he retired to England to write his Memoires sur la Revolution. Mrs Crewe recommends him to her correspondent as a plain, sensible and pleasant man and hopes the two will meet when the Frenchman travels to England in the Spring. He died in 1800.

Discrimination and a more terse and happy mode of expreſsing their meaning on the most trivial Subjects. I observe too they are much more familiar with <u>Scientific Terms</u> than we are, and that Expreſsions which the common People here frequently use, are such as would be thought with us strangely affected and pedantic. For Instance, they are for ever disputing about le <u>Physique</u> and <u>la morale</u> – then a Milliner will tell you that your Ribband is not analogue to your Gown – then they frequently talk of such a Man, or Woman's mind not being <u>bien organiseé</u> – if they say they know any thing – it is often <u>Science</u>, and not savoir, which they have. – Thus they all seem to have more Knowledge than the generality of English, upon a first view of them; tho an unavoidable disgust at their insipid falling off, on a further Inspection, is sure to make one afterwards retract that Opinion. – I have often marked in their Conversation the <u>flattest</u> <u>Truisms</u>! – and <u>general</u> Propositions are the very Soul of them: – they would be quite at a loſs if you was to rob them of their <u>on</u>. which they hack to Death – "on trouve toujours ceci" – "on pense ordinairement come cela"[81] and so on through all the Aſsertions that ever were, or might be made. Now <u>general</u> Propositions are almost always, <u>I</u> <u>think</u>, the Vehicles of Stale Maxims which, as so much has been written and said upon every Subject, one must have perpetually popped upon in a thousand other Places. – Pray remember, however, that when I make such <u>wise</u> Remarks, it is always with Deference to <u>your</u> Opinion, and that I write down what occurs to me just as I should venture to speak to you, were you present. ✗

Saturday Even.ᵍ -

Saturday 14ᵗʰ January 1786

Mr. Crewe and Mr. Burke intend setting off for England on Monday next, and I rather think my Brother Charles will soon follow them, for he says the Life at Paris is but little suited to his Taste. – It is certainly formal in many respects compared with a London one; there are fewer great Houses open for the Reception of Crouds, and the number of ceremonious Visits which are to be paid in an Evening must be considered as a heavy Tax upon the Time of a Stranger, who can but seldom be very much at his Ease during the time they are paying. – Yesterday we had a very pleasant Dinner at the Duc de Nivernois – There was a good mixture of French and English Company, and we staid there till some time after Coffee. I was very well amused with all I heard Monsieur de Boulie[82] and some more Grandees say about the present

83 Sir William Eden, later 1ˢᵗ Baron Auckland – he was representing the British Government in trade negotiations with France. Following the wars in America both countries were seeking to increase revenue through trade. Eden gained an agreement that allowed the staple products and manufactures of the two countries to be traded on easier terms. The duty on hardware was agreed at 10%; pottery, porcelain, saddlery, cotton, muslins and woolens were all charged at 12%. The duty on French wines was reduced and that on brandy was halved. To the benefit of Britain silk was left out of the treaty, but both countries are said to have gained. Born 1744, Eden was trained as a barrister but entered politics and served as under-secretary of state and 1ˢᵗ Lord of the Board of Trade. He was a privy councillor for Ireland and sat in the Irish parliament. He established the National Bank of Ireland. At the time of Mrs Crewe's visit to Paris he had been appointed to negotiate a commercial treaty with France. He went on to become the Ambassador–extraordinary at The Hague during the French Revolution and was created the 1ˢᵗ Baron Auckland of West Auckland, Durham in 1793. He became a joint Postmaster-General for 1798-1804 and President of the Board of Trade in 1806-7. He died in 1814. His Journal and Correspondence were published in 4 volumes, 1860-62.

84 Marie Amelie, Duchesse d'Orleans. Basically a timid and tentative woman, her virtue was in contrast to the coarse philandering of her husband. It was said by the Baronne d'Oberkirch she "always looked sad, sometimes smiled but never laughed" (Goodden, p59). Constantly mis-used and neglected by her husband she was a melancholy creature who could not escape family problems even after his execution, her last years being tainted by financial disputes with her children.

85 mis-spelt by Mrs Crewe – it should be Bouillon.

86 belle esprit: witty.

87 there are several explanations for the term, one of which, according to Leslie & Taylor's Life of Reynolds, is suggested by Mrs Crewe herself, who says that it derived from the attendance of Madame de Polignac, wearing blue silk stockings, at a gathering at Mrs Montagu's. Gatherings at Mrs Montagu's, and other society leaders, sought to attract the most scholarly and intellectual women of the day and the term came to represent such women.

88 Ton: style, fashion, distinction.

89 William Seymour Conway, 1760-1837, 6ᵗʰ son of the 1ˢᵗ Marquess of Hertford. He was the Member of Parliament for Coventry 1783-4, Downton 1785-1790, and Orford 1790-1796. Educated at Harrow and Oxford, he married Martha Clitherow in 1798 and had 2 children Edward and Henry. He voted against the Duke of Richmond's fortification plans on 27 Feb 1786 – which are mentioned elsewhere in the diary.

Politics of England and France. Time only can discover whether M[r]. Eden[83] will be equal to the Task he has undertaken, but it appears to be an arduous one, at least from the Judgment they form here of its Intricacy and the absolute Necessity of his being well versed in the French Language. – We went after this to the Duche∫e de la Valiere's, where there is always much Company on a Friday, and a Supper afterwards, but the last we refused staying for, and, to say the truth, I had enough of the former part of the Busine∫ – so that I was but too happy to get back to this Hotel, where I found a few English People ready for Supper. On Thursday last Madame de Rochfeulle carried me to the Duche∫e D'Orleans',[84] where I was presented in form. We pa∫ed through a great Suite of Rooms, and in the last found her Highne∫ sitting in State to receive her Company with much good humour and good breeding – but a more silent dull meeting is impo∫ible to conceive; and so, they tell me, it always is the early Part of the Evening, when it is nece∫ary to go, if one means to have it in one's Power to sup there. The Chevalier Jernaghan has just been here to invite us to a Breakfast on Wednesday next, where the Duche∫e de Bullion[85] and some very fine Folks are to be. By what I could gather from him the Company he has chosen for that Day is very select, and of the Belle Esprit[86] kind. Their Parties here, I think, in general consist of a mixture of blue Stocking[87] and Frivolite. Every body is talked of as having some Ton;[88] and many People that are walking about Paris keep up a Character, as if they were at a Masquerade for Life. One frequently hears too of some Person having formed himself on such a Model; just as if it were po∫ible to do this effectually: or that Consistency was absolutely nece∫ary or natural in our Whimsical World! This thank God! is not yet so with us, nor is there any thing which I, for one, should think more troublesome. – However, I don't mind what I write – it is at the moment, as I have often told you, and it is therefore very po∫ible I may frequently contradict myself and lay down the most opposite Opinions.

Tuesday Morn.ᵍ.

Tuesday 17ᵗʰ January 1786

M[r]. Crewe and M[r]. Burke left us Yesterday – and M[r]. W. Conway[89] is to set off tomorrow, that he may be in time for the Meeting of Parliament. My stay here will not exceed three Weeks or a Month more; so that I

90 *Angelique Elisabeth, Comtesse de Matignon, died 1833. Her surname before marriage was Le Tonnelier de Breteuil and she was the daughter of the Duc de Breteuil, Minister of the French War Department. In 1772 she married the 18-year old Louis Charles de Goyon de Matignon, Comte de Matignon, who was tragically killed the following year in a hunting accident in Italy. At the time she was five months pregnant (London Chronicle 20 Jan 1774). She is described as "a widow, fresh, pretty, rich and independent". (Farr, p103).*

91 *Louis, Duc de Breteuil.*

92 *Dardanus is an opera by Sacchini, first performed at Versailles in 1784 then again at Fontainebleau in 1785 and in Paris in 1786.*

93 *Louis Philippe Joseph, Duc d'Orleans (1747-93). A member of the King's extended family, Louis Philippe was a grandson of Louis XIV and his own son later became King of France in 1830. He was known as the Duc de Chartres until his father's death in 1785 and in 1792 renounced his title, taking on the name Philippe Egalité. A regular visitor to England, he became an intimate friend of the Prince of Wales and took back to France the English fascination with horse-racing. Rarely on good terms with the French king he was at one stage banished to his chateau. During the revolution he became a strong supporter of the Third Estate against the privileged orders and voted for the death of the King. When his son defected to the Austrians in 1793 he was arrested and guillotined.*

94 *Pierre André de Suffren, 1729-1788. At the time of their meeting he was aged 56 and had behind him a long career of military action at sea, much of it against the British. His experiences helped him develop a strategy aimed at directing a maximum of strength against a fraction of the enemy's line, a strategy that helped him rise to the position of Admiral. Despite Mrs Crewe's jolly description he was also described as a man of violent temper, prodigious energy, explosively choleric and vulgar in his manner.*

must make haste and see all that is to be seen in this grand Capital – Last Night Lady Clermont carried me to Madame de Matignon's[90] where there was what we should call a dull Aßembly, because the Circle of Women lasted the whole Evening, and no attempt was made to break it by Card Tables. They do not understand the management of such Parties at Paris, for they have not been long used, like us, to the Meeting always in great Crouds, and to the laying aside that Quantity of Form which a large Aßembly at first seems to demand. This Madame de Matignon is a very great Lady – She is Daughter to Duc de Breteul,[91] Minister of the War Department, and, besides this, She has twelve Thousand pounds a Year, is a handsome and youngish Widow, and very fond of Splendor. – Lady Clarges and Miß Carter came home with me to Supper, and we found my Mother, Brother Charles and Lady Mornington waiting for us – To day I am going to dine at Monsieur de Caraman's, and in the Evening to Dardanus,[92] which, they tell me, is one of the finest Operas ever seen. To-morrow I am to be presented at the Ducheße de Brisac's, where there is to be a Supper. you see I am perfect Miß Jenny, and indeed many People wonder that I, who decline so, some small Parties, should yet rush into Crouds and not complain of Fatigue. but you are to know that I think the being jumbled with a number of other People is not half so harraßing as an Exertion to keep up regular Conversation with Strangers, besides, my Curiosity is much more gratified by a general View of their Life and manners, when they are exerting all their <u>Graces</u> and <u>Airs</u>, than by hearing Discourses in a Circle which are often dull in proportion to their Plausibility. ~ The Duc de Orleans[93] asked many Questions last Night concerning England at this moment, and whether there was any Chance for a Change in Administration. – He made a little Joke, as they all have done, about Mr. Eden's Desertion and said he wondered that the want of the French Language should have been dispensed with. He brought the famous Monsieur Suffrein[94] up to me to shew the Sword ornamented with Jewels which had been presented to him by the States of Holland. Monsieur Suffrein is a fat round good humoured looking Man. – Monsieur de Boulie was there too, and I saw several other Men I knew, but few Women, as I have shirked them most since I came. ♪

95 Antonio Maria Gasparo Gioachino Sacchini, 1730-1786, was an Italian composer of operas and one of the most gifted of the Neapolitan school. He worked in Venice, Germany, London and finally, from 1783, in Paris. His best known work Oedipe à Colone was first performed at Versailles during Mrs Crewe's trip, which she may be referring to in her entry for Friday 20th January. His works showed influences of the other Parisian favourite Gluck, and are noted for their broad melodies, a style clearly approved of by Mrs Crewe.

96 strophe and antistrophe: stanzas from ancient Greek choral lyric poetry. Choruses were composed in pairs of stanzas, the first pair being the strophe and the second pair the antistrophe.

97 Mrs Crewe was referring to the trombone which, although not a new instrument, was not used as part of the orchestra until the end of the 18th century. The use of trombones in this production of Dardanus is particularly noted in The New Grove dictionary of opera.

98 Caractacus and Elfrida were two pseudoclassical plays by William Mason, 1725-1797, written in 1752 and 1759 but not performed until 1772 and 1776. Horace Walpole described Caractacus as laboured and uninteresting.

99 – fly, where our vengeance calls us.

Wednesday Morn.ᵍ -

Wednesday 18ᵗʰ January 1786

I wish you could have been at the great Opera last Night – A more striking Entertainment, take it for all in all, I never saw. It is certain our Stage almost every year affords one or two Singers which Connoiseurs may think compensate for all droning Recitatives and insipid Dancers, Gestures and Scenery, but indeed, since Sachini[95] and Gluck are the Composers of their Operas here, and since the Performers have left off the Strange and disgusting French Manner of Singing, it is impoſible not to be often delighted with the great Opera at Paris. That which I saw last Night is called Dardanus: a Piece tho not remarkably well written, yet full of Interest – and here I must Venture to observe that, in my Opinion, the Greek Model, which has had so much said for and against it, seems to be quite calculated for an Opera. – The Strophes and Antistrophes[96] last Night had a remarkable Effect upon all the Audience – And as no Opera can ever produce that sort of Sympathy which regulated Tragedies, and other dramatic Representations, being more like reality, are formed to excite, what can be wished for, than to be quite overwhelmed with Sounds of Harmony and influenced by a System, as it were formed "to elevate and surprise" – ? They have a very full Orchestra here, and a new Instrument in it which, I think, is called un Trombeau[97] – it has a mixed sound of Drum and Trumpet and produced a great Effect: The Scenery of this Theatre is remarkably magnificent and the Machinery is managed with infinite Dexterity. As to Dancing, that has always been in the greatest Perfection here, and one is not shocked, as with us, at an Immense Distance between the Leaders and Figurantes. I cannot quit this Subject without expreſsing a Wish that something of this kind of Opera was attempted in our Language. I am aware of Mason's Charactacus and Elfrida,[98] which are both written upon the Greek Model – but they did not go far enough, I think – for such good Poetry should be adapted to Italian music – And surely People would be more affected by Distreſses conveyed in a Language they understand than by mere Sounds, which are all are fine Operas have to bestow upon the generality of Auditors. ✗ There was a moment last Night when every one seemed to be as inclinable to fight as the Actors themselves – it was when the Young Warriors with unexpreſsable Animation sung to their Troops
　　　"Volez
　　　Ou notre Vengeance nous appelle"! – [99]

100 Victor Maurice de Riquet, Comte de Caraman. His wife was a niece of Mme de Mirepoix. Caraman was a soldier for most of his life, fighting in many campaigns between 1743 and 1760. In 1761 he was appointed marechal de camp, then later second-in-command at Metz, lieutenant-general in 1780, and commander for the King in Provence with special powers in 1788 and 1789. Walpole wrote of him in 1765: "He is a very well behaved man and has been learning English… If he is not one of the first families, he is well received and upon as good a footing was any man in Paris. He lives extremely well here and has a good fortune to support it." (Correspondence, op cit, vol 38, p520) Also: "agreeable, informed and intelligent" (Correspondence, op cit, vol 38, p527). The Duc de Lauzun painted a less sympathetic picture of Caraman, describing him as a complete dandy; he said that though Caraman was an excellent officer in the army, full of experience and activity, nevertheless he was fussy, stopping men in the street who's uniforms were not properly buttoned and giving them an earnest lecture on military discipline (Lauzun, p188). He married in 1750 Marie Anne Gabrielle Hénin Liétard. The Caramans and their eight children led a happy domestic life at Roissy, near Paris, where Walpole attended a ball in 1775. In 1787 Walpole returned the favour by inviting Caraman to his home at Strawberry Hill. He emigrated during the revolution, and didn't return to France until 1801.

101 Rose Bertin, 1744-1813: Mrs Crewe describes well the influence on Parisian society of the dressmaker Rose Bertin. Based in the Faubourg Saint-Honoré, Bertin was a round-faced, snub-nosed, small-eyed Norman. It was said that with a Norman's traditional closeness to money, she charged her clients very high prices, justifying the charges by the artistry she put into her creations. When one client complained about the costs she retorted, with reference to a well known painter, "Eh! Do you pay Vernet only for his paints and canvas?" However, Mrs Crewe doesn't seem impressed by her artistry. In the 1780s Bertin had been responsible for encouraging the Queen to abandon the stiffness of formal court dress and to wear loose, simple gowns, a move that encouraged Antoinette's image of unconventionality among the French people. During the revolution Rose Bertin went bankrupt as the aristocracy stopped spending their money. She still did work for the Queen though and was part of the conspiracy for the royal couple to flee the country in 1791. Though the King and Queen were captured Rose Bertin escaped abroad and eventually set up a dress shop in London's St. James's.

102 blondes – Mrs Crewe is probably referring to a French lace, originally of unbleached cream-coloured Chinese silk, called blonde lace; for ganses see note 60.

and I want to know if the whole Audience could have been worked up to any great Pitch of Animation or Enthusiasm, had they first heard the Story in any Language than their own? – Here indeed the Audience, even to the lowest of them, by the Shouts which they frequently send forth, and the many inconveniences which they contentedly suffer on crouded Nights, sufficiently prove how capable they are of tasting this Species of Entertainment – Before I sallied forth to the Opera I dined at Monsieur de Caraman's,[100] where we found a very pleasant Society in a great House. This is one of the few Families who have not adhered to all the French Rules of Education. – Their Daughters have not paſſed their Infancy in Convents, nor their Sons in paltry Academies, but the Attention which they have both bestowed upon their Children is universally acknowledged here, and they are esteemed Amiable and respectable for it, without suffering the least Imputation on the Score of Pedantry, which is so frequently found attached to bold Deviations of this Nature. – Their House is very large, and their Garden what we should in London call very Magnificent even for the greatest Nobleman. But at Paris one sees without end House after House upon this large Scale, and abounding in most of the comforts of Life. One thing I have been much struck with in this bitter Cold Season, and that is the Ingenuity with which they contrive that their stoves shall warm all their Apartments. – In a few such Respects they certainly beat us, but, oh! in how many other Points both of Luxury and what I should term Comforts, are they behind us! Madame de Rochfeulle proposed to me to go with her after the Opera to the famous Milliner's Madam.ᴵᴵᵉ Bertin.[101] I was rather surprised at her choosing such a time of Night, but She told me it was a Fashion here to Visit her on a Tuesday Night when the Dreſſes, which were to figure at the Queen's Ball on Wednesday, are usually displayed. We accordingly went, and were ushered by a Servant into a very large Hotel containing a Suite of Rooms which were all well illuminated. – In the first of them there sat about twenty Women and Girls all hard at Work upon Blondes and Ganses[102] – Madame de Rochfeulle talked to one of them with such earnestneſs about a Dreſs for herself which She had in Agitation for some future Ball, that I concluded this must be the great Woman – but no! She proved only to be "the great Woman's Butler" – "We must march further on, She said, to see her" – and when we did so, it was easy indeed to distinguish her, for She sat upon a sort of Throne, at least an elevated Chair in the Center of a much larger Room surrounded by Persons of all Ranks and Denominations, who were listening to her Dictates upon the Important Article of Dreſs. – She was herself decorated too in a much more splendid Manner than the Rest, having her Fingers covered with large valuable Rings, such as are in great Vogue at present, and having, in short, Watch, and Chains, and Trinkets of infinite Value spread all over

103 Beauty, madam, is not an accessory called for.

104 Adélaide Diane Hortense Delie, Duchesse de Brissac, 1742-1807. Before marriage her surname was Mancini de Nevers. She was the daughter of the Duc de Nivernois. Walpole described her in 1765 as "pretty, with a great resemblance to her father; lively and good-humoured, not genteel." (Walpole, vol 31, pp51-2) In 1791 she had been in Italy for 4 years, gravely ill – so much so that Walpole thought she was near death. She married in 1760 Louis Hercule Timoléon, Duc de Cossé who became Duc de Brissac in 1784. The Duc was a member of the King's guard and the Governor of Paris. He was described in 1792 as rich and cheerful, with Madame du Barry as his mistress and every hope of restoring Paris to Louis XVI as his ancestor had done 300 years earlier to Henri IV. However, following the fall of the Tuileries in September 1792 Brissac was murdered and decapitated as he was taken through the town of Versailles, his head being thrown through a window of Madame du Barry's house.

105 Jacques Delille, 1738-1813, described by Mrs Crewe as L'Abbé de Lisle. Mrs Crewe was clearly impressed by him, as were most of his contemporaries, but his reputation has not stood the test of time and his work is now considered at best to be mediocre and at worst poor. He published Les Jardins in 1782. He was an excellent conversationalist and storyteller, read his poetry with great elegance and endeared himself to society with his frivolity, wittiness and good nature. He made the mistake of marrying a tyrannical woman, just one example, people pointed out, of his inability to take sensible decisions. After the revolution he travelled to Switzerland, Germany and London, where he translated Milton's Paradise Lost. He returned to France in 1802.

her. Madame de Rochfeulle presented me to her with a civil Speech which announced my Admiration of her Fame, and, perhaps, nothing can more strongly prove the Force of Ceremony than my feelings at that Instant! – I had actually the Sensation of awe on being brought into the Presence of Mademoiselle Bertin! I beg you won't laugh at this, for I am persuaded, had it been your Case and you had seen the Respectfull and serious Countenances of both Sexes standing round her, you must have caught the Infection as well as myself. – The Duchess de Castries was waiting in one Corner of the Room for her turn to be spoken to – two Ladies had got Possesion of her Ear at the moment we entered – and several Gentlemen were beguiling the Time in different parts of the Room with her Apprentices or Myrmidons – for really what one should call the People who were in this Drawing Room I know not. – I observed several large Wooden Busts and Statues dispersed about, and upon them various Parts of Dress – and, every thing had on it the Stamp of Science, and, if I might judge from the sort of Ecstacy which was lavished on the chief D'oeuvres of her Art, Mademoiselle Bertin has certainly carried it to the highest possible Pitch of Perfection. What was exposed this Night for the Public Inspection was the entire Assortment of the Duchess de Castries' Habit for Versailles to Night. I only wish you could have heard the Words in which the Raptures it did not fail to produce were conveyed – indeed till then I did not know that such a Subject could have produced them – With us, the Figure, and not the Drapery is predominant: but here, the being decorated with Grace and Refinement is almost every thing, and I have known the most Sensible and the most conversant upon better Subjects not scruple to be eloquant upon this! The Hair Dresser said one Day "La beaute Madame ne'st qu'une accesoire applesant![103]

Wednesday Even:g.

I am busy dressing for the Duchess de Brisac's Supper[104] – This Morning we had a Breakfast at the Chevalier Jerneghan's A l'Angloise. ~ The Party consisted of twelve or fourteen People; among whom was L'Abbé de Lisle,[105] Author of a beautiful french Poem called "les Jardins", which I recollect to have read with much Pleasure a year or two ago. This Man's Appearance is against him, but he received the Praises and Compliments which were lavished on his Poems by the Company with so much Modest Simplicity that one forgot he was an Author invited to be brilliant, and it was imposible not to hear with infinite Pleasure some passages from his own Works which they forced him to favour us with, and which he delivered with great Feeling and Energy.

106 Delille spent 18 months in London translating Milton's Paradise Lost into French. Ariosto was Ludovico Ariosto, an important Italian poet who lived from 1474-1533.

107 Nicolas Boileau-Despréaux, 1636-1711, generally known simply as Boileau. He was better known as the founder of French literary criticism than he was for his poetry, although his works were translated into English and much admired there. Dryden regarded him highly.

108 Francois-Marie Arouet Voltaire, 1694-1778, poet, historian and philosopher, embodiment of the 18th century French enlightenment.

109 John Frederick Sackville, 3rd Duke of Dorset, 1745-1799. Educated at Westminster, Member of Parliament for Kent 1768, he succeeded to his title in 1769. He was made a Privy Councillor in 1782 and Ambassador to France from 1783-1789, being received as a Knight of the Garter in 1788. He was a patron of cricket and the lord steward of the royal household from 1789-1799. His life-long friend Sir Nathaniel William Wraxall wrote of him: "His person was highly agreeable; his manners soft, quiet, ingratiating, and formed for a Court; destitute of all Affectation, but not deficient in Dignity. He displayed indeed, neither shining parts, nor superior Abilities. Yet, as he possessed good sense, matured by knowledge of the world, had travelled over a considerable part of Europe, and had improved his understanding by an extensive acquaintance with mankind, he was well calculated for such a Mission. He nourished a strong passion for all the Fine Arts, and a predilection for men of Talents and Artists; a taste which he indulged…But the Mediocrity of his Estate, when contrasted with his high Rank, imposed limits on the liberality of his disposition… To Marie Antoinette, the French Queen, the Duke of Dorset rendered himself highly acceptable, and enjoyed some degree of her personal favor: a circumstance by no means unessential in his situation."(Wraxall, pp.619-620) However, there was another side of Lord Dorset. He was also known as a great womaniser, causing a great deal of gossip over his affair with Lady Derby, which ended with the break up of her marriage and the birth of an illegitimate child; and then having an affair not only with the Duke of Devonshire's wife Georgiana but also with Lady Elizabeth Foster, dearest friend of Georgiana and lover of her husband.

110 William Harcourt, 1743-1830, Member of Parliament for Oxford 1768-1774. His father wrote in 1770 that if he "was not such a lazy fellow he would send me some accounts of what is passing. But so great is his aversion to writing that without an absolute necessity he never sets pen to paper." He was a soldier, achieving some fame when commanding the 16th regiment of light dragoons in the 1776/7 American campaign; leading a small band of men he captured George Washington's 2nd in command, Maj-Gen Charles Lee, which at the time excited hopes in England of a capitulation of the Americans. He eventually rose to the rank of Field-Marshall, although Mrs Crewe refers to him at this time as General Harcourt. At the age of 66 he became the 3rd Earl Harcourt, succeeding his brother to the title.

The Palais Royal

Cagliostro

Frances Greville by Ozias Humphrey

Lady Clermont by Sir Joshua Reynolds

Mlle Raucourt as Medea

Lady Louisa Clarges by John Downman

Le Comedie Francaise

The poor man is almost blind, and that Circumstance alone would have made him interesting – his intrinsic Merit however is very great – his Genius and Imagination seem to be truly poetic, and he gives some striking Proofs of it; for I do aſsure you, upon some reflective and melancholy Subjects he drew Tears from many of us. For my own part, I was quite refreshed with what I heard – After the Turbulence of last Nights Opera and the barren Importance of Mademoiselle Bertin's Court, and it had the same sort of Effect upon my Mind that the pure Air of the Country has upon one's Senses after a long Residence in a smoaky City – Yet I must own these Parties are in general by no means formed for such Enjoyments – they are too mixed and too crouded – Literary Enthusiasm is of a retired contemplative Cast, and requires Elbow Room – at least, I like very few Witneſses to my Feelings when they are so roused. The Abbé de Lisle repeated to us his Characters of Milton and Ariosto,[106] which form I think, charming Contrasts, and are drawn in the most animated Style – His Conceptions of both seem'd to be delicately just, and convinced me he had felt and seized upon their opposite Beauties. – I was overjoyed at the Reverence with which he mentioned Shakespear – His muse seemed to glow with English Zeal, and indeed I am persuaded She was educated in our School ~ – I never met with French Poetry which gave me such real Pleasure. Boileau[107] and Voltaire[108] – but it does not become me to criticise, and so I finish my Treatise on this subject. ✗

Thursday

Thursday 19ᵗʰ January 1786

The Duke of Dorset[109] gave a Dinner Yesterday to all the English on Account of the Queens Birth Day, but we were lazy, and would not go to so crouded a Place. I called at Lady Mornington's in the Evening, and met there Lord Downe, Lady Clermont, Lady Clarges, Miſs Carter, Mʳ. Harcourt,[110] and some more of our Country, who said his Grace had given a very grand Entertainment on the Occasion – I hear indeed from every one that he lives remarkably well and has very good wines, which always stamp a Man for Elegance in the Subject of Housekeeping at least, I have so often heard a great Streſs laid upon this Article, that nothing Sounds more terrible in my Ears than Complaints amongst Men of Deficiences in this one Point. ✗

111 George Bridges Rodney, Lord Rodney, 1718-92. He spent most of his long naval career fighting the French, defeating them in 1747 off Cape Finisterre, bombarding and blockading Le Havre in 1759-60, taking Martinique, St Lucia and Grenada from them in 1762, and victorious over them off Dominica in 1782. Nevertheless the French were kind enough to accept him as a resident in Paris from 1775-8 and, as Mrs Crewe points out, to present him with £2000.

112 Albinia Hobart, 1738-1816, daughter and co-heir of Lord Vere Bertie, she married George Hobart in 1757. Hobart went on to inherit from his brother the title of 3rd Earl of Buckinghamshire in 1793. Mrs Hobart was notorious for her obesity, her love of dancing, her activity in amateur theatricals, her campaigning at the polls, and the gambling table at her house in St James' Square. Gillray produced cartoons emphasising her size, while Walpole was always amazed at her agility considering her size, describing her once as "all in gauze and spangles, like a spangle pudding" (letters vol 32, p111). Such was the lightness with which she danced Harry Conway declared she must be hollow (Walpole's letters vol 10, p259). She campaigned for Pitt in the 1784 election when Mrs Crewe and the Duchess of Devonshire campaigned for Fox – a fact that might explain Mrs Crewe's critical attitude towards her in the diary. Mrs Crewe is as unimpressed with Mrs Hobart's view of the acting of Madame Raucourt as she is with the actress herself.

113 Anne Julie Francoise, Duchesse de La Valliere, 1713-93. Before marriage her surname was de Crussol. She married in 1732 Louis César de la Baume le Blanc, Duc de Vaujour, 1732; he was made Duc de la Valliere in 1739. Walpole wrote in 1766 that she was "… still miraculously pretty though fifty-three". Lady Sarah Bunbury (Sarah Lennox) described her in a letter in 1765: "The Dss de la Valliere, who is 52, is the handsomest woman I saw, but indeed she is extraordinary. Her face is now as beautiful as an angel, & really looks only 25; her person is bad, but she hides that with a cloak." (Lennox; pp171-2).

Saturday Morn. ͛ -

Saturday 21ˢᵗ January 1786

Yesterday in the Afternoon we paid a visit to the poor old Marechal Biron to thank him for his Civilities about Boxes at the Theatre, which I have proffited from since I came. He has always been remarkably obliging to the English; and they will soon, I fear, feel his Lofs, as he seems to be very near his latter End. – An Event which even here they look forward with Regret. His Generosity and Liberality upon all Occasions have been conspicuous, but on no one more, I believe, than his presenting Lord Rodney[111] with two thousand Pounds to enable him to offer his Services to his Country during our late War with France. I can conceive few Actions more noble, or lefs imputable to unworthy Motives. – It is to this Old Man's Magnanimity, perhaps, that we are indebted for our most brilliant Succefs; – After we had finished this Visit, We proceeded to Mʳˢ. Hobart's,[112] and then to the Duchefse de la Valiere's, where I staid Supper. This is the first time I have Supped out since I came here, but I feel now much stronger and better than I did – I rather think I shall often repeat this sort of Visit, for the Hours at Paris are very good one's, and it is besides impofsible to gratify Curiosity without mingling into their Societies at all Hours. – As to the Sights of a public Nature, the Weather has not hitherto permitted me to see any of them – however before my return I hope to visit some that are the most remarkable. Mʳˢ. Hobart's Fete last Night was really delightful – every Mortal was full of Admiration at the Ingenuity with which it was contrived, tho all She had done to make her Apartments appear to such Advantage was at a very trifling Expence; and a great deal of the Enjoyment, I imagine, arose from the Contrast between her House, and indeed that of every English Person, and those of the French upon such Occasions. I say this, because I am sure nothing can be more formal than all the Parties where I have been in Paris before Supper. The women sit regularly in a Circle, and rise at the arrival of every Mortal; so the Bows, Curtsies, and Speeches on setting off are so much more numerous than with us, that it is next to impofsible for any English Person to like French Society till the form is broken through by a Supper, which certainly does put one tolerably at Ease. The Duchefse de la Valiere's[113] was the fullest House I have yet been in – She stays at home every Friday, and last Night there were so many Strangers, particularly English People, that we had all great Difficulty to get Places. Voltaire made the following Lines upon her when She was Young and handsome.

114   *Woman without jealousy*
       Beauty without coquetry
       A good judge without much knowledge
       A good talker without wanting to
       Neither haughty nor familiar
       Without vanity at all
       This is the portrait of la Valliere
       It is neither complete nor flattering.

115   *Catherine Graeme, 1749-1804, married in 1768 Thomas Hampden (formerly Trevor), who was made 2nd Viscount Hampden in 1783. When Mrs Crewe met the Hampdens in Paris they were returning from a year in Italy, spending some of the time there with Lady Clarges. Sir Horace Mann, who met them in Florence, described Lady Hampden and her sister as among his choicest visitors: "both most amiable women", he wrote (Walpole's correspondence, vol 25, p592). But in Rome Lord Hampden played profligately at cards and lost. Earlier, on their first trip to Italy, in 1771, they had been described by Mrs Home as "the maddest of mad people" (Ingamells), and later George Canning was not much taken with them either: "Lord and Lady Hampden (whom I never saw before and do not much like upon this first sight of them. She seems rather affected, though clever, and he a great puppy and a great fool)". (Journal, p265) She was a noted patroness of singers and musicians.*

116   *Marie Louise, born c1734 and living 1807. Before marriage her surname was Amelot de Chaillou. She married in 1752 Claude Sibylle Thomas Gaspard Nicolas Dorothée de Roncherolles, Chevalier de Pont Saint Pierre to 1752, Marquis de Roncherolles from 1752. George Selwyn liked her "much more than any of the whole set" of French at Richmond. Mrs Crewe describes her as a good sort of agreeable woman, but her first visit sparks off from Mrs Crewe a complaint about the formality of visits in Paris. She sees her on three occasions. She is referred to in Walpole's letters as a good friend of Crauford.*

117 *talkative, chatty.*

118 *talking tediously.*

"Femme sans Jalousie
"Belle sans Coquetrie
"Bien Juger sans beaucoup Scavoir
"Bien Parler sans le vouloir
"Ne'tre ni haute ni familliere
"Navoir point de Vanité
"C'est le Portrait de la Valliere
"Il n'est ni finis ni flattée[114]

This old Duchesse has been long a Friend of my Mother's, and was on that Score particularly kind to me, for She provided a Place which was next to herself; but Lady Hampden[115] and I were scrambling together, and I was great and chose the bad Supper in the Antichamber rather than forsake my company in Distress. It is surprising how the Manners of Paris are changed since I was here before – They then never thought of meeting in crowds, except at public Places, and indeed made it a Rule, unless upon very particular Occasions, not to sit down more than eight People to their little Supper. But now the old People say they can get no general Conversation at their Meals, and that ever since this Queen came to the Throne People's Minds have been dissipated, and that much Confusion has ensued. – I observe nevertheless that much more Attention and greater respect is paid to old Age here than in London – at least, one sees old tottering Women going to all these Places, seeming to enjoy them, and treated both by Young Men and young Women with as much good humour and Chearfulness as if they were their Contemporaries – There is, I do think, much Merit in this, and of the three Capitals I have been in, within the last twelve Months, Dublin Paris and London – the two first have undoubtedly the Preference in this Respect. To day I am going to dine in a quiet Way at Madame de Roncherolle's, and I hope afterwards to get home and rest a little. ✗

After Supper - 11 O'Clock -

Lady Clermont, Lady Mornington and my Mother are gone, and I have taken my pen up from Idleness, for I am not sleepy yet. Our Dinner to Day at Madame de Roncherolle's[116] was very comfortable to one, – The Party consisted of nine People, and I must own, the old are, in my Opinion by far the pleasantest to live with here, indeed they are fond of what they call Causêing[117] to such a Degree that we should sometimes think it degenerated into what we call proseing:[118] however one picks up many little Scraps and Anecdotes among them by this means, and I like nothing better at present than to sit quietly and hear their small chat when they have lost Sight of Forms. – I heard one Anecdote to Night

119 Stephanie Félicité Ducrest de Saint Aubin, Comtesse de Genlis, 1746-1830, m Charles Alexis Brulart, Comte de Genlis in 1762. She was at one stage the mistress of the Duc de Chartres (later the Duc d'Orleans) and governess of his children. When Mrs Crewe met her in 1786 she was already the author of a collection of stories Les Veillées du chateau (1784), but became more prolific after leaving France in 1793. She lived by her pen in England and Switzerland, until returning to France in 1802 when she became feted by Napoleon and popular for her novels, a mixture of history, morals, sentimental romance and sensation. Her Mémoires inédits sur le XVIIIe siecle et la Révolution francaise were published in 1825, in which she reflected some of the scandalous way of life before the revolution.

120 Charles Jerningham, 1742-1814, was a French officer, the Chevalier de Barfort, referred to by Mrs Crewe as Chevalier Jerningham. He was also a Knight of Malta and St Louis. He not only put himself out for Mrs Crewe but also for Lady Clarges and Miss Carter, the latter of whom wrote that he had made their stay in Paris pleasant, procuring for them not only pleasures but comforts without end and that he had been more indulgent to them than even a grandmother (Rizzo, p283). When the revolution came he lost all his property in France and had to cross to England. In 1802 he returned to France to see if he could recover what he had lost but without success, and the following year he was arrested and held prisoner until the eventual restoration of the monarchy (Kirk).

121 it's interesting to note the English had an international reputation as tea drinkers even in 1786.

122 Samuel Richardson, 1689-1761, English novelist, published his novel Pamela in 1740; the Harlowe family featured in his novel Clarissa, published in 1747.

of Madame Genlis[119] which the Chevalier Jernegham[120] had from herself. – It was that She had often disguised herself in order to get at the Manners of the lowest People, and once in particular She had taken the habit of a Cook Maid, and paſed a whole Evening in a Servant's Hall, where some of the Footmen had made love to her. The Conversation at present rolls chiefly upon several Duels which have been lately fought between young Men of the first Distinction; and it is thought they will provoke some Reprimand from the King – – It seems that during the Carnival much Mischief often happens, and they frequently fall a fighting God knows why. – A Number of English People are gone to day to Versailles to see a New Opera there – I cannot say I felt any Inclination to take so cold a Drive. However we talk of going there very soon, to see the Installation, and to stay two or three Days, that we may have time to observe at our leisure what is worthy remarking at Versailles. ✗

Saturday

Saturday 28ᵗʰ January 1786

I have not continued this Journal for some Days past, because nothing I have seen or heard of during that time has been worth your notice. In a Morning I have sometimes gone out to Shops, and in an Evening I have sometimes paid and received Visits – in short my Life has been, what, I think, every Paris one may be called, a regular Confusion – indeed most Lives in Capitals are such when they are formed upon a large Scale, and not closely linked with a small, regular Society. – Last Night Madame D'Andelot (a Lady whose Husband, it is supposed, will be shortly sent Ambaſsador to England) gave the English a Tea drinking at her House – For, you must know, they think here that we are never quite happy unleſs when we meet round a Table for that Purpose,[121] – And really I could hardly avoid Smiling at the old fashioned Way in which this Ceremony was performed. One Lady was placed at the Head of the Table to preside over the Rest, who were all seated round it in the same formal Manner that one has seen represented in some uncouth Frontispieces of old English Romances – And so it is in most other Customs in which they ape us: for, being little acquainted with our Refinements and the Manners of the day, they take them more from Novels than actual Observations, and for that plain Reason, are much more like what we were than what we are. Madame D'Andelot, for example, had certainly read Pamela, or the Harlowe Family,[122] and we were more obliged to Mʳ. Richardson for our fine Dish of Tea than to her. After this Ceremony

123 cicerones – guides.

124 her son John, born 1772, so 13 years old at this time.

125 John Hampden-Trevor, 1749-1824, created 2nd Viscount Hampden in 1776. He was educated at Westminster and Christ Church Oxford before becoming a Member of Parliament between 1768 and 1774. He was a diplomat, the British Minister at Munich in 1780 and at Turin from 1783-1798. (DNB)

was over, more Company came in, and I was presented to many Persons of both Sexes who were very obliging in their Offers of Civility during the Rest of my Stay at Paris. – But, I believe, what I shall see and what I shall do, is already pretty well determined upon. Our Party to Versailles will soon take Place, provided my Mother, who is to day confined with a Cold, recovers soon enough ~ Lady Clermont and Monsieur de Castries are busy preparing Lodgings and Ciceronies[123] for us at that Place – All I dread is the Quantity of Amusement I must swallow, and the poor Pittance of Repose I am likely to get. However I consider it as a sort of Duty to see all that I can see with tolerable Ease before I leave this part of the World: And my Health lately has been so much better than it was upon my arrival at Paris, that I hope to have no Excuse for Lazineſs on that Account. The Duke of Dorset has sent us a second Invitation to dine with him, but it falls out unluckily upon one of the Days which has been long destined for Versailles. ~ This I am sorry for as I wished to have a View of him in his Glory as Ambaſsador. My Brother Charles goes continually to the Versailles Balls, and seems much leſs tired by this Place than he was, which I am very glad of, as I flatter myself he may be tempted to continue with my Mother here sometime after I have left her. – As to myself, I must honestly confeſs to you that I wish to return, for the Sake of seeing my Son[124] after this long Absence – I certainly wish also to see you and a few more friends in England whom I love; but John at present is the Object which I have for ever in my View. If you ask me what I seriously think of the Life at Paris, I will tell you fairly that, were I a French Woman I verily believe I should prefer it to that of London for many Reasons, but more particularly on the important Account of Hours, which are here regular and wholesome ones, tho I think they are not so well proportioned as they might be, and that in point of Morning one is sadly bilked of it, unleſs indeed one determines upon rising much earlier that at this Season of the Year can be expected. Not but the Weather at this Moment is remarkably mild, and we are all wondering what you can mean by writing about Snow and Frost in England. Last night a Party of English supped here after Madame d'Andelot's, and it was very comfortable. To Night we were to have gone to the Italian Comedy, and afterwards to a concert at Lord Hampden's,[125] but my Mother was not well enough to Stir out, and I have taken this Opportunity of being lazy and writing Letters to my Friends in England. To-morrow is Post Day, when I hope in God I shall hear from some of them. I am likewise very impatient to learn what has been done in the opening of Parliament.

126 Doctor Lee is not identified.

127 Frederick St John, 1765-1844, probably the 2nd son of Frederick St John, 2nd Viscount Bolingbroke. He was a General in the army.

128 Not traced. He may be the same Mr Hardy identified by Ingamells (see bibliography), who was in Florence in 1784 and Venice in 1792.

129 On a visit to Paris in 1791 William Windham wrote to Mrs Crewe asking her to send letters to him via "Monsieur Perregaux, Banquier"; this sounds like the same person. In fact he was Alphonse Claude Charles Bernardin, Comte Perregaux, 1750-1808, who, soon after Mrs Crewe's diary was written, began lending money to the Duchess of Devonshire and became one of many to whom she was indebted. His wife was painted by Vigée Le Brun in 1789.

Sunday

Sunday 29ᵗʰ January 1786

My Mother was so very far from well Yesterday in the Afternoon that I persuaded her to let me send for Docᵗʳ. Lee,[126] an English Physician, who has resided here since he left off Practice, and is good enough to give Aſsistance to People of our Country when they stand in need of it. He called at Night and found She had some Fever; which however this Morning is much abated, and I hope She will be soon quite well. This Docᵗʳ. Lee seems a plain good sort of regular Physician – Lady Mornington and General Harcourt both knew something of him before he came here. But, had he been the lowest in our School, he would have been worthy fifty of the French Practitioners, who talk such old fashioned Nonsense, even the best of them, about bleeding in the Foot, a seventh Day Crisis, and a thousand other long exploded notions, as prove them to be very far behind us in this Science. It is not likely indeed the Case should be otherwise for the Profeſsion is treated in so humiliating a Way that no Gentleman can enter into it. There have nevertheleſs been a few Instances of tolerable Skill in some Cases, and, I believe, only a few. – in general they are certainly Bunglers. ✗

Monday

Monday 30ᵗʰ January 1786

The English Post brought no great nor very interesting News, last Night, of any Sort. I find that some beautifull Dresden China, which Frederic Sᵗ. John[127] made me a Present of, was seized at the Custom House, and likewise some Tapestry that I sent over by Mʳ. Hardy[128] – How provoking this is in a little Way! But some good will accrue to me from it, for I shall be extremely cautious respecting such Matters in my own Journey. I have for this Reason already adopted the Advice of Monsieur Perigord,[129] the Banker, who has been obliging enough to undertake the Conveyance of several small Articles which I have to carry as Presents to my Friends. This Precaution is not unneceſsary; for by all Accounts the Custom Houses in England are terribly strict at present. Last Night, as I found towards ten O'Clock that my Mother seemed pretty well, I resolved to go to a Ball, which I had an Invitation to, at Monsieur de

133

130 Daniel Hailes is described by Mrs Crewe as a Secretary at the embassy and a "civil good sort of Softly character". He was appointed as Minister Plenipotentiary to France from April 28 1784 and is also referred to in 1787 in a letter sent by Madame de Sabran to the Chevalier de Boufflers, where she says she likes him very much. (Webster, p230)

131 Louis Marie, Vicomte de Noailles. The Noailles family were one of the grand court families of the 18th century, at a level with the Rohan and Lorraine families. They survived the revolution and despite losing their pre-eminence in royal circles nevertheless maintained a position as a great landed dynasty in the Eure-et-Loir region. The Vicomte de Noailles was related to the Marquis de Lafayette and shared with him his fascination for America and its revolution. Together they planned to go to America to fight for independence – in the end Lafayette went but pressure from family and King prevented Noailles. Noailles became one of a group of courtiers against the court, aristocrats against privilege, those who wanted to replace dynastic with national patriotism. He was a prominent player on the night of August 4th 1789 when the National Assembly proposed the abolition of feudal rights. With an outburst of revolutionary oratory he turned a session that had met with the purpose of restoring order throughout the country into one that dramatically dismantled many of the rights that supported the position of the aristocracy. The kingdom, he said, "floated between the alternatives of a complete destruction of society and a government which would be admired and followed throughout Europe."(Schama, p.438) Public order, he said, could only be re-established if the causes of public revolt were removed. To achieve this purpose he proposed to the Assembly "that taxes be paid by all individuals of the kingdom according to their revenues, that all public charges should in the future be borne equally by all, that all feudal obligations be redeemable by the payment of fixed sums of money.... but that the corvée, mortmain and other personal servitudes be abolished without indemnity". (Barry, p.448) At the time of Mrs Crewe's visit he would have been about 30 years old: she seems irritated by his excessive offers of civility, his great quantity of small talk, and his insistence on sending her two new books to read which arouses in her a "spirit of contradiction". Neither did Vigée Le Brun find him easy: "The Marechal de Noailles had a sharp mind which could be especially cutting. He found it difficult to resist making a sarcastic comment whenever the opportunity arose." (Vigée le Brun, p63).

132 coxcomical - the amusing behaviour of a conceited dandy.

133 Diane-Adélaide, Comtesse de Simiane, 1761-1835. In later years she is referred to in the Burney journals, several times, as someone Burney liked to see.

134 macaronies - 18th century English dandies who affected continental manners and styles.

Caraman's and accordingly, after my Brother Charles and I had supped together, I set out. On my Arrival I met Mr. Hailes (the English Secretary)[130] on the Stair Case, who told me the Company was at Supper, but that did not signify, and he would convey me to the Mistreſs of the House, which he did – She immediately procured me a Seat at her own Table, and, tho I had no Acquaintance with my Neighbourhood, I was very well amused with observing the Beauties which sat near me, and the Stile and Manner in which the fine Folks of Paris appeared in when their Hearts were open; for at a Ball there is always, I think, a kind of Gratitude to the Master and Mistreſs of the House, and a Determination to be pleased which restrains every symptom of ill humour and Sulkineſs. ~ We were an immense while at Table, but when Supper finished we went down Stairs, where the Young People resumed their Dancing, and for the most part appeared to very great Advantage. I was vastly well entertained with the Variety which went on, but I could not help thinking the whole time that I liked a good honest English Ball much better. In the first place, every body with us has more Liberty than is permitted here, for if one is past the Age of Thirty, or should not choose to Dance, one is desired to take a Seat in a particular Place, where one may sit the whole Evening without a probability of speaking to any Person except one's next Neighbour – Every thing indeed is so nicely regulated that it must be formal, and, for my own part, I would most chearfully dispense with much of the <u>Propriety</u> in a French Aſsembly, for the Sake of enjoying a little leſs Restraint. The Dances were all Cotillions, and, as only eight got up at a time, the Ball Room was not, you may suppose, a large one, but rather chosen for its Shape, I imagine, as there was a very large Room near it, in which I observed only two or three old Men who seemed to be walking about to talk over their Politicks. Monsieur de Noailles[131] shewed off very much in his Dance, and acquitted himself very well. He seems to be a leading Figure in the great World of Paris; but his Manners are so Coxcomical[132] that I have heard many of his own Country criticise them. Madame de Simiane[133] was the most remarkable for Beauty at this Ball, and in every other Country She would be called handsome. Madame de Coigny is a little Coquet who is distinguished by her Wit and Repartee; but I have so slight an Acquaintance with her that I can form only a slender Judgment of her Capacity and Cleverneſs. The Dreſses in general struck me as very like those I have seen at the Prince of Wales's Ball – and in point of Dancing, I could discover no Difference from our Cotillions, except that the Men keep on their Hats, and have upon the whole a much better Air than our Macaronies.[134] – It is the Fashion for most young Frenchmen to wear Black Cloathes, even when they are not in Mourning – They say, it answers to them in the Article of Expence, and has always a good Appearance. – I am not sure that this is not a sensible and good Custom,

135 Anne Louise Germaine Necker, 1766-1817, daughter of the financier Jacques Necker, and better known at a later date as the Baroness de Stael. She married the Swedish Ambassador to Paris Eric Magnus, Baron of Stael-Holstein just before Mrs Crewe's visit to Paris and though she had three children by him it was said to be a marriage without affection and they separated in 1798. In later life she wondered if she would not have done better to have married William Pitt, as had been proposed. Soon after Mrs Crewe saw her at the Caraman's ball she established a salon in Paris that became a centre of intellectual activity and political discussion. In 1788 she published a book on Rousseau and went on over the next 30 years to write novels, plays, essays, historical and critical works, and political memoirs. Her views hold a place in the development of French thought which has ensured her a place in the history books. Her father had been a popular Minister of Finance but wasn't liked by the King, who dismissed him in 1781.

136 John Benjamin Laborde, 1734-1794. He was a musical composer and writer on the history of music, born at Paris 1734. He studied under Rameau and was admitted to the court of Louis XV, to whom he was appointed first valet de chambre. He composed several operas, amongst which the most successful was his Gilles Garcon Peintre, which he produced in 1758. On the death of Louis XV in 1774, Laborde resigned his office, married and became one of the fermiers-généraux. In 1780 he published his 4 volume Essai sur la Musique Ancienne et moderne, published at great expense and embellished with a great number of well-executed engravings. The French revolution brought on the ruin of Laborde. A farmer-general could expect no favour from the leaders of the revolution and he perished on the scaffold on the 20th July 1794, five days before the fall of Robespierre. His wife was Rosalie Laborde who was painted by Vigée le Brun in 1774/5.

137 Buxton: a spa town in Derbyshire.

138 coute qui coute: whatever the cost.

139 not quite alone: she had her maid with her!

140 Bridge of Save – she means the Bridge of Sèvres, crossing the River Seine to the south-west of the city.

141 James Greville, one of Mrs Crewe's brothers. Born in Lorraine, France in June 1753, he attended Harrow School and Trinity College, Cambridge, studying for the church and receiving his degree in 1780. He served as Rector of Stockton-on-Tees from 1780-82, Rector of Whickham, Durham from 1782-1816 and Rector of Peasemore in Buckinghamshire from 1816. For further information see the Introduction.

but I leave you to determine that point for me. Monsieur Nechar's Daughter[135] was at this Ball too – She is just married to the Swedish Amba∫sador, and every Body was curious to look at her, and pronounce upon her first Appearance. Mademoiselle Bertin, it seems, told her, "She had prepared a Dre∫s, which would at once expre∫s by It's Ornaments the Genius of her Father, and the Virtues of her Mother"! This curious Speech of their famous Milliner is repeated in all Houses – She may have verified her A∫sertion but, if She did, Genius and Virtue were expre∫sed in a Language that I do not understand. My Brother Charles Yesterday brought my Mother and me a fine Me∫sage from Madame de Polignac to invite us to sup with her at Versailles on Tuesday, and to go afterwards to see the Representation of a new Piece – This it seems is a great Compliment coming from the Queen's Favourite; but the going and returning at Night, after doing so much, sounds very fatiguing, and I have declined it, meaning to content myself with going to Versailles on Wednesday Evening to stay two Days, to see the Installment and other Sights there at my Ease. I pa∫sed this Morning with my Mother till near two O'Clock, and then called on Lady Clarges, on Lady Mornington, and on Madame de Rochefeulle – The last is confined at home at present. M^r. and M^rs. Labord[136] have promised to come and sup with me this Evening in a quiet Way at ten O'Clock. – They are both of them pleasant comfortable People, and there is something in her character and Manner of thinking that would strike you as being in a very superior Stile, if you knew her as well as I do; indeed it struck me from my first Acquaintance with her at Buxton.[137] 𝒳

Wednesday Even.ᵍ.

Versailles ~

Wednesday 1ˢᵗ February 1786

Here am I – God knows why! for I protest I can hardly tell you how it happened that I should have Courage enough to make this Excursion quite alone! The fact however was that People had talked so much of the Installation and of It's being a fine Sight for Strangers, that I said nothing should hinder me from seeing it, so I went on, saying I <u>would</u>

142   Lady Payne: wife of Sir Ralph Payne, Member of Parliament, created 1ˢᵗ Lord Lavington in the Irish peerage, 1795. Frances Lambertina Payne was the daughter of Baron Heinrich Kolbel of Saxony. George Canning gave a description of her: "Ly. Payne is a woman of fashion, more completely answering in every point (except folly and vice) to that description than almost any woman I know. She is a foreigner by birth (a Pole) but married very young, and has ever since (perhaps these 25 or 30 yrs.) lived in England, in the very best company, knowing everybody and universally liked". Canning also reports the Paynes as being friends of Molly Carter.

143   Elizabeth Ann Sheridan, 1754-1792, first wife of Richard Brinsley Sheridan. Reported to be exceptionally beautiful and with a wonderful singing voice she remained on friendly terms with Mrs Crewe even though she either knew or strongly suspected that her husband was having an affair with her friend. In 1791 she had an affair herself, with Lord Edward Fitzgerald. Always delicate in health her life became threatened through pregnancy with Fitzgerald's child and she died a few months after it was born. Her story is told in <u>Sheridan's nightingale</u>, by Alan Chedzoy.

144   Dorothy, Duchess of Portland, only daughter of the 4ᵗʰ Duke of Devonshire and wife of William Henry Cavendish Bentinck, 3ʳᵈ Duke of Portland, who had been Prime Minister in 1783 and went on to become Prime Minister again from 1807-1809. She and Mrs Crewe had worked together to secure the election of Charles James Fox at Westminster two years earlier. Mrs Crewe's brother Charles married, in 1793, Charlotte Bentinck, daughter of the Duke and Duchess of Portland.

145   Hannah Hare, wife of the Foxite MP James Hare. Her husband had come from a poor background but mixed with the wealthy, winning and losing large sums at cards. A great supporter of Charles Fox he had even shared a house with him at one point. His profligacy was rescued for a time when he married, in 1774, Hannah, daughter of Sir Abraham Hume who, it was said, brought with her a very considerable fortune. They had one daughter but he and his wife soon separated and he had several children by subsequent liaisons.

146   Dr Charles Burney, 1726-1814, composer and author of <u>A General history of music</u>, long considered a standard work . As a young man was been employed by Mrs Crewe's father, Fulke Greville, and had been witness at his wedding. A life-long friend to Mrs Crewe he was also her godfather. Well-known and highly considered in his own day his fame was overtaken by that of his daughter, the diarist and novelist Fanny Burney, who also produced <u>Memoirs of Doctor Burney</u>, published in 1832.

147   Mr Tredell: not identified.

148   tiff – i.e. get themselves dressed up (from tiffany).

149   vapour about – to make idle boasts, empty talk.

150   from Shakespeare's <u>King John</u>, Act 1, Scene 1, lines 202-3: "And talking of the Alps and Apenines, The Pyrenean and the river Po –".

see it <u>coute qui Coute,</u>[138] till I found at last that I was engaged to myself, and did not dare put myself off. My Mother is still confined to her Apartment, tho upon the whole much better than She has been for some time – however <u>her</u> coming was out of the Question – Lady Clermont said She would not come – my Brother Charles would not come – and so I was necessitated to come alone to this queer Hotel[139] – But the Hotel is not the worst part of the Business, for as to being at an Inn alone, I never think that uncomfortable provided there is a good Fire, but I find that two Grandees, who were to have <u>the Honor</u> of attending me to the Church tomorrow, were obliged to leave this Place to day, and all I have now for it is to be escorted to the Church by the Master of the Ceremonies at Court – Yet I don't much Care about this Circumstance either – I shall, I hope, see the Sight; and, tho I met with a sad Disaster upon the Road, one of the Horses tumbling down, and my Maid and I being detained upon the Bridge of Save[140] three Quarters of an hour, – both terrified to Death, because we were on so narrow a part of it that every Carriage which came by gave us a Shock, as if it meant to tip us over into the Seine – notwithstanding all this, I say, I feel to have very tolerable Courage for to-morrow's Bustle. This Morning as I was writing Letters for the Post who should walk into the Room but my Brother James[141] – He is going on to travel I don't know where, and means to spend a few days at Paris in his Way. I proposed this little Agreeable Party to Versailles to him, and he seemed to like the Thoughts of it very well – So I hope he will be here time enough to-morrow Morning to set off with me to the Church. – Last Night I sat at home quietly with my Mother, and the same Party which was here the Night before came to sup with me. This I think, is all I have to tell you for the present. As to the Letters I receive, I seldom mention them, as you must know more about their Contents than I can inform you of. My Correspondents have been pretty good upon the whole since I left England, and Lady Payne,[142] Mrs. Sheridan,[143] the Dutchess of Portland,[144] Mrs. Hare,[145] Dr. Burney,[146] Mr. Tredell[147] &c – have at different times sent me very comfortable Prog of various Sorts ~ Good Night! I must be up with the Lark to get my Hair Dressed for this Shew. I begin almost to repent the having taken so much trouble to see a parcel of Men <u>tiff</u>[148] themselves in blue Ribbands – but I am in the Scrape now, you see, and so I'll get through it handsomely – It will, at all Events, serve to vapour about[149] when I get to England – Oh! how I shall shew off amongst you all with "my Alps, my Appenines, and River Po"[150] (or, at least, My Spa, my Brussells, and the River Seine) ✗ Not one of which, however, between you and me, is worth an Evening's Walk over poor Philip's Hill, when one makes some new Remark upon Beeston Castle, and finds out that the Welch Hills are pretty Objects from that Spot. ✗ near Crewe Hall! –[151]

151 Beeston Castle is between Nantwich and Chester, in Cheshire. It was built in 1220 on a massive block of red stone with a sheer cliff on either side, giving it a spectacular position. It was reduced to a ruin during the English Civil War, but from at least the 18th century its wonderful views have made it a favourite spot for picnics. Crewe Hall was the country home of the Crewes.

152 Mrs Zeperfield – no further information about her.

153 Lady Anne Smith was the daughter of Lewyns Boldero Barnard of Cave Castle, Yorkshire, and married Robert Smith in 1780. The Smiths had 12 children, eleven of whom were girls.

154 Louise, Countess Potocka, wife of Comte Ignace Potocki. She had been married previously to Prince Saphieha and after Comte Potocki went on to marry twice more. In 1791 she was painted by Vigée le Brun, when they were both in Rome

Friday
Paris

Friday 3rd February 1786

I cannot say much in favour of my second Expedition to Versailles, For Fate seemed determined that I should meet with nothing but little Disappointments from the time it was first proposed. A Letter, which the Gentleman who was to have conducted me to the Chapel, wrote and dispatched was, by some Mistake, sent to another Inn, so that I did not receive it till an hour after the Time he appointed me to set off – the Streets were then so full of People that I grew frightened about driving alone to the Place where he was to wait for me – My Brother James too – who left Paris early in the Morning in order that he might be in time to accompany me, Mistook the Hotel, and, concluding from not finding me at first that I was gone to the Ceremony, set of by himself for it – so that, in short, with all these Impediments I only saw the Procession of Knights in the Gallery of the Palace. The Irishman in the Jubilee was therefore a Joke to me. I went to the Gallery because my Courage failed me about the Church, and I was conducted thither by Mrs Zeperfield,[152] an old Servant who lived with me formerly and is now settled at Versailles. My Brother James and I after this met at my Inn, and we both returned together to Paris, where we found my Mother very much recovered from her late Illness – I passed the Evening agreeably in her Drawing Room with the Duc de Nivernois and Monsieur de Caramans, who paid her Visits. As to the Ceremony, which I saw so small a Part of in the Morning, I will not attempt to describe it – All I shall tell you is, that the Dresses and Pageantry appeared to me on the whole to be very magnificent. The King and Queen of France looked imposing enough in all their Finery – But I had much rather have heard the Music in the Chapel which they tell me was very fine indeed. ✗

Saturday

Saturday 4th February 1786

We had a very grand Entertainment at the English Ambassador's Yesterday, and as I know you will like a List of the Company you shall have one. ~ The Ladies were Lady Hampden, Lady Clarges, Miss Carter, Lady Smith[153] (Wife to Sir Robert Smith) Mrs Goldburne, Madame Potoski,[154] Miss Payne and Myself. The Gentlemen Lord Hampden,

155 William Gardiner, 1748-1806, a lieutenant-colonel in the 45th Foot (Sherwood Forest) from 1778, who went on to become a special envoy at Brussels, 1789-1792, an MP in the Irish parliament and Commander in Chief of Nova Scotia in 1805.

156 Mr Crosby: not identified.

157 George Byng, 1764-1847. On his return from Paris he later that year joined the Whig Club and Brooks's, determining his future political career. He became the Member of Parliament for Middlesex in 1790 and continued to hold the seat through to 1847. A sympathetic commentator described him in 1813 as "one of the old Whigs, a moderate reformer, and a man who has never acted an equivical, but rather a manly, fair, and open part. It would be well for themselves, and well for the country, if many others possessed the moderation of Mr Byng; but it must also be added, that unless there were others more active, and more ardent, public affairs would receive but little attention."

158 Ignace Potocki, 1750-1815, a Grand Marshall of Lithuania and Polish Ambassador at Berlin. In 1792 he fled the country and was stripped of his estates, but returned in 1794. Handed over to the Russians he was imprisoned for some years in the castle at Schlusselbourg. In 1809 he was made envoy and ambassador extraordinary at Vienna.

159 hazard is a dice game dating back to the 14th century, popular and played for high stakes in 18th century English gambling rooms. The banker sets a stake. The player calls a number from 5 to 9 and then throws two dice. A correct call wins the stake. The player loses for an incorrect call, but there are some combinations which allow the player to continue to throw, whilst neither winning nor losing.

160 presumably "Skreens" – i.e. fire screens.

161 Robert Bisset, 1759-1805, an historian, born in Scotland but moved to London where he set up an academy in Chelsea. He wrote works on Edmund Burke (1798) and George III (1804) as well as two novels: Douglas, or the Highlander in 1800 and Modern literature in 1804. He was also the editor of an eight-volume edition of The Spectator in 1796. His death in 1805 was said to have been caused by "chagrin under embarrassed circumstances" (DNB).

Colonel Gardner,[155] Lord Downe, M[r]. Hailes (the Secretary) M[r]. Crosby,[156] M[r]. Byng,[157] my Brother Charles, Count Potoski,[158] his Father and Brother, the <u>Senator of Rome</u>, and a Man I never learned the name of. The Senator is now the only Person who bears that Character in Rome; he lives, I am told, in the Capitol: and his Office is merely to preserve a Vestige of It's former State. We staid in the Evening some time to play at Hazard,[159], and to talk English with Impunity. ~ There is great comfort, I think, in being now and then released from the Labor of expreſsing one's self in a Foreign Language, which, by the Way, is often not only Fatiguing, but Embarraſsing likewise. - I found my Mother at home receiving Company, and I staid in her Circle till it was time to Sup – I then retired with my Brother Charles, James and a few more English to my own Drawing Room.

Sunday

Sunday 5th February 1786

Yesterday was a day of Presents – Soon after Breakfast I received two pretty Fire Skeens[160] painted upon Silk from the Duc de Nivernois. – This Galanterie was in Consequence of my having last Night wanted one – A few Hours after this Lady Clarges gave me several Strings of Roman Pearls, which She had brought from Italy with her: and when She found that there were not quite enough to set in Buckles as her own were, M[r]. Biſset,[161] who is likewise come from Rome, insisted upon supplying the Deficiency – There would have been something so stiff and so Stupid in refusing this little Offer, that I checked my first Impulse to do so, and shall therefore be rewarded with this Pearl. You will say perhaps, "what Objection could you have to M[r]. Biſset's Present-"? Why, none that I can give any good Reason for. I only think, that it is awkward to be under the least Obligation to People one has but a Slight degree of Acquaintance with, and who are not likely to fall much in one's Way. I have however asked him to Sup here this Evening; and besides feeling gratefull to him for his Pearl, I believe him to be a good sort of Gentleman like Man. You imagine, perhaps, you are now at the End of my Presents – but you are not: for before the Day finished Miſs Carter insisted on giving me a Pair of Ear Rings made of the same sort of Pearl, but much Larger, and Amazingly pretty. My Mother is better than She was but does not go out yet, so that we see a great deal of Company in an Evening – Last Night the Mixture of French and English was by no means unentertaining. ~

162 George John, 2nd Earl Spencer, 1758-1834, brother to Georgiana Duchess of Devonshire. Educated at Harrow and Trinity College Cambridge, he took the Grand Tour in 1778-80 and on his return went into Parliament. Politically associated with the Rockingham and Cavendish Whig factions he played a prominent part in the downfall of North's administration and was rewarded with the position of Lord of the Treasury in 1782. It was a short tenure, though, and that same year he adhered to Fox rather than remain in office under Shelburne. He succeeded to his father's title as Earl Spencer in 1783 and continued to support Fox from the House of Lords. In 1794 he switched his allegiance to Pitt, taking positions as a Privy Councillor 1794, First Lord of the Admiralty December 1794-February 1801, and Home Secretary 1806-7.
Lavinia, Countess Spencer, 1762-1831, daughter of 1st Earl Lucan. According to the <u>Dictionary of National Biography</u> she was a "woman of great beauty and intelligence, brilliance of conversation and charm of character", but her sister-in-law Lady Bessborough held a different view, writing of "her cleverness (which term peculiarly suits her in every way).... coarseness of mind, as well as of expression.... intolerance.... the most extravagant abuse, the most unsparing scrutiny. Nothing escapes: character, understanding, opinions, dress, person, age, infirmity – all fall equally under [her] scalping knife." Lady Bessborough also mentions Lady Spencer's "excellent understanding.... Political Asperity.... exterminating Virtue and stern Piety" (White, The complete peerage). Reynolds painted her portrait on more than one occasion.

163 Louis Athanase des Balbes de Berton de Crillon, 1726-1789. It's interesting that Mrs Crewe should describe him as "a sort of blue stocking wit", a term usually applied to women. Most of the Crillon family went into the army but Louis Athanase took instead to the Church. In 1771 he produced his first book <u>De l'Homme moral</u> and followed it in 1777-9 with the 2 volume work <u>Memoires phliosophiques de M. le Baron de cambellan de sa majesté limpératrice reine.</u>

164 "Oh! my god! madame", said she, "he said this time my pains are no longer of the liver but of the kidneys so he will make another change of medicine."

Wednesday Night.

Wednesday 7ᵗʰ February 1786

Tho I do not Visit or run about half so much as most People here, I really can but seldom find time to sit down to write either to you, or any other of my Friends in England – Indeed and indeed I cannot reconcile myself to Paris Mornings – they are by much too short for Comfort, and certainly for Correspondence, which, perhaps, you will say is not unlucky, Since I Select so few Facts or Anacdotes worth recording – but this Sort of Rebuke now would signify very little, for I have long made up my Mind to the Justice of it, and I can say without Insincerity that my chief Motive for Scribbling as I do is for the Pleasure of conversing with You. Lord and Lady Spencer[162] arrived here Yesterday from Nice, and are, I understand, to stay a Fortnight, but I have not seen them yet. To Night we have Supped at Lady Mornington's – and last Night Mʳ. and Mʳˢ. Laborde, Lord Downe, and a few more English Supped here. The Night before last I went to a new Comedy, which was so entirely devoid of Intrigue, Wit, humour or Merit of any kind, that I hardly thought the Actors would be allowed to get through with it – but it was not quite condemned. I am told, much Partiality and unpardonable Indulgence prevail at present upon this Subject; tho the Modern Productions are indeed seldom such as to admit of any Violent Competition between Authors of any kind. – To Night Monsieur de Crillon,[163] a Sort of <u>Blue Stocking Wit</u>, called on my Mother and told us that, as we had Exprefsed a Wish to see the <u>Lice'e</u> or <u>Lyceum</u> here, we should receive an Invitation from a few of It's Members to go there some Morning before I left Paris – I feel very glad of this, as I shall like to have once seen all that is remarkable here; and if the Lectures we shall hear, turn upon the <u>Belles Lettres</u>, and not on Mathematicks or any of the abstruse Sciences, it is pofsible we may meet with some Entertainment. ~ Apropos to what is unintelligible, I called this Morning upon my little Spa Acquaintance Madame de Rochfeulle, and was very sorry to find her in Bed with a Disorder She has several times Complained of lately – I could not help saying that I feared her Physician had mistaken her Case, and asked her what he really thought her complaint Was " ~ Oh! mon Dieu! Madame (said She) il dit a cette heure que mes Douleurs ne sont plus <u>Hepatique</u> mais <u>Nephretique</u> ainsi qu'il faut encore changer medicine."[164]   I asked her the meaning of both those Words, as you may suppose, because they left me just as much in the Dark as I was before, but I was sorry, for this poor little Woman's Sake, to find that She had no clearer Ideas of them than myself, and that She was likely to continue in total Ignorance about her Complaint, and Consequently quite at the Mercy of her miserable French Physician! – The Fact is, as I have elsewhere remarked, they are

165 Mrs Crewe is probably referring back to Moliere's play Monsieur de Pourceaugnac, which she saw on 4th January. The play contains a famous satirical episode describing a consultation between doctors.

166 Fermier General: someone who had a contract with the Crown to collect certain indirect taxes, on commodities like tobacco, salt, and soap, in return for sums of money advanced to the Treasury. The contracts ran for six years and accounted for as much as one third of all revenues collected by the State. Traditionally the Fermier Generals made large profits on the transactions and were hated by the people for the ruthless manner their uniformed officers entered, searched and seized property. They became an obvious object of hatred during the revolution and many were guillotined, spectacularly so during a mass execution in May 1794. The person she refers to here is probably Monsieur Monregard, who she dines with again on 20th February.

167 Place de Louis Quinze: now the Place de la Concorde, at the eastern end of the Champs Elysées.

168 petite Maitresse: foppish woman.

here sadly behind us in the Art, and if any English Physician happens to be called in, his Superiority is instantly discernible – You see therefore Moliere's Satyre has no good Effect among the Order, in this Country at least[165] – I wonder it has not checked their Pedantry a little – Yet, Why do I wonder? for is not Pedantry in Profeſsions the Companion of Ignorance. ⨯

Saturday

Saturday 10ᵗʰ February 1786

My Mother and I Yesterday dined at the House of a rich Fermier General.[166] And, to say the truth, I was very happy to escape one day from the very fine Parts of Paris, and to see it in a more homely and Genuine Point of View. The Gentleman and Lady of this House are very old Friends of my Mother's, and talked to me about my Brothers and myself when we were Children in Loraine. - They gave us an excellent Dinner, and shewed us several Apartments that the best lodged Peer in London would think magnificent – indeed I am not quite certain that I don't think their Hotel, considering It's Situation (for it stands in the Place de Louis Quinze[167] which is the finest Part of Paris) take it for all in all, is not the most Delightful Habitation I ever saw in any Capital. - We found Mʳˢ. Goldburne here, who, it seems, is very intimate with the Daughter in Law of the House – whom we saw nothing of, for She is now lying in – but what is all this to you? I will change the Subject. We are Busy preparing for Versailles where we are to Sup to Night with the Queen's Favourite Madame de Polignac, and where it is probable we shall sup with the Queen herself. I hope H. M. will come there that I may have it to talk of hereafter, otherwise I should care little about it, for I am inclined to feel quite tired and Disgusted with the Noise She is always making about nothing at All – She certainly is a perfect Mistreſs of the Art of tiring; and so much does She encourage it that, I understand, it is entirely owing to her that One's Attention is forever engaged about Subjects which can be no way interesting after they are first started. – The Effect, for Instance, of Mademoiselle Bertin's Dreſses, the Fashions among the Gentlemen's Buckles, the Comparisons between English and French Fashion – all this, with much more of equal Dignity, has been introduced as Important Conversation by the Queen of France into the Polite Circles. – I have heard several old Persons complain terribly of the height to which Frivolité is carried, merely because her Majesty is much prouder of the Title of <u>petite</u> <u>Maistreſse</u>[168] than of Queen of France. –

169 she was baptised November 28th 1748, so would have been just turned 37 at this time.

170 from John Dryden's Macflecknoe, 1682:
"Thy genius calls thee not to purchase fame
In keen iambics, but mild anagram:
Leave writing plays, and choose for thy command
Some peaceful province in Acrostic Land.
There thou mayest wings display and altars raise,
And torture one poor word ten thousand ways."

171 Jonathan Swift, 1667-1745, English author.

172   "Vile species bold how well you Play
the role of a Queen."
"Why not, my Sovereign?
You often play at mine."
Mademoiselle D'Oliva had a reputation as a prostitute, so the epigram casts a slur on the Queen. For information on the diamond necklace affair see the Introduction, pages 41-44.

To say true, as I am an oldish Person myself[169], I am as tired as they are of so much frivolité; tho I by no means desire or think that it is necefsary to talk on very wise or learned Subjects – I only mean to say, that almost all Subjects are tiresome, if discufsed every day and for Hours together, and that that of Drefs in particular is surely a very barren One after a few things have been said upon it. Besides, the very Idea of Mens being occupied much about their Persons certainly decreases the Dignity they might have in other Respects – The Buttons they often wear would make you quite Sick! You must puzzle for two Hours sometimes about the Name of one of their Common Women. The Anagram is spread all round him, and, look which way you will, this Name or some Motto (which perhaps, When Descyphered, is not fit to be read) you are to talk of Afterwards. – Is this a Sign of Refinement in Taste here ? Does it not rather recall to your Mind all the Criticisms, which you have read in so many good Books, against such Distortions of Reason, Feeling, and common Sense? does it not make one think of "dwelling in Acrostic Land"[170] – in short, of every thing that is opposite to a Natural Grace? The poor old Bagatelle, which Swift[171]praised so much, tho it did not mean much, meant something that was good humoured and chearfull for a little Time – but Frivolité, which they are so fond of here, surely means no Earthly thing that can contribute to one's Happinefs – on the Contrary there is a Sort of Listlefs Dullnefs and a Gloom which it casts over even those People who seem to be It's greatest Advocates. The following Epigram has been lately made upon the Queen and Mademoiselle D'Oliva the Young Woman who personated her in the course of the Strange Intrigue about the Diamond Necklace during the Eveque de Rohan's Affair ~

"Vile espece ose tu bien
"Jouer le Role d'une Reine.
"Porquoi non Ma Souveraine?
"Vous Joue'z souvent le mien.[172]

I left Lord and Lady Spencer and Lady Clermont with my Mother last Night, and went with my Brother and Lord Downe to the Duchefse de la Valiere's, where there was a great Croud as usual. These crouds amuse me, as I have often told you – and last Night I liked my Neighbourhood at Supper very well. ~

12 O'Clock

The Duc de Nivernois sent me some Verses the Day before Yesterday, which are thought extremely pretty, and I am of course very proud of them but I have not time to send you a Copy just now – indeed I hardly

173 Anna Laetitia Barbauld, 1743-1825, a minor English author: she was Anna Letitia Aikin when she published her Poems in 1773 and married Rochemont Barbauld in 1774. The Monthly Review gave her first book a glowing tribute: "We congratulate the public on so great an accession to the literary world, as the genius and talents of Miss Aikin. We very seldom have an opportunity of bestowing praise with so much justice." Samuel Taylor Coleridge walked forty miles to meet her and William Wordsworth admiringly told Henry Crabb Robinson that he wished he had written the final eight lines of her poem Life. Her poems were collected together in The poems of Anna Letitia Barbauld; edited by William McCarthy and Elizabeth Kraft. Georgia U.P., 1994.

174 *For a long time, I took to be a liar*
   The elegant and sensible author
   Who traced this beautiful character
   Where is joined both
   Everything that can have rights
   For attaching as for pleasing
   Reason solid and not severe
   Deep and delicate spirit
   And shining with such sweet light
   That he dazzles less than he lights up
   Pure taste, elegant manners
   Talent that is open without intention
   Swift judgement and always wholesome
   Tender of sentiment and sincere heart
   Everything without exception
   Everything that knows how to enchant us
   Everything that we love or we revere
   Is gathered together in this picture
   And the object appears to me too beautiful
   To not be imaginary
   But I came back from my error
   I saw C[rewe] worthy of her mother
   And I give justice to the author
   He did not paint a mirage

find any Time to bestow upon this Journal now that I mix more in the World; and it is generally while my Hair is Dreſsing that I attempt to give you a faint Idea of our goings on at this Place. The English Lines were quoted from Mʳˢ. Barbold's[173] Poems a Book he borrowed of me during my Stay at Paris. ~

'Of Gentle manners and of taste refined
'With all the Graces of a polish'd Mind
 'Clear sense and truth still shone in all she spoke
'And from her lips an Idle sentence broke
'Each nicer elegence of art she knew
 'Correctly fair and regularly true

 J'ai pris longtemp pour un menteur
 L'elegant et sensible Auteur
 Qui traca ce beau charactere
 Ou se reuni a la fois
 Tout ce qui peut avoir des droit
 Pour Attacher Comme pour plaire
 Raison Solide et non Severe
 Esprit profond et delicat
 Et brillant d'un si doux eclat
 Qu'il eblouie moins qu'il n'eclaire
 Gout pur, elegante maniere
 Talent qui perce sans deſsein
 Jugement prompt et toujours sain
 Sentiment tendre et couer sincere
 Tout enfin sane rien excepter
 Tout ce qui scait nous enchanter
 Tout ce qu'on aime ou qu'on revere
 Est Aſsemble dans ce tableau
 Et L'objet me parus trop beau
 Pour n'etre pas imaginaire
 Mais je revien de mon erreur
 J'ai vu C------ digne de sa mere
 Et je rend Justice a La'uteur
 Il n'a pas peint une Chimere[174]

On Monday next my Mother means to take Poſseſsion of some Lodgings at the Hotel de l'Empereur which are better than those She has here; and as that Hotel is close to the Luxemburgh Gardens, and in a much more Airy part of the Town than this, I mean to go there too for the Remainder of the Time I shall Stay. The Smoke of this Hotel has been intolerable ever since we came. It is very odd that they should submit here so patiently to that Inconvenience for, I am told, there are

175 from Shakespeare's <u>Othello</u>, Act 3, Scene 3, line 323:
"Trifles light as air
Are to the jealous confirmations strong
As proofs of holy writ."

176 – the bon ton: the leaders of fashion and style in society, the aristocratic, rich and famous

177 Yolande Gabrielle de Polastron, Duchesse de Polignac, 1758-1793, a favourite of the Queen. She is said to have been unpretentious and charming, always simply dressed and wearing little jewellery. She was a blue-eyed brunette, with an excellent singing voice, establishing herself as a favourite of the Queen in 1775. Vigée Le Brun captured her good looks. In 1782 she was appointed governess to the King's children and though she was not an ambitious woman she allowed herself to be manipulated by her lover the Comte de Vaudreuil and her own greedy family to gain lucrative offices and status for themselves and their friends. Mrs Crewe says she had loads of honours heaped upon her. But she has had her detractors too. Schama says she was ravishing but dim-witted. In 1789 the King sent her from Paris for her own safety: as she entered the carriage to leave the Queen gave her a purse containing 500 louis d'or and a note, which said "Goodbye, tenderest of friends. What a frightful word. But it is necessary. Goodbye. I have strength only to embrace you". In Vienna in 1793 soon after hearing of the guillotining of Marie Antoinette she contracted a mysterious illness and died within 12 hours, just before her 44th birthday.

hardly any Chimneys in Paris which do not Smoke very much at Times – But as to their Workmanship, they are sad Bunglers compared with our Artisans, and tho they have some shewy pieces of Cabinet Work, one may almost always perceive a Want of Finishing and Correctneſs in them. – This may, I conclude be imputed to the poverty of the Tradesmen, who cannot, like our's, employ many Hands at once. The Windows here are Clumsy Casements, which never shut Well; and I thought I perceived in the Carving upon some of them, as well as upon their Tables and other Articles of Furniture, some Resemblance of those Parts of Crewe Hall which were modernized in the last Century. We are to dine to-morrow at the Marechal de Castries before we leave Versailles. I will tell you all how and about it either there or after my Return. Adieu for the present. God grant the Horses we are to have may not frighten us this Time! ~

Versailles
Sunday - near 2 O'Clock in the Afternoon

Sunday 11ᵗʰ February 1786

I am busy Dreſsing my Hair as fast as I can to be in readineſs for the Dinner at Marechal de Castries in an Hour's time, so that I shall set down what I have heard and seen in a still more Confused Manner than usual – But it is better to write as near the Moment as one can, for otherwise the "Trifles light as Air"[175] which I treat of would many of them vanish from my Memory, and be left untold. – My mother and I with our two Maids and two Men left Paris soon after we had dined. We came to the Hotel I put up at last time, and found tolerable Lodging Rooms. About half past Nine We sallied forth with Lady Clermont to the Ducheſse de Polignac's great Supper where the Bon Ton[176] of France always meets on Saturdays and Wednesdays, because the Queen is frequently to be met with there. There were two Rooms full of Supper Tables, and as much Confusion the whole Evening as generally Arises in such large Companies at Meal time. Madame de Polignac[177] is one of the most gentle, pleasing Women I ever saw – She has a Beautifull Countenance is about six or seven and Thirty, and was thought ten years ago the Handsomest Woman here – She must have also a charming Character, and just Manner of Feeling, to have continued so Meek and Modest as She has done, and so much the Favourite of every Body, tho

178 Daughter of the Duchesse de Polignac, she was betrothed to the Duc de Guiche at the age of 12. Because she came from a background that was not wealthy her mother sought a dowry for her from the Queen and was granted 800,000 lives, which caused some offence at court. At some time she was seduced by the King's brother the Comte d'Artois, who later became Charles X. The public long looked upon her as one of his easiest conquests. It was during his reign, 1824-1830, that the Duc and Duchesse de Guiche became two of the most fashionable couples at court. Her brother Jules also had great success after the revolution, becoming Charles X's ambassador to London and eventually head of government in 1829-30.

179 Lady Grimstone: she refers here to Harriot Grimston, 3rd Viscountess Grimston, 1756-1786. She died later that year, in November 1786, aged only 30.

180 – she was, in fact, 30 the previous November, being born 2nd November 1755.

She has been for a long time confeſsedly the first Favourite at Court; and has had such Loads of Honors heaped upon her. The Ducheſse de Guiche[178] her Daughter is but Eighteen Years old, and yet has a Child four Years of Age. Is not that very Singular? Soon after we arrived at Madame de Polignac's we underwent Presentations without End! – and, to say the Truth, I was in so melancholy a Mood that, when my Choice was given me by the Mistreſs of the House to belong to a little Party in her Room, or to venture to the great Table, I preferred the latter, because I could be lost there. The Ducheſse de Guiche then led me to a Seat next to her own, and I sat for an hour or two very well satisfied with looking at what presented itself before my Eyes in the Shape of Cookery or Desert. This poor little Ducheſse de Guiche had a sad Headake the whole time, and this occupied me a good deal; for there was something that struck me as quite charming in her whole Appearance and total Unconsciousneſs of her Beauty; which is nevertheleſs very great. After Supper we all walked into another Room, and as I was making my Way towards my Mother, whom I Spied at the End of it, a Lady of my Acquaintance told me I had better stay a Moment where I was till the Queen had finished her Conversation with a Monsieur something – "Why where is the Queen?" said I – "Next to you," She answered – I looked and there She was – But really in this Sort of Party which consists, I suppose, of about Eighty or an Hundred People, it is impoſsible to distinguish Any Person Immediately one is not much used to see. Her Majesty then walked by, and I was not near her again the whole Evening, but I met my Mother who told me She had talked to her a good deal. All this Time I don't believe I have told you what Sort of Woman this Queen of France seems to be – in the first Place then, her Face is, I think, very like Lady Grimstone's[179] – it is not what one can call handsome and yet has something in it which, for a Queen at least, is very good – Her Figure was fine formerly, but it is become clumsy to a great Degree and, tho She is under Thirty,[180] She has on this Account been obliged to give up Dancing, which She was very fond of. As to her true Character it is quite impoſsible for me to give it you – the Young and the Idle seem most fond of her, amongst those I have met with here, and from this I conclude there is not much Solidity in her Composition. ~

181 *from Milton's* <u>*Il Penseroso*</u>, *line 157*
"And love the high embowèd roof,
With antique pillars' massy proof,
And storied windows richly dight,
Casting a dim religious light.
There let the pealing organ blow
To the full-voiced quire below,
In service high, and anthems clear,
As may with sweetness, through mine ear
Dissolve me into ecstasies,
And bring all heaven before mine eyes."

182 *it's not that he doesn't have goodness on his face but that he has a shortage of it.*

183 *not found; it may be a saying she heard from a friend or acquaintance.*

184 *at this time "curious" referred to objects whose true meaning was obscure enough to require some thought before intellectual satisfaction could be achieved by arriving at its correct interpretation. This might refer particularly to allegory and metaphor in literature, painting and architecture. See* <u>*The Tudor and Jacobean house*</u> *by Malcom Airs, Bramley Books, 1998, p6.*

185 *a common ordinary was a meal prepared at a fixed rate for all comers.*

186 *Charles Gravier Vergennes, 1717-87, Foreign Minister who negotiated the Peace of Paris in 1783.*

Monday –
Paris –

Monday 12th February 1786

I went to the King's Chapel to hear high Maſs Yesterday Morning – The Music was fine, but the Drums and Fiddles in my Opinion spoiled the Effect which good Choirs ought to have – It was indeed far from "Diſsolving the Soul in Ecstacies" – or bringing "all Heaven before our Eyes"[181] However it was Harmony for all that, and good in its Gothic Way. We went afterwards to the Apartments where we were noticed in a civil Manner by her Majesty and Comte D'Artois. The King spoke also to Lady Clermont, and I had then a good Opportunity of Examining his Countenance and Manner, which struck me as good humoured and Unaffected – But I find here sad Complaints of his Want of <u>Grace</u> and <u>Bow</u> – They are for ever saying he is a good Prince, qu'il a la Bonte' point sur sa Physionomie mais qu'il manque <u>cela</u>[182] And as often as I hear this, so often it reminds me of a Lady's Wisdom who, observed that "to be sure her Sister's was a <u>happy Marriage</u>, but her Diamonds were all <u>Roses</u>"![183] After this we walked into H.M. private Apartments, which are filled with every Sort of Ornament that is curious[184] or costly – His Library looked plain and Comfortable I thought, and we were all pleased at his having dedicated one Part of it to small statues of the most famous Warriors, Statesmen, and Authors of the last and present Age. Having viewed all these things, we returned to our Inn to prepare for the Marechal de Castries' Dinner, to which we went soon after two O'Clock, and were presented by the young Duc and Ducheſse to the old People. The Marechal is Secretary at War, which is a Post of much greater Splendor here than with us. People poured in very fast, for he keeps a Public Table; so that we had an Opportunity of seeing many of the Most Distinguished Characters at the French Court. The Apartments however which he occupies are very small, and the Sort of Scramble which they all seemed to make for Place's reminded me very much of a common Ordinary at a Race.[185] – I wish we had had Time to visit at Monsieur de Vergennes[186] for I should like to have seen that great Minister; but this was impoſsible as we were both determined to get back to Paris as soon as we could for the Sake of the English Post – You may perceive therefore by this that we do not forget you all, and, considering what a Life we lead here with Marechalls, Ducs, and Grandees of every kind you ought I think to consider this in the light of a great Compliment. ~

187 *Emma was her daughter – see the Introduction, pages 33-34 and her portrait facing page 154. It's interesting to note this is the first indication her daughter was with her.*

Hotel de l'Empereurs

9 O'Clock Monday Night

Here we are in our new Lodging which, tho it is not so magnificent as our other was, is much more agreeable in many Respects. We are just returned from Dining at the Duc de Nivernois; before which we went to the Royal Academy ~ but I am so fatigued with what I have done to day that I must defer my Account of it all till to-morrow – Lady Clarges who lives in this Hotel has just sent to desire I will Sup in her Apartment and I think I will. Good Night – Tomorrow I will be Circumstantial, if I can get any time for You. ~

Tuesday Morning –

Tuesday 13ᵗʰ February 1786

In the first Place, I must tell you that, This Hotel is so well Situated and the Air one breathes here is so much purer than that we have left, that I already feel the good Effects of it. Our Rooms do not Smoke too, and this is a vast point. The Luxemburgh Gardens are so near us that I shall be able to Pop in and out of them without getting into those odious French Coaches, and paſsing through a hundred narrow Streets, which we have hitherto been forced to do. All this I rejoice at on little Emma's Account[187] more than my own – but I have no busineſs to prose about it, and so you shall have the History of Yesterday according to my Promise. The Crouds which were expected at the Academy made it neceſsary for us to give up dining at the usual Hour, and the Duc de Nivernois ordered a Dinner to be ready for us and a few more of his Friends at six O'Clock. – About one we Sallied forth with Lord Downe and three French Ladies to the Louvre where the Academy is – Their Room, they tell me, is as large as our House of Commons, but I confeſs it did not appear to be so to my Eye. We found Crouds of Carriages making up to the great Gate of the Palace, with some Difficulty arrived there, and with more Difficulty got tolerable Places afterwards. Having waited upwards of two Hours for them an universal Buzz announced the arrival of the <u>Forty Members,</u> some of whom are such Favourites that they received loud Applauses as they paſsed by; amongst those was the poor little Abbe de Lisle, whose Poetry I have before mentioned to you, and, by the bye, remember I shall never forgive you unleſs you get His Poem upon Gardens,   and are as charmed as I was at the Beautifull

188 Jean Francois Marmontel, 1723-1799, French author of successful tragedies. comedies and comic operas. At the time of Mrs Crewe's visit he was Secretary to The Academy.

189 Jean-Francois, Marquis de Saint-Lambert, 1716-1803. He was a poet and contributor to L'Encyclopédie, one of the great literary monuments of the 18th century. He is also remembered as successor of Voltaire in the affections of Madame de Chatelet and as the rival of Jean-Jacques Rousseau in those of Madame d'Houdetot.

190 Le Marechal Beveau – not identified.

191 Cardinal de Luines – Paul d'Albert de Luynes, 1703-1788, successively Bishop of Sens, Cardinal, Abbot. of Corbie, and Chaplain of the King's mother. He was a member of the Academie Francaise and an honorary member of the Academie des Sciences.

192 Guibert, Jacques Antoine Hippolyte, Comte de Guibert   He was 39 at the time of Mrs Crewe's visit and had made his reputation 12 years earlier with publication of his analysis of warfare Essay on tactics. His ideas were to prove the greatest influence on French military ascendancy through the period of the French Revolution. He had at one time been the lover of Julie de Lespinasse hostess of one of the most brilliant and emancipated of Parisian salons and the author of several volumes of passionate letters. Published in 1809 her Lettres show intensely experienced emotions of love, remorse, and despair. She died broken hearted in 1762 as a result of her unrequited affection for Guibert (Encyclopædia Britannica). Guibert is described by Schama (pp257-259) as one of the prodigies of French intellectual life, sometimes gripped by black fits of dour Romantic melancholy but shining in public and disconcerting gatherings with his encyclopedic grasp of science, philosophy and literature. In 1788 he reformed the French army, making it more efficient, thinning out the layers of officers, making it more disciplined, finding money to pay more to the ordinary soldier but at the same time saving about 30 million livres.

193 not identified.

Paſsage in it respecting the Man from Otaheite, many other Parts are tiresome. Monsieur Marmontel,[188] Monsieur Guibert and Monsieur S^t. Lambert,[189] Author of the Seasons, and several more got vast Applause before they took their Seats at a long Green Table in the Middle of this large Hall. The Duc de Nivernois, Le Marechal Beveau,[190] Le Cardinal de Luines,[191] and several more Members of great Rank paſsed by with them, and it was Satisfactory and pleasant to get a full View with a little Trouble of the most remarkable Men in this Country for Talent and Literary Reputation. – Monsieur Guibert[192] then took his Seat for the first time as President at the Academy in the Room of Monsieur Thomas, and in a most Masterly Speech replete with Eloquence and Feeling returned thanks to his Brother Academecians for having placed him there. His Eulogy upon Monsieur Thomas was admirable, and that, together with his Unaffected Humility in taking the Chair, raised a Sort of Murmuring Approbation much more flattering than all the loud and Undistinguishable Applauses he had excited on his first Appearance. If there was any Fault in Monsieur Guiberts Speech, it was, in my poor Judgment, in the Profusion of Imagery which made it "not only Sweet but Luscious" – in fact, his Oration was throughout so warm and Luxuriant the Mind had no breathing Time, I thought, – I know that to accuse an Orator of this Fault may be considered as Flattery disguised; but I really think it one for ought not Eloquence, like Gardening, to – admit of Intervening Slopes and Lawns to relieve as well as gratify the Eye? – dispersing Objects at proper Distances would produce the happiest Effects – It is not indeed a Maſs of Perfection that we look for, if we are reasonable in our Desires, it is only so much as our poor limited Faculties can go along with comfortably. – I know nothing about the Principles of Oratory, but it appears to me those Parts which are mere narrative should be kept almost clear from Ornament – however this was not the Case, I think, in Monsieur Guibert's fine Speech – Neverthelеſs I wish you had heard it, for, in spite of all I have remarked it was a very Capital one, and had an Effect upon all the Audience. Monsieur S^t. Lambert answered him, but he is an old Man with so Weak a Voice that I could with great Difficulty hear him – Monsieur Duſsy[193] then read some Verses which he had made on Monsieur Thomas – They were affecting because they turned chiefly upon those Melancholy Topics which the Loſs of Friends naturally present to the Mind, and had a turn, I fancied, something like Grey's – They were besides animated by happy Allusions to Domestic Circumstances, which, tho they contributed little to our Gratification, who knew him only as a Writer, must have brought him much nearer to the Minds of those who had been his Friends or Acquaintance. We waited a great while before we could get away, and were very happy to find our good Dinner ready for us at the Duc de Nivernois: where two or three Women and two or

194 It had been the custom since the end of the 16th century for strolling players to set up booths at the fairs held in Paris during the winter in the Saint-Germain quarter. The speciality was opéra-comique, or romantic comedy interspersed with song and dance, as well as other popular comedy

195 Mr Pittoux is Mrs Crewe's attempt at spelling the name of Mr Pidow; others had the same problem, as pointed out by Ingamells(see bibliography), describing him as Pidou, Piton and Pedon. Mr Pidow is described by Mrs Crewe as "the gentleman who travels with" Lord Downe – it had become common practice in the 18th century for young men to complete their formal education with a grand tour of Europe's major cultural centres, and to be accompanied on their travels by a tutor, popularly known as a bear leader. In his book Liberal Education, published in 1789, Vicesmus Knox described a bear leader as a grave, respectable man of a mature age, with 'that natural authority and that personal dignity which command attention and obedience. In addition to his duties as teacher, mentor and guide, he would have to watch over the morals and religion of his pupil", both of which would be constantly in danger of being "shaken from the basis and levelled with the dust before the end of the peregrination". Mr Pidow was filling this role for Lord Downe and Mrs Crewe was keeping an eye out for somebody to accompany her son John when he reached the right age. When Mrs Crewe's husband had carried out his grand tour in 1760 he was accompanied by John Hinchliffe, who not only went on to become the Bishop of Peterborough but also married his pupil's sister, Elizabeth Crewe. Besides accompanying Lord Downe, Mr Pidow was also the bear leader for Lord Grey, 6th Earl of Stamford, 1765-1843, who toured Italy in 1787-8, and for the 5th Duke of Manchester, 1771-1843, who went in 1791-2.

three Men we knew very well, made up the Party. Monsieur de Boulie was there, and I hope you will know him when he is in England this Spring, for I am persuaded he will strike you as being a plain Sensible and pleasant Man. We found Lady Clarges Singing with Sachini, and supped very comfortably with her. The Hampden's and a few more – And so finished our Day. There are a Thousand little Circumstances which I should dwell upon, if I had time, and, believe me, I should have much Pleasure in communicating them to you! – but really it has been as much as ever I could do to Scratch off the loose Sketches you have of my Life here. ~

Friday Morning

Friday 16ᵗʰ February 1786

The Day after the Academy we dined at Madame la Marechalle de Mirpoix; where there were very few People – This Visit has left nothing on my Memory worth recording. In the Evening of that Day (which I think was Tuesday) Lady Mornington and I went to one of the small Theatres at the Foire Sᵗ. Germain,[194] where we got but baddish Places – however we Scraped up an Acquaintance with some odd People that sat near us; and you must know I like peeping about this Town in so easy a Way very well – I mean if poßible, to get a Sight of other Places, which, they say, are much better because they do not aim at so much as this did. They talk to me a great deal about a Sort of Theatre which one may call, I think, a live Puppet shew. Lady Mornington and some others were there a few Nights ago, and declared they could never have discovered the Deception – I am informed that the Idea is borrowed from the Greeks, who conveyed Sounds to the Stage from a Different part of the House – It Succeeds amazingly here that is certain – but I have not yet told you what I knew about it – The Performers are Children, who Act in dumb Shew, nay even so accurately as to move their Lips whilst People behind Speak for them. On Wednesday Lord Downe Mʳ. Pittoux[195] (the Gentleman who travels with him) and Dʳ. Lee dined with us. I like the Appearance of Mʳ. Pittoux very well, and I hear so good a Character of him that he runs in my Head as likely to suit John hereafter, in case he goes to reside abroad, and is boarded in some Province Town. As to London, Paris, Bruße Brußells or indeed any Capital, God preserve him from them for some Years to come! But I have not time to enter into all this at Present – This new Hotel is at a great Distance from the Society

196 voiture: a carriage or coach.

197 cabriolet:: a gig or cab – a much smaller vehicle than a carriage.

198 Kensington Garden: in Central London, attached to Kensington Palace and adjacent to Hyde Park.

199 Le Lycée: Mrs Crewe must have attended one of the first lectures ever given since the Lycée was only founded in 1786. It continued under that name until 1803 when the name lycée was used to describe secondary schools and the name Athénée was adopted. It's reputation deteriorated over the next 40 years and it finally folded in 1848. Mrs Crewe gives an excellent description of its aspirations and its reception.

200 Jean-Francoise de La Harpe, 1739-1803, dramatist, journalist and critic. He was a disciple and friend of Voltaire, producing indifferent tragedies – his best work came in his literary criticism, much of which was given in the form of lectures at the Lycée, such as that attended by Mrs Crewe. These were collected together and published 1799-1805 as <u>Lycée, ou Cours de littérature ancienne et moderne</u>.

201 Joseph Addison, 1672-1719, essayist and major contributor to <u>The Spectator</u> and <u>The Tatler</u> between 1709 and 1714.

202 Hugh Blair, 1718-1800, a Scottish church minister, who was part of a distinguished literary circle.

we chiefly paſsed our time with at the other. Paris is certainly in many Respects a much more inconvenient Town to move about in than London – The Streets are so narrow that one for ever is stopped and obliged to back one's Coach – to be sure the Coachmen drive safely enough, but it seems to be a strange Clumsy Busineſs, and at first I was often flurried by the Shocks which Carriages I met with gave to my Wheels – Most of the Gentlemen here, who cannot afford to keep a regular Voiture[196] drive about all Day in things with one Horse, which they call Cabriolets,[197] which to my eye are nothing more than the common sort of English Buggies – It is really sometimes very unpleasant to meet them when the fine Young Men are Chariotteers and choose to make Awkward and Dangerous Imitations of our English Skill in Coachmanship. – People seem to live at an immense Distance from each other in this Town, and it is therefore Impoſsible to get common Visits over half so soon as in London. I always conceived that their Fauxburg Sᵗ. Germain might be compared to <u>our</u> Sᵗ. James's End of the Town – but this is not so – the Persons of Fashion here are about all over the Town; and for that Reason they have always many Contrivances about their Arrangements for the Evening. ✗

near dinner time ~

I have taken a very pleasant Walk in the Luxemburg Gardens this Morning, and there is much more Appearance of Spring than there is even with us at this time of the Year. Several People tell me that Paris is three Weeks forwarder than London – Is that so pray? or is it only my Fancy that makes it much warmer this February than usual? – Kensington Garden is a better Garden[198] than this near us; but very few of us dream of going to walk there at this Season, or conceive any other Garden as very pleasant; and yet to day I saw Numbers sitting upon Benches, and basking themselves in the Sun as if it had been July. They always look very good humoured and chearfull in this Town, and I wish you could come To-morrow and peep at it all. – Yesterday as soon as we had Breakfasted my Mother and I went to the Lice'e[199] to hear Monsieur de la Harp[200] give his first Lecture upon Epic Poetry – He is a famous Author, and his Poetry is held in much Esteem by his own Countrymen, tho, I believe, it is little known in England, at least I have not met with, or heard of his Works till I came here. He began with a Diſsertation on the Ancient and Modern Languages, which was richly Ornamented by Style and Anecdote. – He read with very great Simplicity and good Taste, and several Rules which he laid down, and Opinions which he advanced had great Force; but I believe they were not very new; at least I thought I had before met with several of his Arguments in Addison,[201] Voltaire and Doctʳ. Blair,[202] and other Writers upon this Subject. He

203 kindness rather than wittiness.

204 from Alexander Pope's <u>Epistle to Richard Boyle, Earl of Burlington</u>:-
  "Oft you have hinted to your brother Peer,
  A certain truth, which many buy too dear:
  Something there is, more needful than Expence,
  And something previous ev'n to Taste — 'Tis Sense:
  Good Sense, which only is the gift of heav'n,
  And tho' no science, fairly worth the seven:
  A light, which in yourself you must perceive;
  Jones and Le Notre have it not to give."

205 from Abraham Cowley's <u>Ode: of wit</u>:-
  "Some things do through our Judgment pass
  As through a Multiplying Glass.
  And sometimes, if the Object be too far,
  We take a Falling Meteor for a Star."

206 tags: loose-ends.

207 Corporal Trim is a character in Laurence Sterne's <u>Tristram Shandy</u>, first published 1760-67.

was very much Applauded several times – I observe it is in the Fashion here for People to clap their hands upon slight Impulses of Admiration. – This I dislike very much, for Applause should not, I think, be so commonly mounted to it's highest Pitch, because it must necefsarily cease to have that Effect which it may have if <u>chastely</u> bestowed. This Lice'e, as they call it, is a new Institution here, and it is very much the Fashion for fine Folks to Subscribe to it – There are Courses of Lectures upon Anatomy, Chimistry, History, and the Belles Lettres every Day, in a long Room Kept for the Purpose. If the Women only attend the two latter, I should think the Plan would turn out to their Advantage and Amusement; but what, for God's Sake, have We poor Women to do with <u>Chimistry</u> or <u>Anatomy</u>?. or rather what have We, or even the <u>other</u> Sex, to do with <u>five</u> or <u>Six</u> Sciences at once? It is indeed very extraordinary to observe the Present Rage for both <u>Frivolite</u> and <u>belle</u> Esp<u>rit</u>. Monsieur de Boulie the other Day at Dinner said, that he wished some of them would think it worth their while to cultivate the <u>bon</u> <u>Esprit</u> rather than the <u>belle</u> <u>Esprit</u>,[203] for that in the end he was persuaded it would answer their Purpose, better, even with Respect to Vanity – And so I verily believe – Do you remember Pope's Lines,"
        "G<u>ood</u> <u>Sen</u>se which only is the Gift of Heaven,
        And tho no Science fairly worth the Seven."[204]
I always liked them, and am sure you do, for we always think alike upon this Subject – but I digrefs Strangely – have I finished all I had to say about this Lice'e? Why, if I should not, there is no great harm, for you will hear from every Body that it is an Institution Paris is very proud of, tho some People think it is too lazy and Confused a Way of getting at Knowledge; that the <u>wise</u> People will not become wiser by it, because the Lectures are not deep, and that other's will only change their Ignorance for Superficialnefs, and fancy they have got a <u>great Way</u> when they shall take "a falling Meteor for a Star"[205] – You'll think I am mad this Morning with my Tags;[206] – Do you know there are Days when I find my Memory too much for me; and other Days again when I can recollect nothing, if I would give the World for it – ! My History of this Lice'e is like Corporal Trim's History of the King of Bohemia and his seven Castles[207] – I verily believe I have begun it Fifty times, and never gone further than he did. One good Reason indeed for my not giving you very accurate Information is that I am greatly in the dark myself – for all I know I can tell you is that, upon the whole I liked the neatnefs of Monsieur de la Harp's Discourse, tho, you may be sure, I did not like to hear him abuse our Language without Mercy, and say that it was a Combination of Sounds <u>scarcely</u> human! and that it might be compared to the <u>Hifsing Noise of Animals</u> more than any other. I never heard before that it was so difsonant to the Ears of Foreigners – But if the Whistling and Hifsing in it are so offensive as he afserts, I am sure <u>we</u>

208 <u>Le Roi de Cocagne</u> *was a light piece of comic fantasy by Marc Antoine Legrand (1673-1728). Legrand had been an actor at the Comedie Francaise. In the sense given here burlesque referred to parody or satire.*

209 *Louis XV, 1710-1774.*

Emma Crewe
By Thomas Gainsborough

The Palace of Versailles

Rose Bertin

The Marquis de Lafayette

Self portrait, c. 1781
Elisabeth Louise Vigee Le Brun

Frances Anne Crewe
by Nathaniel Dance-Holland

might with some truth retort that the French Language has a constant nasal Sound which our Ears are as little delighted with. When all this was said, there was a general Buzz and Laugh all over the Room, and the Eyes of the Aſsembly were fixed upon the Corner where we English People sat. In consequence of which several Men were so civil as to come up to us afterwards, and talk <u>loudly</u> to the Chevalier Jernegham and others upon the <u>Injustice</u> of what had been advanced – however, I fear, this was merely the Effect of French Politeneſs. It is certain that no one can bear Attacks on their Country upon very Eſsential Points, but as to others, I by no means think it unpleasant to get behind the Curtain here, and to learn their real Opinions when they do not mean to be Complimentary. ✗

Sunday

Sunday 18ᵗʰ February 1786

We go on leading an odd sort of confused Life which paſses away like a Dream, and will leave much the same Sort of Impreſsion, I fancy – however it is the only one that ought to be led for a short time in such a Place as this, where one comes to take a Cursory View of <u>things in general</u>. Last Night I paid a Visit to the Marechal Biron to thank the poor old Man for his Boxes at the Theatre – There was nothing to be seen at his House worth mentioning – He was playing his good comfortable Rubber at Whist; and after I had staid a little while I returned to my Mother's Apartment, where much Company arrived, and several English People supped – She is much better Lodged here than she was before – It will besides be a great Comfort to me to leave her in so good a Neighbourhood as Lady Clarges and Miſs Carter. – The Night before last Miſs Carter and I went to see a Burlesque Piece somewhat in the Style of Midas called Le Roi de Cocagne[208] – They are all very fond of it here, and it seems it has several Allusions in it to the Court of Louis the fifteenth[209] – but they are lost upon me, so that I may well be Forgiven for not admiring it as I otherwise ought to do – I will tell you however what happened between the Acts – You must first understand tho that Disapprobation is here frequently expreſsed in the same Manner as Applause with us. – in short, clapping the hands is often made to indicate both Praise and Dispraise – The Noise of this

210 *her little girl's maid was probably Dolly, who is mentioned later.*

211 *from Shakespeare's* <u>Othello</u>, *Act 3, Scene 3, lines 183-5:*
" 'Tis not to make me jealous
To say my wife is fair, feeds well, loves company,
Is free of speech, sings, plays, and dances well;
Where virtue is, these are more virtuous. "

212 *the passage in italics has been crossed through in the diary but can still be read.*

213 *mis-spelt by Mrs Crewe, she refers here to George Steevens, 1736-1800, who,*
with Samuel Johnson, published a fully annotated edition of Shakespeare in 1773.
He also assisted Johnson with his <u>Lives of the Poets</u> *and contributed to Reed's*
<u>Biographia Dramatica</u> *and throughout constantly quarrelled with literary associates.*
After his death his second-folio Shakespeare was bought for George III and is now in
The British Library.

214 *Edmond Malone, 1741-1812, a friend of Johnson, Reynolds, Burke and*
Boswell. He published an edition of Shakespeare in 1790 which was important for
seeking to establish the order in which the plays were written and for making first use
of several contemporary records. Malone was not unknown to Mrs Crewe some years
later: in 1793 William Windham wrote to Mrs Crewe: "by the way, your friend and
admirer, Mr. Malone, is going somewhere into your neighbourhood, and would be very
glad, I am persuaded, of any encouragement to make you a visit. Will you authorize
me to give him such, or, what would be still more gracious, write him a line
yourself."(<u>The Windham Papers</u>, *vol.1, p.159)*

215 *umbras: shadows.*

Sort in the Pitt was, at one time between the Acts, so violent that we could not at all gueſs at a Reason for it – at last a Centinel came to our Door, and whispered something to a Lady who sat near us, which occaſioned her immediately to turn to me and desire that I would remove my Cloak, which hung over the Front of the Box – I did so with great eagerneſs, as you may imagine, when I found myself the Object of the Whole Pit! – I have since thought their Etiquettes are cruel in the Case of Strangers who can never learn them but by such Experience as mine! My little Girl's Maid,[210] for Instance was the other Day ordered out of the Luxemburg Garden by a Soldier, because She had a <u>Short</u> Gown on, which is a Dreſs prohibited in that Place – Nor is it at all uncommon for Gentlemen who sit in the Highest Boxes in the Theatres here to be ordered from the Pitt to take off their Hats – But it must nevertheleſs be confeſsed that upon the whole the generality of the lower Claſs of People are more civil and obliging in their Manners than with us. ~

Tuesday

Tuesday 20ᵗʰ February 1786

We are to dine to day again at Monsieur Monregard's the rich Fermier General's – Madame M. is a pure jolly Dame – "feeds well, loves Company.

"Is free of Speech" &cc[211]
All of which as Othello says "where Virtue is these are most virtuous," – A Strange Compliment to us Females, who might probably have thought Desdemona's Character preferable to that, tho She <u>had</u> prefered Caſsio to him. Whoever, in short, liked this Paſsage? – I mean what <u>Woman,</u> or indeed the Circumstance of Othello's being a Black? – [212]*For my own Part whenever M*ʳ*. Stevens,[213] or M*ʳ*. Malone[214] or any other of Shakespear's Editors applies to me on the Score of Criticism I shall have a long Chapter on the last Article, and desire him to Discover by his Researches that he was only a Mullatto – and he Ought too to poſseſs these Sentiments and that good Taste which are inseperable to a great Soul – He maybe as blind as the Poet pleases but he must still be a Gentleman.* – To return however to Madame Monregard – She "feeds well, I tell you, loves Company, is free of Speech, and, I believe, "Sings, Plays, and Dances well" – and of Course encourages a great deal of Festivity and good cheer at her House. – To day, I understand, is her day for <u>Authors</u> and their <u>Umbras</u>.[215] I'll tell you after my return how it has paſsed off – I mean I shall have Time; for want of which a Thousand little things, which at the Moment struck me as having been made on purpose for

216 Louise Marthe, Marquise de Coigny, 1759-1832. Born Louise Marthe de Conflans she married the Marquis de Coigny in 1775. She was described by the Duc de Lauzun who, like many others, fell in love with her, as clever and charming. Madame de Coigny, never much in sympathy with the court, eventually associated herself entirely with the Orleans party. At the Revolution she fled to England where she mixed with the Whigs and the "constitutional" party of the émigrés, while her husband followed the fortunes of Louis XVI, who rewarded him by making him a general. They divorced during the Emigration, and Madame de Coigny returned to France in 1801, where she proclaimed herself a fervent admirer of Napoleon. She remained devoted to Lauzun and he to her until his execution in 1794, though opinions are divided as to the exact nature of their relationship. The letters she wrote to him from England in 1791-92 were published in 1884.

217 La Reine des Roquets: the queen of pug-dogs.

218 Hartshorn and Sal Volatile – hartshorn is an ammonious substance obtained from the horns of a hart, usually sold as an aqueous solution; sal volatile is ammonium carbonate, especially in the form of a scented solution in alcohol used as smelling salts.

this Journal, have since escaped my Memory. You must know I have had so many Letters to write by the two last Mails to England that it has not been poſsible for me to note down accurately every Circumstance and Adventure during the past Week – Yesterday Morning Madame de Coigny[216] came and paid a very long Visit for She forgot the Dinner Hour, and we thought She never would go. – This little Woman, I can aſsure you, is a very Principal Personage in this Town, for She has chosen a line of Conduct unlike that of any Woman here – Her House is open all Day long to the fine Young Men of Fashion and, tho She does not behave in any Way that can cause the least Scandal to her Reputation, She contrives to get very much hated by the other Women, nay even by the Queen, who likes to see all the Fashionable World at Versailles, and calls Madame de Coigny, <u>La Reine des Roquets</u>.[217] – My Brother Charles dines there continually, and there are twelve or fourteen of them who call in, at all Hours, to dine in their Boots and Spurs; because they think here that is our <u>English Fashion</u>, which, thank God it is not yet: But this Madame de Coigny is a little odd Sort of Excentric Woman that People like very much – She has very entertaining Ideas, they Say, and flashes them off like Lightning when She is in Spirits – which, I fancy, She was Yesterday for She did talk at a most prodigious Rate indeed! When I attempted to Answer her, I felt I protest as if I was playing Minuet Time only to a Jig – Oh! it was Rapid Work! and, I don't know how you feel about it, but Such a Woman as Madame de Coigny, would, I think, give me an Asthma if I lived with her any time! She came to invite us to her Ball next Saturday, and it is to begin with Children's Dancing. I have asked leave to carry little Emma. But I must really throw my Pen down – This lively Visitor has quite jaded me with her quick Transitions from one Subject to another, her pointed Allusions which required much Use of the French Language to seize upon; and in Short, with her <u>Hartshorn</u> and <u>Sal Volatile</u>[218] Discourse! – She is certainly one of those People who are too much to <u>live</u> with, tho they do admirably to Taste now and then – But you will begin to think I have Stolen some of her own Conceits to kill or rather <u>maim</u> her with her own Weapons. ✗

219 Guibert's Tactique – <u>Essai général de tactique</u>, published in 1773.

220 from Shakespeare's <u>Merchant of Venice</u>, Act 2, Scene 2, line 65:

"Talk not of Master Launcelot, father; for the young gentleman, according to Fates and Destinies and such odd sayings, the Sisters Three and such branches of learning, is indeed deceased."

221 Corneille's <u>Cinna</u> was produced in 1640-41 and concerns a plot by Cinna and his lover Aemilie to assassinate the Roman Emperor Augustus. Maxime, a co-conspirator who is secretly in love with Aemilie, betrays Cinna, but Augustus, weary of bloodshed, forgives all three and wins their future allegiance.

Wednesday Morn..ʸ.

Wednesday 21ˢᵗ February 1786

Yesterday we dined at Monsieur de Monregards with the great Monsieur Guibert, Mʳ. and Mʳˢ. Goldburne, Monsieur and Madame (I forget what), the Son and Daughter of the House, and another French man whose name I have likewise forgotten. – Monsieur Guibert told us he intended being in London in May, so that you will probably see him there, and I need not therefore take so much trouble to describe him as I should otherwise do: –You must know however that, tho' I am very well aware he is one of the most remarkable People of this Age, tho' I formerly heard of nothing but his Tactique[219] amongst Officers in Camps, tho' this Capital rings with his Ability, and tho' I heard him make a very Elegant and Beautiful Oration at the Academy the other Day, – nay even tho' he took Pains to be Chearful and Agreeable Yesterday, he has not the Honor to hit my Fancy near so much as many People, certainly beneath him in Capacity, have done here. He seems to be very Impatient of Contradiction upon some Points, and it appeared to me that he carries with him a Sort of Consciousneſs of being always in the Right, and that this makes him Indolent concerning those Arguments of the Moment with which he Strives to convince those who Disagree with him. He appears to love talking very much too, and I observed he took the Opposite Side of almost every Question – this, of Course brought on Disputes; and they were hardly fair one's, because Monsieur Guibert was always but too ready to cut them Short with his own Decisions, that he might fly to other Subjects of which he was equally the Master. Mʳ· Goldburne is not a very wise Man, I believe, however he deals in "the Sisters three, and such little Branches of Learning"[220] and so, can't please you, he entered the Lists with Monsieur Guibert upon the Comparative Merits of Shakespear and Corneille – at first, Monsieur Guibert said (with much truth, I think,) that neither Englishmen nor Frenchmen could be fair Judges, but that however he himself was quite certain that in all Shakespear there could not be found a Scene to equal Corneille's Dialogue in Cinna between Antony and Cinna, nor a Character so finely Delineated as that of his Emilie[221] – By the bye let us some day when we have time look at those two Parts – Not but that I take it for granted much of the Merit in a French Dramatic Author must be lost upon Us – however we shall see some of Corneille's Powers, and very few Frenchmen indeed with their Imperfect Knowledge of our Language can be as just to Shakespear. But to return to their Argument – Mʳ·

179

222 fumier: dung, trash.

223 Elizabeth Montagu, 1720-1800, an English writer and leader of society. She was the first of the intellectual women known as blue-stockings and wrote <u>An Essay on Shakespeare</u>.

224 three characters from Shakespeare, Falstaff from <u>Henry IV</u> and <u>The Merry Wives of Windsor</u>, Dogberry and Verges from <u>Much ado about nothing</u>.

Goldburne admitted that the Dialogue alluded to, was a very fine One, but would not admit that the Character he alluded to, was equal in Point of drawing after Nature, to that of Othello, because <u>Nature</u> had in a manner been quite neglected. Monsieur Guibert grew very warm at this, and said that Corneille had done <u>more</u> than Paint mere <u>common Nature</u>, for he had Painted <u>Roman Nature</u>, and had – therefore described Emilie not only as She <u>was</u> Originally, but as She was <u>become</u> by Force of <u>Custom</u>, and this at the same time, and in the <u>same Speeches</u>. – But, tho' this may Sound Plausibly, I cannot think it quite fair, for surely tho' there may be more Art and more Ingenuity in painting Nature with her <u>Exact Drapery</u>, so as to have no fault found with what Painters call the Costume of a Piece, there must be more Creative Fancy in tracing, (as Shakespeare does) a Character which resembles Nature in <u>all Climates</u> and <u>all</u> Nations. The elevated Sentiments of a Roman, form one Style only, and are at this Time Familiar with no People; – Shakespeare is at <u>Home</u> wherever he is understood, and must be so to the End of the World – And indeed Monsieur Guibert was so Condescending as to confe∫s after all that he thought Shakespeare a more <u>Universal</u> Genius than Corneille – but he finished with declaring that, after laying aside the <u>Fumier</u>[222] of <u>our</u> Poet, and several Faults likewise in the French one, he <u>must</u> give Corneille the Preference for being the greatest Writer of the two. – I did not like all this, you are to know, much, but I am neverthele∫s glad I heard it. As to <u>my</u> Idle thoughts upon such Matters, they ought certainly to go for Nothing even with myself, but my <u>Feelings</u> are what I cannot Struggle against, and they tell me that in what Voltaire and Monsieur Guibert call the <u>Fumier</u> of Shakspeare they might, as I think M^{rs}. Montague[223] observes, find many Pearls of Inestimable Value, if they knew how to look for, or how to Distinguish them from what is <u>really</u> Rubbish. – Indeed it will be a great while before they will be able to understand Shakespeare, even the <u>wisest</u> of them here; for I observe they hardly even attempt to learn the <u>Familiar</u> Parts of our Language, and such as are used in Conversation even now – How then for God's Sake, can they Seize upon the Pith of several Sentences which hang, perhaps, upon the Spelling of one Word, and at which We ourselves often only gue∫s from the Context? The Duc de Nivernois is Translating English into French all day long, and several I have met with talk of <u>reading</u> it with <u>Facility</u>, but I have remarked that they are in general quite behind hand when something Occurs out of the common Course of their Reading, and must be <u>caught</u> at rather than received from any Conviction in their Minds. – Monsieur Guibert said he had read a great deal both of Prose and Poetry in our Language, but that he had no Sort of Skill in Speaking it – And yet this Man Decides upon <u>Dramatic Dialogue</u>; and thinks he understands Falstaff, Dogberry, and Verges,[224] and every <u>Clown</u> in Shakespeare! Pray send his Laborious Editors to

225 Burke and Fox: Edmund Burke, 1729-97, and Charles James Fox, 1749-1806. Both were intimate friends of Mrs Crewe and renowned for their debating skills in the House of Commons.

226 ame de louage: soul for hire.

227 Thomas Gray, 1716-71, English poet.

Monsieur Guibert. – However this Frenchman is himself a great Character, and I liked him for the Eagerneſs with which he talked of coming to England, and of Visiting our House of Commons – We told him he would there hear Speeches in his own Style of Eloquence, but he had the Modesty to confeſs that he wished to be Impreſsed upon the Models of a Burke and a Fox,[225] and he added that the Difference between the English House of Commons and the French Academy was this, the former being of real Importance, they talked in it upon <u>Something</u>, in the latter, upon <u>Nothing</u>. Upon the whole I rather think you will like him, for he seems to have a great deal of Soul, and Feeling that really belongs to himself. I say this because I do aſsure you that not half of the Extacies one meets with here are <u>Genuine</u> and I think my Mother's Idea therefore of their having an <u>Ame</u> de <u>Louage</u>[226] is perfectly good and Applicable to many. Monsieur Guibert from what I can judge, if he has any Fault, it is that of being Embarraſsed with too lively an Imagination – the Images and Allusions in his Speech the other day Crouded too thickly, I thought, upon each other, Nevertheleſs they were Pure and such as you will approve of, when you read it, for it is Printed, and I mean to carry it with me to England. You will then agree with me that he Deserves to be Ranked in the first Claſs of Merit here. He talked of the Abbe' de Lisle with the same kind of Enthusiasm with Which we talk of Grey,[227] and he says He is the First French Writer Inspired with true Poetic Fire! I incline to think so too, tho' it would be Arrogant in <u>me</u>, perhaps, to go so far – but indeed I have a very high Opinion of Abbe' de Lisle, and only wish you could hear him repeat his Character of Milton and Ariosto – You would be Charmed if you did, and in the mean time, for God's Sake, read part of his "Jardins" – There <u>are</u> Imitations in it that is certain, of many of <u>our</u> Poets; but surely such Imitations as his which often, if not always, Improve upon the Originals are Sins one may readily Pardon. *x x*

Wednesday Morn.ᵍ –

Wednesday 21ˢᵗ February 1786 continued

Nothing shall keep me here longer than next week, that I am determined upon – I long to see you all very much – I long to Breathe the Air of old England again – I long to Feel at <u>home</u> – to make Enquiries after old Crewe Hall – to Prepare for the Journey thither in Summer, when I shall Shew off with my Paris Fashions, and make you all believe any thing I please! my Mother intends coming to England in April, and my Regrets

228 John Markham, 1761-1827, son of the Archbishop of York and a naval officer, rising to the rank of Admiral. He joined the Navy at the age of 14 in 1775, but then spent some years travelling between 1786 and 1793. Subsequently he went back to the Navy, serving in Europe and the West Indies before returning to England to serve as the Member of Parliament for Portsmouth. When Mrs Crewe met him he would have been 24 years old.

229 There was a great scandal at this time because the Prince of Wales had, on 15th December 1785, secretly married Maria Fitzherbert, six years his senior, twice married, twice widowed and a Roman Catholic. The marriage was denied by the Prince and his supporters. Mrs Fitzherbert lived with the Prince until 1803, despite his official marriage in 1795 to Princess Caroline of Brunswick.

230 George, 1st Earl Macartney, 1737-1806, Governor of Madras 1781-85, a 3rd cousin to Mrs Greville. He was created Baron Macartney of Lissanoure (Irish peerage) in 1776, and Earl Macartney in the English peerage in 1794.

231 the Sèvres china works, famous for the quality of its production.

are lessened on leaving her since I have been assured of this. Last Night the Hampden's, Lady Clarges, Colonel Gardner, Lord Downe, M^r. Crosby M^r. Bissett, and others all Supped with us at Lady Mornington's Hotel – To Night we are to meet again at Lady Hampden's – You can't think how comfortable we all are when we English People meet at Night to talk over what we have seen in the Day, to Discard all Candour, and Unanimously to determine that <u>our own Country</u> is the only one to live in! – Most of us are Sincere enough too, I believe; but there is certainly a Spirit of Contradiction and even a Gratification of Vanity and Selfishness in the doing it so often, and to the Degree which many do ~ ~ ~

After Dinner

I have been this Morning to see M^{rs}. Laborde, and we have agreed to go to a Play, or Puppet Shew, or something tomorrow Evening together, for we live now at the Extremities of Paris, and therefore hardly ever Meet – I saw M^r. Markham,[228] the Archbishop of York's Son, at her House, he lives with M^{rs}. Laborde, and seems to be a well bred good Sort of Young Man, I think. Every Body we meet now Pesters us with Questions concerning the Strange Story about the Prince and M^{rs}. Fitzerbert[229] – but what can the English know of it here? For my own Part I very soon tire of Conjectures and Speculations upon Points one has not the smallest Clue to be guided by. The Mails bring us no News that is Satisfactory respecting Politics – There is a Report, I find, of our old Friend Lord Macartney's[230] returning to India; but there I confess I am Weak enough to feel very Selfish, for should he leave England, there must be an End to the Wishes which I had formed about him. – However from a Letter I have lately received that Matter seems to be Doubtfull.

Thursday

Thursday 22nd February 1786

This Morning we are going to see the Save Manufactory of China,[231] which is about five Miles from hence. – If I indulged my Fancy there as much as I feel inclined to do, I certainly should not have Money enough to carry me home to England – The Bisquit Figures, and the Beautifull Pieces of China made here are indeed to say the Truth, the only things I have seen which tempt me much: for as to almost every thing else, to <u>my</u> Eye at least, they are behind us – Their Jewels are not half so neatly set,

232 or mouler: cast or moulded gold.

233 Elisabeth Louise Vigée le Brun, 1755-1842. Her painting was described as charming rather than skillful, but won her great popularity in Paris prior to the revolution. She painted a great many portraits including more than 20 of Marie Antoinette, a result of a great friendship between the two. She left Paris at the outbreak of the revolution and toured Europe before arriving in Britain, where she painted the Prince of Wales and Lord Byron among others. She returned to France in 1805. See The sweetness of life: a biography of Elisabeth Louise Vigée Le Brun, by Angelica Goodden, Deutsch, 1997.

234 Lord Ogleby was a character in a play The clandestine marriage, written by David Garrick and George Colman. It was a comedy, first performed at Drury Lane in February 1766

235 Sarah Siddons, 1755-1831. Though she acted in her father's travelling theatre company from childhood it wasn't until her appearance at Drury Lane in 1782 that she achieved success. She went on to build a reputation described as unsurpassed by any player of any age or country. She is described as having a gloriously expressive and beautiful face, a queenly figure and a voice of the richest power and flexibility

236 this would have been Medée by Pierre Corneille

and their Trinkets of all kinds are Clumsy compared with our's, However, they tell me, I must see their Or Mouler[232] before I go; and I mean it – And likewise I am to peep at Mademoiselle le Brun's[233] Portraits – but I know before hand from the <u>Family</u> <u>Pictures</u> I have already seen at Different Houses, that Her Stile of Painting will not please me. It is very odd that they should so continually make use of the word <u>Simplicity</u>, and yet have so Imperfect a Idea of its Sense! – But it is with every thing as with their Gardens, they must undo a vast deal before they can arrive at what pleases us – Was a Reformation in their Taste left to an English person, he would, I believe, lay their Heads and their Country Waste, before he arrived at Instructing the one or Ornamenting the other. – He would be like Lord Ogleby[234] and say "You must Fling the House into the Canal, and so get Rid of two bad things at once" – Lord Spencer called last Night to take leave of us – They are going to Day. Miſs Payne and her Polish Friends set out before me, the Hampden's at the same time, and Lord Downe and my Brother very soon after, so that the English Party is breaking up very fast.

Friday

Friday 23ʳᵈ February 1786

I last Night saw Madamoiselle Rocourt (the Mʳˢ. Siddons of Paris)[235] in the Character of Medea.[236] – The House was amazingly Crouded, which is always the Case when She Acts, and, I find, they consider her here as by much the most Admirable Female Performer they ever had. She excells in the Violent Stile, such as that of last Night, and <u>her</u> Acting was as <u>Correct</u>, I think, as poſsible – Yet Notwithstanding, I could not help wishing throughout the Play for a greater Variety of Shades, such as Mʳˢ. Siddons always contrives to Introduce – Mʳˢ. Hobart sat next to me, and was in such Raptures with Mademoiselle Rocourt that She said several times, "it was great Pity Mʳˢ. Siddons could not see some of her <u>Attitudes</u> in order to Improve by them" God forbid She should! thought I; for I do aſsure you, those Attitudes which make the House ring with Applauses, are the Attitudes which belong to the Grace of a Dancing Master; and for this Reason Mademoiselle Rocourt's Muscles seem not at all Dependant upon the Feelings, but the <u>Attitude</u> of the Moment – Nor do I think it Arrogant in me to aſsert this, for it is the Eye, and that of every common Observer as well as the wise, which is to decide upon this Point. Pronunciation and Delivery admit of Rules, to which the Ignorant must bow; but <u>Action</u> is the Language of Nature, we all Speak it, and of course we understand it when spoken by Another – Bad

237 Mademoiselle Raucourt, the stage name of Francoise Marie Antoinette Josèphe Saucerotte, 1756-1815, who had made her debut at the Comédie-Francaise in 1772, at the age of 16. She was seen on that occasion by Elisabeth Louise Vigée le Brun, who recorded the event in her memoirs: "The most brilliant debut I remember was that of Mlle Raucourt in the role of Dido. At most she could only have been eighteen or twenty. Her beautiful face, figure, voice and diction all bespoke perfection as an actress. To all these advantages she fused an air of astonishing dignity and had a reputation for wisdom far beyond her years; consequently she was sought after by our great ladies. She was given jewels and stage costumes as well as money; her father also benefited from the latter and made sure he never left her side. Later her manners changed drastically; it was said that the first happy mortal to conquer her many virtues was the Marquis de Bièvres and when she left him for another lover he cried, 'That ungrateful woman has robbed me of my fortune'. If Mlle Raucourt did not remain wise, she did remain a great tragic actress. Later her voice became so harsh and strident that if one closed one's eyes, one might think it was a man speaking. She remained in the theatre until her death and ended her career playing the parts of elderly mothers and queens with unparalleled success." (Vigée Le Brun, p50). Her early fame reached the ears of London's famous actor Garrick, who wrote to his two nieces, at that time living in the French capital: "....the Moment You think you can understand & Enjoy a tragedy, I hope Mad De Combes will let You see Mad^lle Raucourt, who makes such a noise in Paris...."(McIntyre: Garrick, p498) At one stage of her career she led a wild life, got into debt and lost the affection of her Paris audience. She left for Russia and was only reinstated in 1779 with some difficulty by Marie Antoinette. An ardent royalist she and a number of other performers were imprisoned during the revolution and she came close to execution. In 1796 she grouped together a company for a second Théatre Francais at the Théatre Louvois. With the closure of the Louvois in 1797 she moved to the Odéon in 1798, and rejoined her former colleagues in 1799. In 1807, Napoleon gave Raucourt the task of organizing a French company for Italy, performing in Milan, Turin, Genoa and Venice, which lasted until 1814. Fifteen thousand people attended her funeral in 1815, but the curé of the Église Saint Roche would not accept her body into the church until the King gave orders that she receive full Christian burial. Mrs Crewe clearly saw Mlle Raucourt in her more strident period and had little good to say of her.*

238 Sir Joshua Reynolds, 1723-92, English portrait painter, and first President of the Royal Academy founded in 1768. He painted Mrs Crewe, her husband and their children on many occasions.

Action has therefore the Effect of Jargon upon us, or, if you will, of a Foreign Language, which we listen to, perhaps with Pleasure, but do not Comprehend. – The Eye is pleased with Mademoiselle Rocourt[237] but the <u>Heart</u> is untouched, we therefore <u>Applaud </u>her – Mrs. Siddons would make us Weep, or Rage, in Short just as She chose to Affect us. I have told you Mademoiselle Rocourt was perfectly <u>correct,</u> and so She was, for I'll be sworn She had Authority for every Tone of her Voice, and every Posture of her Limbs – but is not this wrong? – There must, I know, be <u>Machinery</u> in every thing, but ought we to see it? If not, why is an Actreſs to take so much Care to convince us that She has devoted a great deal of time and Infinite Pains to the Acquisition of Gestures, which neither Medea, nor any other Creature upon Earth, besides a French Dancing Master, could have put herself into? What Sir Joshua Reynolds[238] somewhere says of Drapery, is exactly what I think of Imitation, "It should not be woollen, or silk, or Linen, it Should be <u>Drapery</u>, it should be nothing <u>more</u>" – An Actreſs should not be Italian, or French, or English, She should be a <u>Woman</u> and nothing more – How pleasant it is to write to you upon all this! and certain I feel that you will explain to me much better what I really think upon this Subject – To say the Truth you were often in my Head when I wrote my Spa and Bruſsells Journal, but as I knew other People would see them I did not feel quite so secure as I do now – I had not half the Pleasure in Communicating every Idle Thought which flitted acroſs my Fancy. – They contain however a pretty good Number and indeed, if I do write, I must always write what Occurs to me; the only Excuse I can offer for the blotting so much Paper. – Every Body is now reading Cagliostro's Memoirs, written in the Bastile where he is now confined on Account of this Affair of the Cardinal De Rohan's – People had done talking of that Prelate when we arrived here, but these Memoirs have awakened the public Attention to him. This Cagliostro had a Strange Suspicious Character till he put out the Account of his Life, which is so Interesting and Melancholy that every one seems Shocked at his having been placed in the Bastile so Precipitately. – His poor Wife, who can no way have been complicated in all this, is likewise in some other Corner of the Prison. The very Name of the Bastile always struck me with Horror, and since the other Morning that I drove round It's Dreary Dyke and Walls that Chill the Blood, I have found the mention of it still more terrible! –

239 laudanum was a solution containing morphine and prepared from opium, commonly used at this time as a painkiller.

240 Colonel Barry St Leger, who in 1776 founded the now famous horse race.

Sunday Evening

Sunday 25ᵗʰ February 1786

I have been Ill these two Days with a Feverish Cold which Dʳ. Lee has been so good as to attend me for. – My Mother is very much Indisposed too, and, I understand, the sudden Cold Weather Affects every Body here. I feel sorry not to have been at Madame de Coigny's Ball last Night, because it was expected to turn out a pretty Fete; but, I believe I must now bid Adieu to what are called the Pleasures of Paris, otherwise I shall not get Strong and well enough to undertake my Journey to England so soon as I wish. ✗

Tuesday Even.ᵍ -

Tuesday 27ᵗʰ February 1786

The Weather has continued Intensely Cold, and every Mortal here has been the worse for it as well as myself. Since I last wrote, I have been confined to my Room by the Strict Orders of Dʳ. Lee. There seems to be a prevailing Folly and Imbecility in all the Medical People in Paris, and even I have Suffered a little by it, for the Apothecary, who was ordered to send me a Soporific Draught the Night before last, chose to infuse but <u>half</u> the Quantity of Laudanum[239] Specified in the Prescription; the Consequence of which was, that instead of procuring me my Rest, it Disordered my Head and prevented my getting one Wink of Sleep! Dʳ. Lee went to him to Reprobate his Conduct, but he could get no Excuse and only this Reason, that it was a Medicine never used in such large Quantities <u>here</u>, and that upon that Account he had resolved to lower the Dose. – My Brother Charles talks of setting out with Colonel Sᵗ. Leger[240] about the same time that I shall go, which I feel sorry for, as I could wish him to stay with my Mother 'till She hears of my safe Landing; but indeed he is so willing to Accommodate himself to us both in all Respects and has done it in so many Instances already that it would be cruel to Interfere with any of his Plans at Present. My Original Day for going was Sunday next, and I flattered myself that I should have had Lord and Lady Hampden as Safe Guards, but this Indisposition must Retard me a little longer Still – I Ardently hope not more than two or three Days, as I really feel now much better than <u>I have</u> done lately. ✗

241 *Marechalle de Mirepoix: born Anne Marguerite Gabrielle de Beauvau Craon she had first married the Prince de Lixin, who was killed in a duel with the Duc de Richelieu. Then in 1739 she married Charles Pierre Gaston Francois, Marechal de Mirepoix, who Horace Walpole described as "hard, polite, dry and civil" (Webster, p19). She had been described as 'the little cat' (Cronin, p63), but Walpole found her "the most agreeable woman of the world, when she pleases — but there must not be a card in the room" (Webster, p20). Her passion for gambling led her into dire straits from which she was rescued only by soliciting help from the King's favourites Madame de Pompadour and Madame du Barry. She was sister to the Prince de Beauvau and the Marquise de Boufflers (also see pp81-3 Craveri).*

Thursday Afternoon

Thursday 1ˢᵗ March 1786

We are going on very quietly in this Hotel, and recovering tho' rather slowly, from this Influenze or whatever is is that has Disordered almost all Paris. – The Weather continues so bad that I am carried in an odd Sort of Vehicle acroſs the Court in an Evening to my Mother's Apartment, where People drop in till ten O'Clock. There are no regular Sedan Chairs in this Town, which is a great Inconvenience, I think, – at least, I always prefer them to a Coach at this Season of the Year in London, when one is often full Dreſſed, as Silk Shoes, and long Trains suffer so much by Sloppy Weather. – There is this to be said, however, in favour of Coaches here, one is always under cover in Alighting from them, and not as with us, obliged to Wade through Part of a Street or up a Flight of Steps. ~ The Duc de Nivernois talked a great deal about the Cardinal de Rohan's Affairs Yesterday – He seems to think the Queen has behaved with too much Severity upon the whole, but that She does not deserve the Abuse that is heaped on her by many People. La Marechalle de Mirpoix²⁴¹ was more Unreserved, and spoke indeed with very great Violence against her the other Day, accusing her of wanting Common Humanity in keeping him in the Bastile 'till his Trial, which is to come on in Time – So there you have both their Opinions. Lady Clermont called Yesterday, and told us She had been at Versailles the Night before to make Tea for the King and Queen at Madame de Polignac's – that the Rooms were Ornamented with Garlands and Wreathes of Flowers – that a little Fête of Dancing and Music went on at the End of one of them – and that the Tea Table at which She Presided was placed in a Sort of Arbour or Bower, which She was ordered to sit in – that the King then followed her, undertook the Management of part of the Tea Equipage, particularly that of the Lamp and Tea Kettle, which in the hurry Occasioned by his Civilities he threw Down; Spilling the Water upon her Gown, and the Oil upon the Floor – that several Courtiers flew to her Aſſistance, much of the Company was alarmed: but the whole ended very Fortunately in the Amusement of the Aſſembly. And as Courts, however Lavish of other Entertainments, must always act with some Æconomy in the Case of Jokes, this Story, it seems, has been made the most of at Versailles eversince, and told also all over Paris for the Amusement of those who were not Fortunate enough to belong to this Fête – The Carnival is now quite over, thank God! for the three last Nights of it have been Distracting even to me in this Confinement. The People in the Streets have gone Hallooing and Singing long after Midnight, and from my Room I have frequently heard

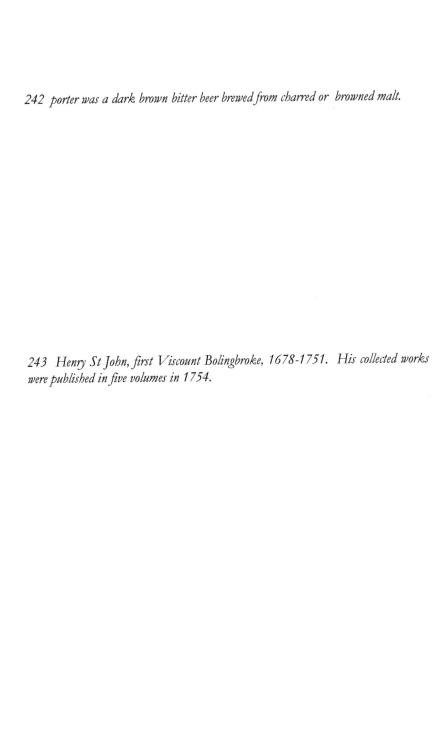

242 porter was a dark brown bitter beer brewed from charred or browned malt.

243 Henry St John, first Viscount Bolingbroke, 1678-1751. His collected works were published in five volumes in 1754.

Noises and Riots, which have Sounded quite Alarming. – Particularly since they informed me that two Harlequins, several Punches, and other Masques were found dead in Consequence of Quarrels. You may laugh as much as you please, but it is Shocking Work to be so near such Horrors for all that. I am told that many are killed every year during the Carnival. For the French not having any Idea of our good old English Fashion of settling Disputes by Boxing Matches, a Knife or some Awkward Fencing frequently terminate the Fray. Drunkennefs is besides in Paris Produced by Spirituous Liquors which do not Deaden their Anger so much as our thick Porter[242] would – In Short by all the Stories I have heard lately, I by no means conceive their Police to be, as is afserted, much Superior to our's, in those Cases at least. But you are to know there is a little Policy working at such times at the Carnival, and it is actually a Measure of Government, not merely to Wink at Excefses, but even to furnish the poorer Sort with Money to produce them; for the more Debauched Men are, the more Abject and the more Contented under their Slavery they become, and, deluded by the false Glare of Riot and Intemperance the lefs likely are they to form Reflections which in the End might be Dangerous to their Tyrant! I know it is the Fashion to say that the lower Clafses of People in France are happy and Contented – I own I have my doubts about it – There is a Sort of <u>Rivalship</u> in Gaiety, and much of their Happinefs is only <u>External</u>, and probably the Effect of Habit; but they have many <u>actual</u> Wants, and tho' they Sing away their Cares, it is like the moaning Song, perhaps, of a poor Weak Child, who puts himself to Sleep that way. Pray does not Lord Bolingbroke[243] say this Somewhere? or is it an Idea of my own? ~

Sunday

Sunday 4ᵗʰ March 1786

Wednesday next is fixed for my Departure, and I now begin to flatter myself that upon that Day I shall really and truly Commence my long wished for Journey. My Brother Charles and I had agreed to go Separately, because our Manner of Travelling is so Different – He likes to go like the Wind Night and Day, and I, who have a Child with me, can never travel at that Rate, tho' I were ever so much Inclined to it. We had therefore, as I tell you, Determined upon not going Together till Yesterday when he desired he might Accompany me as my Health was still in too weak a State to venture quite alone. It is therefore settled that next Wednesday we are to set off for Chantilly, where we are to take leave of some of our Paris Friends. To Day my Mother and I dine at Dʳ. Lee's – We never have seen his Wife in our Lives, but that does not

244 *devoirs: courteous or formal attentions; respects, i.e. pay one's devoirs to.*

245 *vieille Cour: old heart.*

Signify – The Doctor has said very often he has set his Heart on our Dining with him, before I go, and I am sure his Attention to me during the Illneſs I have had here, claims every Return in my Power. I am Puzzling my Brains to find out what sort of Present I should make him or his Wife, and will do all I can to discover her Taste with Respect to China &c at Dinner to Day. The Duc and Ducheſse de Castries have just sent to invite me to a Ball, but I must send my Excuses there as well as to every other Place, for my great Object now is to get quite Strong against the Approaching Journey. ✗ – I conclude that as you are now in the Country, you will hardly be returned before I arrive; and, to say the Truth, I am not certain that I do not like it better, for my Head will be at first Strangely Embarraſsed with Devoirs²⁴⁴ and Duties and tiresome Etiquettes, which are all Unavoidable after such an Absence. – One __must__ be glad to see this Body, and __must__ be Inquisitive after that Busineſs, neither of which really and truly can be Interesting to one – Between you and me, it is very hard upon us all, that we must Aſsume not only Virtues; if we have them not, but a Number also of little __indifferent__ Qualities which have not the Honor to be Claſsed either on the Side of Virtue or of Vice – __little__ Curiosities, little Anxieties about nothing, and about a hundred and fifty __little Affectations__, which are, Neverthelſs absolutely Neceſsary to the Correct Behaviour of all People of the World. __Here__ they are adopted in a much greater degree than in London; and I verily believe that __this__ Sort of Society require that a Vast deal more Ceremony should be Supported – It throws a Veil over Peoples real Feelings when they are Crouded together and packed up so Incommodiously as to render Neighbourhood uncomfortable. The Vieille Cour²⁴⁵ however, dealt so much more in Ceremony and Etiquette with Respect to many Points, that the Young People Rebelled, and have carried it too much, perhaps, the other Way; for there are sad Complaints of __them__ and of the English, whose Manners some flatter themselves they have Imported. The Old and Middle Aged Gentry still lay a Streſs upon Visiting, but I confeſs I think I should grow tired of their Evenings upon this Account – They begin calling on each other from the Hours of five till ten, when Supper is served every where, and each retires to his particular Society – during these Visits no Cards go on, and this it is, I think, which makes the Life so heavy – for tho' I seldom play at Cards myself, I think it is pleasant to see others at them, and to have the Circle broken in such a Manner, as may enable one to talk to whomsoever one pleases. They go very much here to the Theatres, but there is an Uncomfortableneſs in their System concerning that which an English Person cannot Submit to. – three, or four, more People Subscribe together and it is quite Chance and Accident whether they can have Places upon those Nights that they wish to go or not – Nay I have heard them sometimes Say – "I must go such a Night

246 *"He speaks to me who never had a Son": quote not identified.*

247 *Sittingbourne is a town in Kent on the road between Dover and London.*

248 *Goody: a depreciative, meaning weakly, moral and religious; although Mrs Crewe uses it in the sense of a good, motherly woman.*

because it happens to be in my Power"- not because it is a Favourite Piece – Strangers too find great Difficulty about the Theatres, Women I mean, for as to Men, they have the Balcony always open – if one wishes to see a particular Piece, one must take a whole Box or fill it, both of which Circumstances are inconvenient to many People. I think too that being always under an Obligation for one's Place is equally Distreſsing. – Miſs Carter said the other Day that there was so much trouble about every Sort of Amusement at Paris, and so much to be done about every other thing, that She thought what we often all Complained of here ought to be called the Day Mare. I protest it is so apposite to what I have forever felt in Paris, that I was quite charmed with the Idea. ✗

Tuesday Morn.ᵍ –

Tuesday 6ᵗʰ March 1786

Such a Quantity of Snow has fallen within these two Days that the Roads we are to take are Unpaſsable. – Nothing can be more tiresome than this Delay! – My letters to my Friends to tell them when to expect me have been sent some Days ago – my Cloaths are all packed up – my Bills all paid – my Farewells all made; and yet here I am without a gueſs whether it is for a Fortnight longer, or in short, when I am to be released. There is Something in Snow which is, I think, more particularly trying to the Patience, at least the Hindrances which it has occasioned me have been more Perplexing than other Impediments; but it may be however, because it Snows at present that I think so. – Poor Charles is as much Disappointed as I can be he says – but I do not believe him. "He speaks to me who never had a Son"[246] – No one could feel more certain than I did Yesterday about seeing John at Sittingbourne[247] on Sunday or Monday next at farthest! To Night a whole Parcel of English People have been long engaged to sup in this Hotel to take leave of us – but we are now like Strolling Players – for God only knows when it will be "poſitively our last time of Appearing" – I begin to wish now that there was some given time for the Remainder of our Stay, as Uncertainty teizes and Fatigues my Spirits more than actual Disappointments – Many People I know had rather have their Hopes and Fears played with than not, and I think you and I have sometimes Argued this Point together – I most aſsuredly like to know what I am to abide by always concerning every thing. Our Dinner at Dr. Lee's was very Comfortable in It's Way. Mrs. Lee seems to be an amiable sort of Old Fashioned sensible Goody;[248] in which Claſs of Persons there is generally, I think, something Interesting, tho' the Voice of their poor Fame is seldom heard to rise

249 Sir Robert Waller, 1768-1826, eldest son of Sir Robert Waller of Lisbrian. He succeeded his father as 2nd Baronet Waller at the early age of 12. He married twice, firstly to Mary Bernard in 1796 and secondly to Elizabeth Biddulph, widow of John Willington, in 1806. Mrs Crewe describes him as a decent, well-behaved young man who has been travelling in France and Italy for some time. He returned to Italy again in 1791-2.

250 one of the judges who condemned Charles I to death in 1649.

251 Mr Bruce – not identified.

252 Robert Smith, 1752-1838, of Bulcot, Nottinghamshire. He was a member of Parliament and a partner in his family's banking firm. In 1797 he was created Baron Carrington. The English Chronicle wrote about him in 1781: "Mr Smith is a gentleman whose conduct, both in public and private life, every way justifies the high opinion his constituents entertain of him. In Parliament he is uniform and uninfluenced; in private life upright and benevolent. He takes no part in political business out of the House, from an apprehension perhaps that too much zeal might prove injurious to his domestic connexions and convenience, having an extensive concern in a private bank, in partnership with Messrs. Payne and Smith, the essential constitution of which species of commerce manifestly implies the necessity for as many friends as possible. As an individual, therefore, he wishes to stand fair with men of all denominations, but is by no means so much devoted to interested considerations, or to be governed in his parliamentary conduct by any sinister influence. He is far from being defective in original understanding, though he has never thought proper to exert it in the way of oratorical declamation; is very attentive to duty in the House, and may be justly esteemed a valuable member of the British senate." However, according to Wraxall he possessed "no parliamentary talent". (Namier and Brook: House of Commons 1754-1790) His wife Anne was part of the English contingent Mrs Crewe met in Paris and Sir Robert travelled out to be with her.

253 macao: a card game, similar to vingt-et-un or pontoon.

254 the Duke of Richmond, in Pitt's government as Master of the Ordnance, had presented to Parliament plans for the fortification of the dockyards at Portsmouth and Plymouth. When it came to a vote on the plans the House split evenly with 169 votes for and 169 against. The Speaker of the House had the casting vote and voted against the Government. One of the MPs voting against the government was William Seymour Conway who Mrs Crewe met several times during her stay in Paris, the last being 17th January when she reported he was leaving in order to be back for the meeting of the House of Commons.

255 Charles Jenkinson, 1727-1808 - in 1786 he was made President of the Board of Trade.

much above a whisper. But pray who is more a Friend to Human kind than what is Vulgarly called a good Motherly Woman? I protest I never hear the Words that they do not create in me a Sensation of Reverence, and a kind of Confused Gratitude, which many and many People who have excited my Admiration, and even po/se/sed my Friendship, never yet produced! a Mr. Waller[249] (a Descendant from Sr. H. Waller one of King Charles's Judges)[250] dined at Dr. Lee's, and so did a Mr. Bruce.[251] They both seemed to be decent will behaved young Men, and as they have been Travelling in Italy and France some Considerable time, it was Amusing enough to hear their Accounts of Different things which they had met with. – Poor Lord Downe has been very ill, and is Still Confined to his House. *x*

Wednesday

Wednesday 7ᵗʰ March 1786

"Ala/s! Ala/s! it Freezes at a Woeful Rate indeed, and the Ground is covered with Snow; So that, I fear, we have not the Shadow of a Chance for setting off soon. – Sr. Robert Smith[252] however returned from England Yesterday, and, it seems, he says he was not stopped by the Snow, but that more has fallen on the Calais Road since. so that every Body here advises us not to Venture. We were a very large Party of English Yesterday Evening at Lord Hampden's. – We Supped at two Tables, and played at all sorts of Gambling Games, Macao,[253] Hazard, Vingt et une &c. Every Body was Enquiring about Letters and News from England! for the late Division against Ministry upon the Duke of Richmond's Plan of Fortifications must be a great Triumph to Opposition, whether it Shakes the Cabinet or not.[254] Can it be po/sible that Mr. Jenkinson[255] (whose very Name is hardly ever mentioned by any Party without Contempt, I believe) is it po/sible that he should now be advanced to the Heighth of Secretary of State? – One loses much Intelligence at such a Distance from the Scene of Action; but I often think that Distance sometimes gives one a more Impartial View of things, and a more just Outline. – The marking every Step of a Measure, and thus going along with it through every Shade of the Colour, prepares you Gradually not more Favourably for the Completion of it, than in Abrupt Disclosure, which brings the Affair before you at once in a Mature form. ~

256 *Sir Horace Mann, 1701-1786. He was the British envoy to Florence from 1740 to 1786 and died in the year Mrs Crewe's diary was written. He was a great correspondent with Horace Walpole.*

257 *a chaise was an open carriage and an imperial was a case or trunk for luggage.*

258 *a laquais de louage was a hired footman.*

259 *his brother was Louis-Sébastian Mercier, 1740-1814, a dramatist and critic.*

12 O'Clock –

D^r. Lee has just called – He say the Sun is Powerful, that there certainly is a Thaw, and that it is just poſsible we may go Tomorrow – Here is Miſs Payne –

2 O'Clock

Sir Horace Mann[256] has been here for above an Hour. – He came two Days ago to Paris, sets off To-morrow for England. The Snow, he says, is not of Consequence enough to prevent any Body from going Safely, but he will enquire of all the Post Masters, and let me know. We had a great Batch of Politics, and it was pleasant to hear the high and hearty Encomiums he paſsed upon Charles Fox's Political Character; He spoke pretty freely concerning the King, and made the usual Lamentations upon this Unfortunate Reign. ✗

Friday Morn.^{g}.

Friday 9th March 1786

I was more tired Yesterday with the mere Subject of our Departure than I should have been had I Travelled a Hundred Miles. Some People were wise about the Weather; others wise in their Advice to me concerning the Roads I must take – Some telling me to Venture, and some not to Venture because of my late Illneſs – all talking at the same time, and putting it Effectually out of my Power to follow any of their Opinions: which determined me at last to do no more than get the best Information I could from Monsieur Deſsein, the Master of the Inn at Calais, who was just arrived – What he said, and what Monsieur Perigord the Banker said upon the Subject fixed me in the Resolution to set off to Day – It is now past Eleven O'Clock – I have been ready some time, But my Brother Charles is not – The Chaises and Imperials[257] &c are at the Door – the Laquais de Louage,[257] the Coachman I have Employed here, the Master of this Hotel (who, by the bye, is brother to the famous Monsieur Mercier Author of the Plays)[258] and about Fifty more People of one Sort or Another are coming in to make the Customary Speeches. ✗

260 Marechal de Beauveau: not identified. He could be the same person as the Marechal de Beveau, already mentioned, who hasn't been identified either.

261 Lord and Lady Geo Cavendish: George Augustus Henry Cavendish and Elizabeth Cavendish. He was son of the 4th Duke of Devonshire and she was the daughter of the 7th Earl of Northampton.

262 – traineaus: sledges.

263 flambeau: a flaming torch.

Chantilly - same Evening -

We left Paris about Twelve this Morning, and have found the Roads very good thus far. The Weather is Colder than I ever felt it in England, but so easy a Day's Journey has rather done me good – indeed nothing but leaving my poor Mother made me feel any Regrets on quitting Paris – The Life we have lately paſsed there, has been on the whole very Tiresome, and my Lodgings were much too Inconvenient to have been Inhabited with tolerable Comfort for a long time. – The Marechall de Beauveau[260] the Ducheſse de Castries, and several more fine People called Yesterday to take leave – a Ceremony which I think the most Awkward in the World with every one, Friend or Foe, and at every time. The poor Duc de Nivernois very good naturedly presented me with a warm Peliſse to defend me from the Cold, but he has been Confined to his Room with a Fever for several Days, and I have not seen him since. Lord and Lady Geo– Cavendish[261] Arrived in Paris two Days ago to stay two Months. He called on us Yesterday Morning, and we were very glad to meet to talk over the late great Political Event. You see that I have had nothing at all Curious to Communicate to you lately even of my own Trifling Sort. To say true, I have upon that Account more than upon my own been sometimes very much concerned at not being able to go to many Places, an Account of which might have amused you. It has been the Fashion during these few Days past for large Parties to paſs all over Paris in Traineaus[262] upon the Ice. I have not been lucky enough to see any, but I am told they are very Showy Equipages. The Gentlemen drive; the Ladies have fine Furr Dreſses of different Sorts, and the latter wear Masques. At Night they go with Flambeaus,[263] and have Bands of Music following them. – However from what I can learn it is a Prettier Amusement for Spectators than for those concerned, who generally a laid up with Colds the next Day. The Queen Paraded it all over Paris the other Morning; and Madame de Coigny had another Party which began and finished at her own House, and was talked of as having been as Splendid. ~ We mean to get to Amiens To-morrow. ✗

Boulogne - March
Monday Evening 6 O'Clock -

Monday 12ᵗʰ March 1786

We arrived here to Day soon after two O'Clock: have dined, and seen the Captain of a Packet with whom we are to Embark at nine, for the Wind is very fair, it seems. The Roads were good during our whole

264 *from Shakespeare's* Measure for measure, *Act 3, Scene 1, line5*
"*Be absolute for death; either death or life*
Shall thereby be the sweeter.
Reason thus with life.
If I do lose thee, I do lose a thing
That none but fools would keep. A breath thou art,
Servile to all the skyey influences,
That dost this habitation where thou keep'st Hourly afflict."

265 *Chantilly, about 23 miles north of Paris, along what is now the N16 road.*

266 *Amiens is a further 50 miles from Chantilly, along the D916 and N1.*

267 *St-Just-en-Chaussée.*

267a *i.e. Breteuil*

268 *Thomas Lewis O'Beirne, educated as a Roman Catholic he later adopted Protestant views and wrote controversial Whig tracts, pamphlets and periodical articles. Walpole wrote in November 1780 "There is a new comedy, called the Generous Impostor, which Mrs Crewe and all Sheridan's protector's protect, though he did not write it, but I hear it is most indifferent." The play was O'Beirne's, first acted at Drury Lane and attended on the first night by Mrs Crewe, the Duchess of Devonshire, Lady Duncannon, Lady Craven and other fashionable ladies. When the play was published in 1781, O'Beirne dedicated it to Mrs Greville and Mrs Crewe. He was made Bishop of Ossory in 1795 and Bishop of Meath in 1798. The DNB says he retired to Aubigny in 1783-5, but Mrs Crewe says clearly that he was on his way there in March 1786, intending to stay for 12 months*

269 *Aubigny-sur-Nere, about 50 miles south-east of Orleans.*

Journey, but I cannot say we met with nothing like an Accident, for my Brother Charles and I were Overturned on Saturday last without being either of us hurt, tho' the Shock it gave me, was so great that it Disturbed my Rest all night, and has made me full of Tremors ever since! – Were I a French Woman, I should say the Physique, and not the Moral, occasioned all this, for it is certain that a small Portion of Reason may inform one that it is not very likely such a Event should happen twice in so Short a Journey as we have come. However I must remark here that Men are never Sufficiently Candid on the Subject of Female Weakneſs upon such Occasions – It is allways attributed to the Poverty of their Minds, and not to that Unfortunate Delicacy of Frame which renders them more than the other Sex "Subject to every Skyey Influence,"[264] and an easy Prey to Nervous Imaginations. And yet Men can be sufficiently Indulgent to their own weakneſses, witneſs Intoxication, under the Prevalence of which, what Folly and Absurdity are they not guilty of? But does not Fear Intoxicate the Mind? and therefore why is not poor weak Women to meet with some Quarter on the same Score? – Nevertheleſs I own for the Credit of Men of Sense, that they are leſs Inclinable to inveigh against our Understandings, which after, after all, can never Cope with theirs)than Persons whose own Capacities are rather Doubtfull. For my own Part, I like to listen to the unaffected Absurdity which such People advance upon many Subjects, as well as their Favourite one; for, do you know, listening to Nonsense I often think opens one's Mind to the Truth as much as any thing, it certainly Inclines it to Reflections which it might not otherwise have Stumbled upon. – Besides, I do not think the old Proverb, about Swallowing a Peck of Dirt before one Dies", quite inapplicable here. – Well, so it was however; I had my fears, and for several Stages after our Accident I hardly could bear the Appearance of a Hill, or the Sensation which the Chaise gave me when Inclined at all on one Side. But Heaven be praised! a good Night's Rest and a little Exertion of Mind have restored me again to the State I was in, and I feel now even equal to encounter Waves and Winds! We left Chantilly[265] at about ten O'Clock on Saturday Morning, and lay at Amiens[266] that Night. At a Small Post House called St. Juste[267] on this Side of Breteul;[267a] while we were Changing Horses, who should we see but Mr. O'Beirne[268] the Clergyman, stepping out of a large Family Coach, and coming up to us.I immediately alighted, and desired Mrs. O'Beirne to do so too, and we all went and Conversed upon various Topics in a Sort of Ale House, while the Horses were putting to. They are going to live for a twelve Month at the Duke of Richmond's Chateau at Aubigny,[269] and are to Stop at Paris for a few Days in their way to it. It was just after this Adventure that we were overturned, and I thank God it was not before, for I never should have been able to have concealed it from them, and I have since determined

270 the only reference in the diary to her servant Toby.

271 an indication here that she had two maids – later she refers to one of them being for her daughter.

272 Abbeville is about 26 miles from Amiens along the N1 and Montreuil about 25 miles further on.

273 Mrs Crewe was born at Newton Toney in Wiltshire, about 10 miles north of Salisbury.

274 – from a poem by Edward Dyer, 1540-1607:
> *"My mind to me a kingdom is,*
> *Such perfect joy therein I find,*
> *That it excels all other bliss*
> *That world affords or grows by kind:*
> *Though much I want which most would have,*
> *Yet still my mind forbids to crave."*

275 prate: chatter, talk too much, talk foolishly.

not to let my Mother hear of it till after our Arrival in England. Pray remember that, if you should ever Travel this Road, you must not have a very heavy Carriage, or you must be Peremptory with the Postilions concerning the use of a Drag Chain, for it was the want of that which we had to rue! If the Horses had been able to sustain the Weight of my Carriage in going down Hill, it is probable we should have escaped – the Third Horse for they drive three abreast in this Country) pulled and pulled so hard that the Postilion could not prevent his Swerving towards a small Pit into which we were Tumbled! My Brother Charles contrived very Skillfully to save me from receiving the Additional Shock of his Weight, and his Servant in a Moment rode up, got him out, and they very soon Afterwards got me out too. My Servant Toby[270] was gone on to order Horses – however we did very well, for the two Maids[271] left my Brother's Chaise for us to get into it, and we took the Child with us, leaving them all with a few Plowmen to rear up the Carriage – We then went on and Dined at Breteul, which we were about a Mile from, and there had the Comfort of <u>talking the Affair over</u>. Yesterday we dined at Abbeville and lay at Montreul,[272] where we arrived about ten O'Clock. It was the clearest Moonlight Night I ever saw, and the fine open Downy Country We pa∫ed through filled my Head with a thousand pleasing Reveries, and recalled to my Mind my Youthful Days in Wiltshire and Hampshire.[273] Recollection I think, generally Cloaths the Objects it recalls to one's View in their <u>best</u> Attire, and I feel very Greatful for this; tho' I believe it is a kind Office which it performs for every other Person who, in Reverting to the past Scenes of his Life, sees only, or at least most Distinctly the Pleasureable Side of it. For what Reason, let Philosophers determine – I am contented with the <u>Fact</u>, and with being able truly to adopt that old Line

"My Mind to me a Kingdom is" –[274]

The Inn we are now at is kept by English People, and the Landlady is so much inclined to Prate[275] that my Brother Charles and I have been amusing Ourselves with her – She Says there are one thousand and four hundred English Persons in this Town – a Colonel Woollaston and his Family are settled here, and likewise Lord Newark and Lady Somebody his Daughter in Law, who was Lady Tyrconnel, and a Colonel Bullock and <u>his</u> Family are settled here too – and that some of the Families live in a <u>genteel</u> <u>Stile</u> <u>enough,</u> but that for <u>the</u> <u>most</u> <u>Part</u> the English who come here are not <u>good for much,</u> and that they never can agree among each other. We asked her why She chose to settle herself in a foreign Country? – and if She was not Sometimes tempted to see her own native one? She answered that "<u>sure enough</u>" She had gone once or twice over to pay Visits to her Friends, but that She had been so long Established abroad now that She never wished to fix any where else, and that London always Frightened her because of the frequent Fires and Robberies – "The Fires (says she) have happened every Day since this

Insurance Office was set on Foot, and I know a Woman myself who set her own House on Fire for no other Reason" – This good Woman Prosed on a great deal more upon various Subjects in this Way, which indeed there is no Violent Reason that you should be bored with. But pray tell me what you think on the Subject of Fires, for I confeʃs to you, that I have my Fears too, and wish much to learn whether what She has advanced is really <u>so</u> or <u>not</u>. *x x*

Dover. Tuesday Afternoon

One O'Clock -

Tuesday 13ᵗʰ March 1786

We had a very good Paʃsage of four Hours, and arrived here about two O'Clock this Morning without Let or hindrance. My Brother and little Emma slept all the Way, but the rest of Us were, as usual, very Ill, and I am now hardly recovered from a cruel Head ach which I had all Night. One of the Custom House Officers came on Board the Moment we reached the Harbour, and we were obliged to leave all our Trunks, and every thing we did not wear, in his Poʃseʃsion till this Morning. Mʳ. Payne the Master of the Inn, came and Conducted us from the Shore to his House – He told us that the Roads were still so Dangerous that he could not advise our Venturing from hence to Canterbury so soon as this Morning; but I was too much Fatigued to stay Parleying with him about all this before I went to Bed. *x*

Near three O'Clock

My Brother Charles went off this Morning, but I did not see him first. I have been busied all Day in settling every thing with Respect to my Journey to Sittingbourne to-morrow; I hope you will allow that I am very good for not having Stormed and Raved to you before this upon meeting with such Cruel Impediments at a Time when I am so little able to bear them! I have sent a Letter to John by my Brother Charles, and I do hope that I have now Arranged Matters very safely for seeing him To-morrow. Mʳ. Payne's Histories are so Dismal tho' about <u>Mails</u> <u>returning</u> <u>to him</u> <u>without their</u> <u>Boys</u> – about Stage Coaches having been

276 from Shakespeare's <u>Measure for measure</u>, Act 2, Scene 2, line 110:
        "Could great men thunder
        As Jove himself does, Jove would ne'er be quiet,
        For every pelting, petty officer
        Would use his heaven for thunder; nothing but thunder.
        Merciful heaven!
        Thou rather with thy sharp and sulphurous bolt
        Splitt'st the unwedgeable and gnarled oak
        Than the soft myrtle; but man, proud man,
        Drest in a little brief authority,
        Most ignorant of what he's most assur'd,
        His glassy essence, like an angry ape,
        Plays such fantastic tricks before high heaven
        As make the angels weep".

277 from Shakespeare's <u>Hamlet</u>, in the famous "to be or not to be" speech:
        "For who would bear the whips and scorns of time,
        The oppressor's wrong, the proud man's contumely,
        The pangs of dispriz'd love, the law's delay,
        The insolence of office, and the Spurns
        That patient merit of the unworthy takes… ?"

Dug out of the Snow – and about <u>Treacherous</u> Places on the Downs which the most Vigilant Drivers cannot always avoid that I verily believe I should not Mind Waiting Another Day at this Place, were it not for my strong Desire to see my Dear John at Sittingbourne To-morrow. ~ My Maid tells me I have had very great luck at the Custom House, for that during the Examination several things were about to be Condemned, and that nothing but a great deal of usual Dexterity neceſsary on such Occasions could have saved them. – There is something by no means unentertaining in the Flurry and Confusion which all this Creates at the Moment – and I must fairly own a very Sensible joy which I feel in Secreting any little Contraband Piece of Goods from those rough Custom House People. – At the same time, I admit there is nothing to be <u>proud</u> of in such Feelings, but I cannot restrain them, and I am sure, I am not the only one by many who has them, for I hardly ever saw that Person who had not rather a Hankering after Conspiracies of <u>this Sort</u> when they fell in his Way. Many too whom I know, with a vast deal of Merit in other Respects, have yet no Sort of Objection to Cheat those they <u>really love</u>: but this I have an utter Abhorrence to, even tho' the Affairs be of the most trifling Nature – The more Unsuspected too, and the leſs Chance there may be of a Discovery, the more disinclined I feel. ~ Nor is there any Victory to be attained for it is like Shooting at one's Canary Bird in his Cage! – But enough of this – and as to Custom House Officers, Dreſsed in their "little brief Authority;"[276] and attacking one with all "the Insolence of Office,"[277] in resisting them one seems to be acting more upon the <u>Defensive</u> than otherwise, and only defeating by Art and Management the <u>Oppreſsion</u> of a Power too Strong to be openly Resisted. ~ Besides the little Man in a Black Wig strutted with so Imperious an Air that, if I had naturally detested the Idea of Smuggling, I should at the Sight of <u>him</u> have Cheated the Revenue of thousands, had it lain in my Power. I seems that the Lenity of others has deprived them of their Places, and that the Strictest orders are sent to their Succeſsors every Day ~

After Supper.

This has been a Day of great Repose, and, it has therefore suited me vastly well. Mr. Payne thinks the Road between this Place and Canterbury still so Suspicious from the Drifting of the Snow, that he advises me to get into a Lighter Carriage than my own; and this Plan I like very well, because my Maid, the Child and I shall feel much safer when we follow the Track of our own Chaise, and are able to stop Short in time, if that should come to any Accident. – Dolly I have sent to

278 *there were two maids, one for Mrs Crewe and one for her daughter. She writes that she will follow behind with her maid and the child, while Dolly has been sent on to London. This indicates that Dolly was the child's maid.*

279 *Mr Mackenzie: probably a school master, or somebody employed to take care of her son.*

London to Night by the Stage[278] – She good humouredly offered to go first in the Post Chaise and Brave all Dangers, but the thoughts of this quite Shocked me, whilst I was taking such good Care of my own and my Child's safety. It is now Eleven O'Clock and time to go to Rest – The Wind is very high, and I hear the Sea roaring at a great Rate – However all this, I believe, has no meaning in it, for I understand the Weather on the whole is tolerably good. ✗

Wednesday
Sittingbourne

Wednesday 14ᵗʰ March 1786

Here am I as happy as Heart could wish! having found Letters from John and Mʳ. Mackenzie[279] to say they will be here the Moment I send for them – I have accordingly Dispatched a Post Chaise, and hope to see them in about two Hours. We have travelled very safely to Day, but it has been sad heavy work with the Snow, which still covers the Ground, and renders the Roads quite Dangerous in some Parts. Mʳ Payne made us take a light Carriage and send our Chaise on before till we came to Canterbury. – And, as I heard there but an Indifferent Account of what we were to expect this Stage, I pursued the same Method again. – The Truth is I am become a sad Coward since my Overturn, and when I get quiet and more settled I will take myself to task for it, and make use of all the Reason I can Muster; for there are no Misfortunes in Life worse than such little Plagues as these. and when they once get into Poʃʃeʃsion of one's Mind they Interfere with every Enjoyment, and we are not happy, because we may be otherwise – Wretched Philosophy – and as wretched Policy it argues, I think – but however, before the Wise paʃs Sentence upon me, let him be as Nervous as I am, and then let them be Overturned into the Pit near Breteuil! – The Inns upon this Road, tho' they are not the best in the World, look like little Paradises compared with those abroad – It is true there is in general much more Space in the latter, and that there is in many other Respects a great Air of Magnificence – but Magnificence is not what one requires on a Journey – It is Comfort, a word they have not, and all their Gilding, Glaʃses, bad Pictures, and Damask Curtains are not, in my Opinion, worth one Door that Shuts, or Bell that rings, or Carpet that keeps one warm, or Shutter that defends the Window: none of which Comforts are hardly even to be met with in France or Flanders; nor do any Foreigners that I ever met with seem to think them neceʃsary Points, as we do, towards good Accommodation in Travelling. ~ Before we left

215

280 Lord John Russell, 1766-1839. He became the 6ᵗʰ Duke of Bedford on the death of his brother in 1802.

281 George Byng, 4ᵗʰ Viscount Torrington, died 1812.

Dover this Morning Lord John Ruſsell's Servant[280] came to Embark with Letters for Lord Torrington[281] at Bruſsells respecting the Marriage – It seems that Belgioiose, the Imperial Minister there refuses to let it proceed till another half-hundred of his Titles and Epithets were done Justice to; so that this Miserable Servant has been near lost in the Snow merely for the purpose of having the Broth made more <u>thick</u> and <u>Slob</u> to suite his Excellency's Palate. Could you have Supposed it poſsible for human Weakneſs to have Degraded a Man so much? To-morrow I must be off very early to get to London before Robberies begin. This does not Suite me quite as it is now late, and I wished to have a little time to converse with John and M^r. Mackenzie – I will now get an English News Paper, write a Letter to my Mother, and by the time I have finished them I hope my Guests will arrive. They will find a very good Supper for I have desired we may have One at nine O'Clock, as I was in too much haste to dine in a regular Way at Canterbury. ~

And here end my Canterbury Tales.

Appendices

Ode for indifference, by Mrs Greville

Oft I've implor'd the Gods in vain,
And pray'd till I've been weary;
For once I'll try my wish to gain
Of Oberon, the fairy.

Sweet airy being, wanton sprite,
That lurk'st in woods unseen,
And oft by Cynthia's silver light
Tripst gaily o'er the green;

If e'er thy pitying heart was mov'd,
As ancient stories tell,
And for th' Athenian maid, who lov'd,
Thou sought'st a wondrous spell,

Oh! deign once more t' exert thy power;
Haply some herb or tree,
Sov'reign as juice from western flower,
Conceals a balm for me.

I ask no kind return in love,
No tempting charm to please;
Far from the heart such gifts remove,
That sighs for peace and ease.

Nor ease nor peace that heart can know,
Which, like the needle true,
Turns at the touch of joy or woe,
But, turning, trembles too.

Far as distress the soul can wound,
"Tis pain in each degree;
Bliss goes but to a certain bound,
Beyond is agony.

Take then this treacherous sense of mine,
Which dooms me still to smart;
Which pleasure can to pain refine,
To pain new pangs impart.

Oh! haste to shed the sovereign balm,
My shatter'd nerves new string;
And for my guest, serenely calm,
The nymph, Indifference, bring.

At her approach, see Hope, see Fear,
See Expectation fly;
With Disappointment, in the rear,
That blasts the promis'd joy.

The tears which pity taught to flow,
My eyes shall then disown;
The heart which throbb'd at other's woe,
Shall then scarce feel its own.

The wounds which now each moment bleed,
Each moment then shall close,
And peaceful days shall still succeed
To nights of sweet repose.

Oh, fairy elf! but grant me this,
This one kind comfort send;
And so may never-fading bliss
Thy flowery paths attend!

So may the glow-worm's glimmering light
Thy tiny footsteps lead
To some new region of delight,
Unknown to mortal tread.

And be thy acorn goblets fill'd
With heaven's ambrosial dew,
From sweetest, freshest flowers distill'd,
That shed fresh sweets for you.

And what of life remains for me
I'll pass in sober ease,
Half-pleas'd, contented will I be,
Contented, half to please.

Extract from *The Indian Emperor* by John Dryden
first performed 1665; published 1667

Act 1, Scene 2

Montezuma:	I sent thee to the frontiers; quickly tell
	The cause of thy return; are all things well?
Guyamar:	I went, in order, sir, to your command,
	To view the utmost limits of the land:
	To that sea-shore where not more world is found,
	But foaming billows breaking on the ground;
	Where, for a while, my eyes no object met,
	But distant skies, that in the ocean set;
	And low-hung clouds, that dipt themselves in rain,
	To shake their fleeces on the earth again.
	At last, as far as I could cast my eyes
	Upon the sea, somewhat, methought, did rise,
	Like blueish mists, which, still appearing more,
	Took dreadful shapes, and moved towards the shore.
Montezuma:	What forms did these new wonders represent?
Guyamar:	More strange than what your wonder can invent.
	The object, I could first distinctly view,
	Was tall straight trees, which on the waters flew;
	Wings on their sides, instead of leaves, did grow,
	Which gathered all the breath the winds could blow;
	And at their roots grew floating palaces,
	Whose outblowed bellies cut the yielding seas.
Montezuma:	What divine monsters, O ye gods, were these,
	That float in air, and fly upon the seas!
	Came they alive, or dead, upon the shore?
Guyamar:	Alas, they lived too sure; I heard them roar.
	All turned their sides, and to each other spoke;
	I saw their words break out in fire and smoke.
	Sure 'tis their voice, that thunders from on high,
	Or these the younger brothers of the sky,
	Deaf with the noise, I took my hasty flight;
	No mortal courage can support the fright.
High Priest:	Old prophecies foretel our fall at hand,
	When bearded men in floating castles land.
	I fear it is of dire portent.

Extract from *The Spectator*
number 557, Monday 21st June 1714
written by Joseph Addison

The old English plainness and sincerity, that generous integrity of nature, and honesty of disposition, which always argues true greatness of mind, and is usually accompanied with undaunted courage and resolution, is in a great measure lost among us. The dialect of conversation is now-a-days so swelled with vanity and compliment, and so surfeited (as I may say) of expressions of kindness and respect, that if a man that lived an age or two ago, should return into the world again, he would really want a dictionary to help him understand his own language, and to know the true intrinsic value of the phrase in fashion; and would hardly, at first, believe at what a low rate the highest strains and expressions of kindness imaginable, do commonly pass in current payment; and when he should come to understand it, it would be a great while before he could bring himself, with a good countenance and a good conscience, to converse with men upon equal terms, and in their own way.
I have by me a letter which I look upon as a great curiosity, and which may serve as an exemplification to the foregoing passage, cited out of this most excellent prelate. It is said to have been written in King Charles the Second's reign by the ambassador of Bantam, a little after his arrival in England.
"Master,
The people, where I now am, have tongues further from their hearts than from London to Bantam; and thou knowest the inhabitants of one of these places do not know what is done in the other. They call thee and thy subjects barbarians, because we speak what we mean; and account themselves a civilized people, because they speake one thing, and mean another : truth they call barbarity, and falsehood politeness. Upon my first landing, one who was sent from the king of this place to meet me, told me, 'That he was extremely sorry for the storm I had met with just before my arrival.' I was troubled to hear him grieve and afflict himself upon my account ; but in less than a quarter of an hour he smiled, and was as merry as if nothing had happened. Another, who came with him, told me, by my interpreter, ' He should be glad to do me any service that lay in his power'. Upon which I desired him to carry one of my portmanteaus for me; but, instead serving me according to his promise, he laughed, and bid another do it. I lodged, the first week, at the house of one, who desired me, 'To think myself at home, and to consider his house as my own.'
Accordingly, I the next morning began to knock down one of the walls of it, in order to let in the fresh air, and had packed up some of the

household goods, of which I intended to have made thee a present: but the false varlet no sooner saw me falling to work, than he sent word to desire me to give over, for that he would have no such doings in his house. I had not been long in this nation, before I was told by one, for whom I had asked a certain favour from the chief of the king's servants, whom they here call the lord-treasurer, ' That I had eternally obliged him.' I was so surprised at this gratitude, that I could not forbear saying, ' What service is there which one man can do for another, that can oblige him to all eternity? However, I only asked him, for my reward, that he would lend me his eldest daughter during my stay in this country; but I quickly found that he was as treacherous as the rest of his countrymen.

At my first going to court, one of the great men almost put me out of countenance, by asking 'ten thousand pardons' of me, for only treading, by accident, upon my toe. They call this kind of lie a compliment; for when they. are civil to a great man, they tell him untruths, for which thou wouldest order any of thy officers of state to receive a hundred blows upon his foot. I do not know how I shall negotiate anything with this people, since there is so little credit to be given to them. When I go to see the king's scribe, I am generally told that he is not at home, though, perhaps, I saw him go into his house almost the very moment before. Thou wouldest fancy that the whole nation are physicians, for the first question they always ask me, is, 'How I do?' I have this question put to me above an hundred times a day. Nay, they are not only thus inquisitive after my health, but wish it in a more solemn manner, with a full glass in their hands, every time I sit with them at table, though, at the same time, they would persuade me to drink their liquors in such quantities, as I have found, by experience, will make me sick. They often pretend to pray for thy health also in the same manner; but I have more reason to expect it from the goodness of thy constitution, than the sincerity of their wishes. May thy slave escape in safety from this double-tongued race of men, and live to lay himself once more at thy feet in thy royal city of Bantam."

The School for Scandal
A portrait
Addressed to Mrs Crewe, by R.B. Sheridan

Tell me, ye prim adepts in Scandal's school,
Who rail by precept, and detract by rule.

Lives there no character, so tried, so known,
So deck'd with grace, and so unlike your own

That even you assist her fame to raise,
Approve by envy, and by silence praise !

Attend! – a model shall attract your view –
Daughters of calumny, I summon you !

You shall decide if this a portrait prove,
Or fond creation of the Muse and Love.

Attend, ye virgin critics, shrewd and sage,
Ye matron censors of this childish age,

Whose peering eye and wrinkled front declare
A flx'd antipathy to young and fair;

By cunning, cautious; or by nature, cold,
In maiden madness, virulently bold ! –

Attend, ye skill'd to coin the precious tale,
Creating proof, where innuendos fail !

Whose practised memories, cruelly exact,
Omit no circumstance, except the fact ! –

Attend, all ye who boast, – or old or young, –
The living libel of a slanderous tongue !

So shall my theme as far contrasted be,
As saints by fiends, or hymns by calumny.

Come, gentle Amoret (for 'neath that name
In worthier verse is sung thy beauty's fame);

Come – for but thee, who seeks the Muse ? and while
Celestial blushes check thy conscious smile,

With timid grace, and hesitating eye,
The perfect model, which I boast, supply: –

Vain Muse! couldst thou the humblest sketch create
Of her, or slightest charm couldst imitate –

Could thy blest strain in kindred colours trace
The faintest wonder of her form and face –

Poets would study the immortal line,
And Reynolds own his art subdued by thine;

That art, which well might added lustre give
To Nature's best, and Heaven's superlative:

On Granby's cheek might bid new glories rise,
Or point a purer beam from Devon's eyes!

Hard is the task to shape that beauty's praise,
Whose judgment scorns the homage flattery pays!

But praising Amoret we cannot err,
No tongue o'ervalues Heaven, or flatters her!

Yet she by fate's perverseness – she alone
Would doubt our truth, nor deem such praise her own.

Adorning fashion, unadorn'd by dress,
Simple from taste, and not from carelessness;

Discreet in gesture, in deportment mild,
Not stiff with prudence, nor uncouthly wild;

No state has Amoret ; no studied mien;
She frowns no goddess, and she moves no queen.

The softer charm that in her manner lies
Is framed to captivate, yet not surprise;

It justly suits the expression of her face, –
'Tis less than dignity, and more than grace!

On her pure cheek the native hue is such,
That, form'd by Heaven to be admired so much

The hand divine, with a less partial care,
Might well have fix'd a fainter crimson there,

And bade the gentle inmate of her breast –
Inshrined Modesty – supply the rest.

But who the peril of her lips shall paint ?
Strip them of smiles – still, still all words are faint.

But moving Love himself appears to teach
Their action, though denied to rule her speech;

And thou who seest her speak, and dost not hear,
Mourn not her distant accents 'scape thine ear;

Viewing those lips, thou still may'st make pretence
To judge of what she says, and swear 'tis sense:

Clothed with such grace, with such expression fraught,
They move in meaning, and they pause in thought!

But dost thou farther watch, with charm'd surprise,
The mild irresolution of her eyes,

Curious to mark how frequent they repose,
In brief eclipse and momentary close

Ah! seest thou not an ambush'd Cupid there,
Too tim'rous of his charge, with jealous care

Veils and unveils those beams of heavenly light,
Too full, too fatal else, for mortal sight ?

Nor yet, such pleasing vengeance fond to meet,
In pard'ning dimples hope a safe retreat.

What though her peaceful breast should ne'er allow
Subduing frowns to arm her alter'd brow,

By Love, I swear, and by his gentle wiles
More fatal still the mercy of her smiles

Thus lovely, thus adorn'd, possessing all
Of bright or fair that can to woman fall,

The height of vanity might well be thought
Prerogative in her, and Nature's fault.

Yet gentle Amoret, in mind supreme
As well as charms, rejects the vainer theme;

And, half mistrustful of her beauty's store,
She barbs with wit those darts too keen before: –

Read in all knowledge that her sex should reach,
Though Greville, or the Muse, should deign to teach,

Fond to improve, nor timorous to discern
How far it is a woman's grace to learn;

In Millar's dialect she would not prove
Apollo's priestess, but Apollo's love,

Graced by those signs which truth delights to own,
The timid blush and mild submitted tone:

Whate'er she says, though sense appear throughout
Displays the tender hue of female doubt;

Deck'd with that charm, how lovely wit appears,
How graceful science, when that robe she wears I

Such too her talents, and her bent of mind,
As speak a sprightly heart by thought refined:

A taste for mirth, by contemplation school' d,
A turn for ridicule, by candour ruled,

A scorn of folly, which she tries to hide;
An awe of talent, which she owns with pride!

Peace, idle Muse I no more thy strain prolong,
But yield a theme, thy warmest praises wrong;

Just to her merit, though thou canst not raise
Thy feeble verse, behold th' acknowledged praise

Has spread conviction through the envious train,
And cast a fatal gloom o'er Scandal's reign!

And lo! each pallid hag, with blister'd tongue,
Mutters assent to all thy zeal has sung –

Owns all the colours just – the outline true,
Thee my inspirer, and my model – CREWE!

Appendix five

May 27 1775

To Mrs Crewe
By the Honourable Charles Fox

Where the loveliest expression to feature is joined,
By Nature's most delicate pencil designed,
Where blushes unbidden and smiles without art,
Speak the sweetness and feeling that dwell in the heart;
Where in manners enchanting no blemish we trace,
But the soul keeps the promise we had from the face,
Sure philosophy, reason and coldness must prove
Defences unequal to shield us from love.
Then tell me, mysterious enchanter, O tell
By what wonderful art or by what magic spell,
My heart is so fenced, that for once I am wise
And gaze without madness on Amoret's eyes:
That my wishes which never were bounded before,
Are here bounded by friendship and ask for no more.
Is it reason? No, that my whole life will belie,
For who so at variance as reason and I.
Is't ambition that fills up each chink of my heart,
Nor allows to one softer sensation a part?
Ah! no, for in this all the world must agree
That one folly was never sufficient for me.
Is my mind on distress so intensely employed?
Or by pleasure relaxed or variety cloyed?
For alike in this only enjoyment and pain
Both slacken the springs of the nerves which they strain.
That I've felt each reverse that from fortune can flow,
That I've tasted each bliss which the happiest know,
Has still been the whimsical fate of my life,
Where anguish and joy have been ever at strife.
But though versed in th' extremes both of pleasure and pain
I am still but too ready to feel them again.
If then for this once in my life I am free,
and escape from a snare might catch wiser than me;
'Tis that beauty alone but imperfectly charms,
For though brightness may dazzle, 'tis kindness that warms.
As on suns in the winter with pleasure we gaze,
But feel not their force, though their spleandour we praise;
So beauty our just admiration may claim,
But love and love only our hearts can inflame.

These lines were printed at Strawberry Hill in June 1775. "I think you will like the ease and frankness of the lines, though they are not poetic; in that light and as characteristic, they are pretty original, so they are far being love-verses without love, the author's reason for not having which, is the worst part, and if poetry was preromptory logic, the inference would be that you must be in love with a woman before you can desire her: at least she must be in love with you, which I take to be seldom the case."

From *Horace Walpole's correspondence with William Mason*; edited by W.S. Lewis, Grover Cronin Jr and Charles H. Bennett. Yale UP, 1955.

Extracts from letters sent by Madame Du Deffand to Horace Walpole,
relating the visit to Paris in 1773 of Mrs Crewe and Mrs Greville.

"Tuesday 1st June 1773
I supped the day before yesterday, Sunday, at the [Place de] Carrousel;
on returning home, I learned that Mrs Crewe had arrived: all my servants
had been occupied preparing the lodgings for her and her attendants.
The following day, with great difficulty they rose, and with
encouragement from me, the mother and the daughter fixed to go to the
Parc-Royal; after dinner they went to the Opera-Comique with
Mesdames de Bussy and de Roncee, and came back all together for
supper at my house.

Wednesday
Yesterday I interrupted you; I'll begin again my narration. I rushed
supper at the [Place de] Carrousel; the Duchesse having learned of the
arrival of Mrs Crewe, sent inviting the mother and the daughter; they
raged about the Comedie-Francaise; on return they [drank???] at my
house and we smoked all three of us at the Duchesse's home, where we
found only her daughter, Monsieur d'Entragues and Monsieur de Rose.
Until now, all those that I have seen, and who have seen Mrs Crewe,
have found her perfectly beautiful: but it is this evening that she
undergoes the greatest scrutiny, and that the security of her success will
be decided; people strike a parallel between her and Lady Georgiana;
they both passed the evening at my house; I had fifteen or sixteen people
to supper, and many others who, under the pretext of owing me a visit,
came to see. It was difficult to know after some time who suffered
most, because of our new arrangements the newcomers amongst the 13
or my own people amongst the 18. You have to put up patiently with
this waiting. Mrs Greville and I are perfectly good together, without
infatuation for each other; I ignore the impression I make on her, I have
received attentions from her, politenesses; I have responded to her with
my best attentions, and by giving her at the same time the biggest
freedoms; I have often passed entire days in her company. She is strong
friends with Lady Spencer, they don't give much away about each other.
They are great friends with the company of Mesdames de Mirepoix, de
Caraman, de Bussy, du Chatelet, de Roncée, etc., Mrs Greville has
hardly acknowledged the Marquise de Boufflers, and she has seen very
little of the Comtesse.
Lady [Spencer] leaves on the 10th for Spa where she and Mrs Greville
will wait till the beginning of July for her husband; her daughter leaves
the same day to return to London; and so finishes the history of the
English. But I have something more to say about your countrymen: that
I do not intend to speak any more of Mr Crauford while he's still in this
world; he owes me a response from three months, he has written once to
Lady Spencer and once to Mr Frances, he will have to pray to allay my

anger, he told me he would write immediately, as well as to Madame de Roncherolles, who is the person in the world he loves the most."

[The Carrousel referred to is the Place de Carrousel, near The Tuileries – see note in Madame de Deffand and her world, by Benedetta Craveri, p474, note78][it's still there today]

[Mr Crauford was John Crauford of Auchinames, a close friend of Fox. Nicknamed The Fish (short for selfish) – see Georgiana by Bessborough, p14,n1; and Craveri, p405]

From Madame du Deffand, Saturday 12 June 1773.

"The Spencers leave tomorrow, they are going to stay at Roissy; Mrs Greville and her daughter will accompany them there, and remain there three or four days after the Spencers leave. The Spencers go Monday or Tuesday to Hautefontaine to the home of the Archbishop of Narbone, afterwards to Liancourt, and then to Brussells to the home of Madame d'Arembourg, and don't arrive at Spa till the first days of July. Mrs Greville goes at the same time, and her daughter takes the route to London; and so finishes the history.

It is not doubted that if one has not seen here such a picture as Lady Georgiana and Mrs Crewe, she had here every chance; but the first opinion of her held; her height, her expression, her liveliness, her dress, her good grace has charmed everybody. The other is little animated, her height is mediocre, and she needs to be scrutinised to be found beautiful; I believe that she has spirit, but she speaks little; she knows our language well. So that is all that I fear you can say; her mother I adore. Since she doesn't stay with me any more, I haven't seen much of her; I flatter myself to be good with her, but we won't make a great friendship."

I don't find it clear here if she prefers Mrs Crewe or Georgiana

p373
Sunday 20 June 1773
"Mrs Greville and Mrs Crewe leave today at eight, I don't think they'll be missed."

Appendix seven

Calendar of the visit

1785

Sat 24 Dec	Arrival in Paris. Dinner at home. Visit from Lady Clermont
Sun 25 Dec	Spent at the Hotel du Rome. Visits from friends and acquaintances
Mon 26 Dec	Spent at Hotel du Rome. Visit from Mrs Hobart
Tue 27 Dec	Visit to Palais Royal Gardens. Mr Labord came to dine. Received other visitors
Wed 28 Dec	Another visit to the Palais Royal. Visited Madame de Caraman and Madame de Cambis. A number of people came to visit her in the evening. Talked with the Duc de Guines about animal magentism.
Thu 29 Dec	Had breakfast at Lady Clermont's. Received two invitations to dine. Stayed home during the evening – Richard Burke called and they read a book together on animal magnetism. Other visitors also called. Dined alone in the evening.
Fri 30 Dec	There is no report for this day except for visits from seven different people in the evening. She feels in a "weak state of health".
Sat 31 Dec	Several people called in the evening. Not feeling well and confesses she can "discover nothing very delightful or curious in Paris life".

1786

Sun 1 Jan	Several people called in the evening. More people called in the evening and talked of Ettrennes – New Year's gifts. Lady Clermont dined with her. She complains of spending all morning with tradespeople sent by Lady Clermont.
Mon 2 Jan	Visited the Hotel de Jabac and then a China Shop. Madame de Roncherolle visited after dinner and then they went to Mrs Hobart's rout.
Tue 3 Jan	Sent two books by the Vicomte de Noailles.
Wed 4 Jan	During the afternoon she and her mother made four visits and in the evening went to the

	French Comedy. Afterwards they went to Lady Hampden's before returning home for supper.
Thu 5 Jan	Most of the day spent preparing to go to Versailles. On the journey to Versailles one of their horses fell down. Saw the King and Queen at Versailles; also Lafayette.
Fri 6 Jan	Returned from Versailles at 3 o'clock in the morning. Visited the opera in the evening.
Sat 7 Jan	Visited the Italian Theatre.
Sun 8 Jan	Visit from the Duc de Nivernais in the morning. Had supper at home with some English friends.
Mon 9 Jan	Dined with Madame de Roquefuelle. Expressed a wish to hear from her "friend". Visited the theatre to see an opera.
Tue 10 Jan	Dined at the Duc de Guines' house. Visited Madame de Roncherolles and then went home to write to her son.
Wed 11 Jan	nothing recorded
Thu 12 Jan	Was taken by Madame de Roquefeuil to the Duchesse D'Orleans.
Fri 13 Jan	Had dinner with the Duc de Nivernais. Visited the Duchesse de La Valliere, but went home to supper.
Sat 14 Jan	Visited by the Chevalier Jerningham who invited her to breakfast on the Wednesday following.
Sun 15 Jan	nothing recorded
Mon 16 Jan	Her husband and Mr Burke left Paris. Lady Clermont took her to Madame de Matignon's. Had supper at home with English friends.
Tue 17 Jan	Dined with Monsieur de Caraman and in the evening went to the theatre to see *Dardanus*. After the theatre went to the famous milliner's Mademoiselle Bertin.
Wed 18 Jan	Breakfasted with the Chevalier Jerningham. Attended a dinner party at the Duke of Dorset's. Called at Lady Mornington's. Visited the Duchesse de Brissac and stayed for supper.
Thu 19 Jan	nothing recorded,
Fri 20 Jan	Paid a visit to the Marechal Biron in the afternoon. Attended a fete at Mrs Hobart's and went on to the Duchesse de La Valliere's for supper.
Sat 21 Jan	Dined at Madame de Roncherolle's.

Sun 22 Jan	nothing recorded
Mon 23 Jan	nothing recorded
Tue 24 Jan	nothing recorded
Wed 25 Jan	nothing recorded
Thu 26 Jan	nothing recorded
Fri 27 Jan	Had tea at Madame d'Andlau's; Had supper at home with some English friends.
Sat 28 Jan	Stayed home in the evening because her mother was not well. Sent for Dr Lee in the afternoon.
Sun 29 Jan	Reports her mother to be much better. Attends a ball at Monsieur de Caraman's with her brother Charles
Mon 30 Jan	Received post from England. Stayed home with her mother all morning. In the afternoon visited Lady Clarges, Lady Mornington and Madame de Rochefeulle.
Tue 31 Jan	Spent time with her mother at home. Same party for supper as the evening before.
Wed 1 Feb	Wrote letters – visited by her brother James. Accident on the way to Versailles with one of her horses tumbling.
Thu 2 Feb	At Versailles – a disappointment. Travelled back to Paris with her brother James – her mother very much recovered. Spent the evening with her mother – visits from Duc de Nivernais and Monsieur de Caraman.
Fri 3 Feb	Attended an entertainment at the English Ambassador's – long list of people there. Played some cards. Afterwards visited her mother before going to her drawing room with her brothers Charles and James and a few more English people.
Sat 4 Feb	Given two fire screen prints by the Duc de Nivernais, several strings of pearls by Lady Clarges, more pearls by Mr Bisset and a pair of ear-rings by Miss Carter. At home in the evening with her mother and a mixture of English and French company.
Sun 5 Feb	Had Mr Bisset to supper.
Mon 6 Feb	Went to the theatre to a new comedy
Tue 7 Feb	Lord and Lady Spencer arrived from Nice. Supped at home with Mr and Mrs Laborde, Lord Downe and a few more.

Wed 8 Feb	Called upon Madame de Rochfeulle and found her ill in bed. Supped at Lady Mornington's. At home had a visit from Monsieur de Crillon who invited them to visit the Lyceum.
Thu 9 Feb	Received some verses from the Duc de Nivernais.
Fri 10 Feb	She and her mother dined at the house of a rich Fermier General. Met Mrs Goldburne. Left Lord and Lady Spencer and Lady Clermont with her mother in the evening and went with her brother and Lord Downe to the Duchesse de La Valliere's.
Sat 11 Feb	Travelled to Versailles. Supper at the Duchesse de Polignac's, attended by the Queen.
Sun 12 Feb	Heard Mass at the King's Chapel. Visited the Royal Apartments at Versailles. Dined with the Marechal de Castries. Travelled back to Paris.
Mon 13 Feb	Moved with her mother to the Hotel de l'Empereur. Visited the Royal Academy and dined with the Duc de Nivernais.
Tue 14 Feb	Dined at the Marechalle de Mirpoix's. In the evening went with Lady Mornington to a theatre at the Foire St. Germain.
Wed 15 Feb	Had to dinner Lord Downe, Mr Pittoux and Dr Lee.
Thu 16 Feb	Had breakfast with her mother then visited the Lyceum.
Fri 17 Feb	Walked in the Luxembourg Gardens. Saw *Le Roi de Cocagne* with Miss Carter.
Sat 18 Feb	visited Marechal Biron; had supper with her mother
Sun 19 Feb	nothing reported
Mon 20 Feb	Visited by Madame de Coigny
Tue 21 Feb	Dined with Monsieur Monregard. Supped at Lady Mornington's
Wed 22 Feb	First talks of returning home. Visited Mrs Laborde and arranged a visit to the theatre; Visited Lady Hampden's.
Thu 23 Feb	Visit to the Sevres china factory. Visit to the theatre.
Fri 24 Feb	Nothing reported.
Sat 25 Feb	Unwell with a feverish cold – misses a ball at Madame de Coigny's.
Sun 26 Feb	Unwell with a feverish cold.
Mon 27 Feb	Still unwell – confined to her room

Tue 28 Feb	Still unwell. Talks of leaving the following Sunday.
Wed 1 Mar	Still unwell but received the Duc de Nivernais and Lady Clermont.
Thu 2 Mar	still unwell
Fri 3 Mar	nothing reported
Sat 4 Mar	nothing reported
Sun 5 Mar	Talks of now leaving next Wednesday; Dines at Dr Lee's.
Mon 6 Mar	Reports that snow has fallen
Tue 7 Mar	More snow has fallen. Supper at Lord Hampden's. Played cards.
Wed 8 Mar	Weather still bad. Receives a visit from Sir Horace Mann.
Thu 9 Mar	Awaiting an opportunity to leave.
Fri 10 Mar	Leaves Paris – travels to Chantilly
Sat 11 Mar	Travelled to Amiens – coach overturned on journey.
Sun 12 Mar	Travelled to Montreul.
Mon 13 Mar	Arrived at Boulogne.
Tue 14 Mar	Crossed from Boulogne to Dover – stayed overnight.
Wed 15 Mar	Travelled to Sittingbourne. Diary ends

APPENDIX EIGHT: FAMILY TREE OF THE CREWE FAMILY

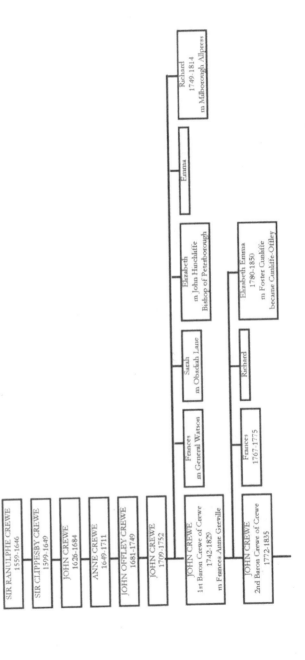

SIR RANULPHE CREWE
1559-1646

SIR CLIPPESBY CREWE
1599-1649

JOHN CREWE
1626-1684

ANNE CREWE
1649-1711

JOHN OFFLEY CREWE
1681-1749

JOHN CREWE
1709-1752

JOHN CREWE
1st Baron Crewe of Crewe
1742-1829
m Frances Anne Greville

Frances
m General Watson

Sarah
m Obadiah Lane

Elizabeth
m John Hinchliffe
Bishop of Peterborough

Emma

Richard
1749-1814
m Milborough Allpress

JOHN CREWE
2nd Baron Crewe of Crewe
1772-1835

Frances
1767-1775

Richard

Elizabeth Emma
1780-1850
m Foster Cunliffe
became Cunliffe-Offley

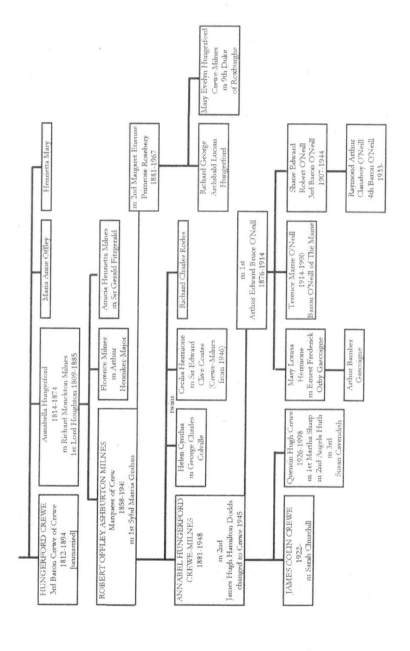

APPENDIX NINE: FAMILY TREE OF THE GREVILLE FAMILY

Fulke Greville 5th Baron Brooke d 1710

Algernon Greville m Mary Somerset

Frances Greville d 1710

William Greville 7th Baron Brooke d 1727

Frances Greville 1st Earl of Warwick 1719-1773

George Greville 2nd Earl of Warwick 1746-1816

Fulke Greville 6th Baron Brooke d 1711

Mary 1715-86

Hester 1716-95

Fulke Greville 1717-1806 of Wilbury Wilts m Frances Macartney

Frances Anne 1748-1818 m John Crewe 1st Baron Grew of Crewe

see Crewe family tree

Algernon Greville 1750-1756

William Fulke Greville 1751-1837

Charles Greville 1762-1832

Henry William Greville 1801-1872

Charles Cavendish Fulke Greville 1794-1865

Algernon Frederick Greville 1789-1864

James Greville rector of Whickham, Co. Durham 1753-

Henry Francis Greville 1760-1816

Brooke Greville 1798-1884

Henry Francis Greville 1796-1864

George Macartney Greville 1793-1834

Algernon Greville 1791-1857

Richard Greville 1787-1866

APPENDIX TEN: FAMILY TREE OF THE MACARTNEY FAMILY

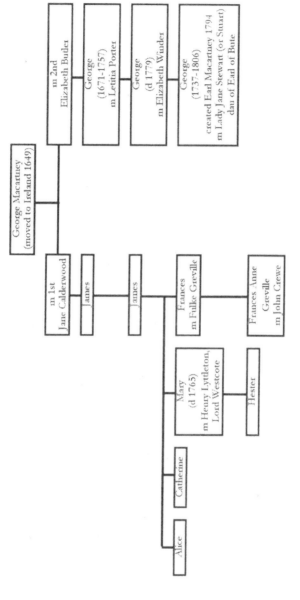

George Macartney
(moved to Ireland 1649)

m 1st
Jane Calderwood

m 2nd
Elizabeth Butler

George
(1671-1757)
m Letitia Porter

George
(d 1779)
m Elizabeth Winder

George
(1737-1806)
created Earl Macartney 1794
m Lady Jane Stewart (or Stuart)
dau of Earl of Bute

James

James

Frances
m Fulke Greville

Frances Anne
Greville
m John Crewe

Mary
(d 1765)
m Henry Lyttleton,
Lord Westcote

Hester

Alice

Catherine

Information taken from: *A genealogical and heraldic history of the landed gentry of Great Britain & Ireland*, by Bernard Burke. 2 vols, 1894

Bibliography

Ackroyd, Peter   London: the biography. Chatto & Windus, 2000.
Airs, Malcolm   The Tudor and Jacobean house. Bramley Books, 1998.
Allen, Michael   The Dickens/Crewe connection IN *Dickens Quarterly*(USA), December 1988.
Asquith, Annunziata   Marie Antoinete. Book Club Associates, 1974. (Great Lives series)
Ayling, Stanley   A portrait of Sheridan. Constable, 1985.
Ayling, Stanley   Fox: the life of Charles James Fox. John Murray, 1991.
Banham, Martin   The Cambridge guide to theatre. Cambridge University Press, 1995.
Barbauld, Anna Letitia   The poems of Anna Letitia Barbauld; edited by William McCarthy and Elizabeth Kraft. Georgia University Press, 1994.
Barry, Joseph   Versailles: the passions and politics of an era. Gollancz, 1972.
Bethell, David   Portrait of Cheshire. Hale, 1979.
Bingham, Madeleine   Sheridan: the track of a comet. Allen & Unwin, 1972.
Black, Clementina   The Linleys of Bath. Martin Secker, 1911.
Black, Jeremy   The grand tour in the eighteenth century. Sutton, 1997.
Brewer, John   The pleasures of the imagination: English culture in the eighteenth century. HarperCollins, 1997.
Brewer's dictionary of phrase & fable; millennium edition, edited by Adrian Room. Cassell, 1999.
Burke, Bernard   A genealogical and heraldic history of the landed gentry of Great Britain & Ireland by Sir Bernard Burke; edited by his sons. Harrison & Sons, 2 vols, 8th ed., 1894.
Burke, Edmund   The correspondence of Edmund Burke. Cambridge University Press and Chicago University Press, 10 vols, 1958-78.
Burke's genealogical and heraldic history of the peerage, baronetage and knightage; edited by Peter Townend. Burke's Peerage, 105th edition, 1970.
Burney, Fanny   **Memoirs of Doctor Burney,** by his daughter Madame d'Arblay. Edward Moxon, 3 vols., 1832.
Burney, Fanny   Evelina. Oxford University Press, 1982.
Burney, Fanny   The journals and letters of Fanny Burney (Madame D'Arblay); edited by Joyce Hemlow and others. Oxford University Press, 10 vols, 1972-82.

Cambridge biographical encyclopedia; second edition, edited by David Crystal. Cambridge U.P., 1998.

Campbell, John   The lives of the Chief Justices of England. Murray, 4 vols, 3rd ed., 1874.

Canning, George   The letter-journal of George Canning, 1793-1795; edited by Peter Jupp. Camden fourth series volume 41. Royal Historical Society, 1991.

Carter, Mary   Mrs Mary Carter's letters. Printed by Clayton & Co., nd. British Library ref no 010902.e.7.

Chambers biographical dictionary.   edited by J.O. Thorne. Chambers, revised edition, 1969.

Chedzoy, Alan   Sheridan's nightingale: the story of Elizabeth Linley. Allison & Busby, 1997.

Chronicle of the French revolution, 1788-1799. Longman, 1989.

Colville, Cynthia   Crowded life: the autobiography of Lady Cynthia Colville. Evans, 1963.

The complete peerage, vol 12, Part 1; edited by Geoffrey H. White. St Catherine's Press, 1953

Connell, Brian   Portrait of a Whig peer; compiled from the papers of Second Viscount Palmerston, 1739-1802. Deutsch, 1957.

Craveri, Benedetta   Madame du Deffand and her world. Peter Halban, 1994.

Crewe, Frances Anne   Travel diary of Frances Anne Crewe. ms. British Library Add.37,926

Crewe, Quentin   Well, I forget the rest. Heinemann, 1991.

Cronin, Vincent   Louis and Antoinette. Collins, 1974.

Cruickshank, Dan   Life in the Georgian City by Dan Cruickshank and Neil Burton. Viking, 1990.

Dakin, Douglas   Turgot and the Ancien Regime in France. Methuen, 1939.

Devonshire, Georgiana, Duchess of   Georgiana: extracts from the correspondence of Georgiana, Duchess of Devonshire; edited by the Earl of Bessborough. John Murray, 1955.

Dickens, Charles   The letters of Charles Dickens. Pilgrim edition. Oxford University Press, 12 vols, 1965-2002.

Dictionary of National Biography.

Dolan, Brian   Ladies of the grand tour. HarperCollins, 2001.

Dumas, Alexandre   The Queen's necklace. 1849.

Farr, Evelyn   Before the deluge: Parisian society in the reign of Louis XVI. Peter Owen, 1994.

Foreman, Amanda   Georgiana Duchess of Devonshire. HarperCollins, 1998.

Fortescue, Thomas, Lord Clermont   A History of the family of Fortescue. Printed for private distribution, 1869.

Fraser, Antonia   Marie Antoinette. Weidenfeld and Nicholson, 2001.

Gascoigne, Bamber   World theatre. Ebury Press, 1968.
Gillray, James   The satirical etchings of James Gillray; edited by Draper Hill. Dover Publications, New York, 1976.
Gladden, Ray   A history of Crewe Hall. Ms.
Goede, C. A. G.   The stranger in England. 1807.
Goodden, Angelica   The sweetness of life: a biography of Elisabeth Louise Vigée Le Brun. Deutsch, 1997.
Greville, Charles   The Greville memoirs. 8 vols, 1874-87
Greville, Charles   Greville's England: selections from the diaries of Charles Greville, 1818-1860; edited, introduced and annotated by Christopher Hibbert. Folio Society, 1981.
Greville, Fulke   Maxims, characters, and reflections, critical, satirical, and moral. 1756.
Grove   The Grove dictionary of instruments. 1994.
Grove   The new Grove dictionary of opera. 1992-4.
Hardman, John   French politics 1774-1789. Longman, 1995.
Haydn, Joseph and Ockerby, Horace   The book of dignities. W.H. Allen, 1890.
Helm, W. H.   Vigée-Lebrun, 1755-1842: her life, works and friendships. Hutchinson, [1916].
Hibbert, Christopher   The grand tour. Book Club Associates, 1997.
Hinchliffe, Edward   Barthomley. Longman, Brown, Green, and Longmans, 1856.
Ingamells, John   A dictionary of British and Irish travellers in Italy 1701-1800; compiled from the Brinsley Ford Archive by John Ingamells. Yale University Press, 1997.
Jay, Douglas   Sterling: a plea for moderation. Sidgwick & Jackson, 1985.
Kelly, Linda   Richard Brinsley Sheridan: a life. Sinclair-Stevenson, 1997.
King, Norah   The Grimstons of Gorhambury. Phillimore, 1983.
Kirk, John   Biographies of English catholics in the eighteenth century. 1909
La Tour du Pin, Henrietta-Lucy, Madame de   Memoirs: laughing and dancing our way to the precipice. Harvill, 1999.
Lauzun, Armand Louis de Gontaut Biron, Duc de   Memoirs. Routledge, 1928. (The Broadway Library of XVIII century French literature)
Lefebvre, Georges   The French revolution from its origins to 1793. Routledge, 1971.
Lennox, Sarah   The life and letters of Lady Sarah Lennox, 1745-1826; edited by The Countess of Ilchester and Lord Stavordale. John Murray, 1902.
Leslie, Charles Robert and Tom Taylor   Life and times of Sir Joshua Reynolds. Murray, 2 vols, 1865.

Lever, Evelyne   Marie Antoinette, the last Queen of France. Piatkus, 2000.

Leveson-Gower, Granville   Private correspondence of Lord Granville Leveson Gower (First Lord Granville) 1782-1821; edited by his daughter-in-law Castalia Countess Granville. John Murray, 2 vols, 1916.

Lonsdale, Roger   The new Oxford book of eighteenth century verse; chosen and edited by Roger Lonsdale. Oxford U.P., 1984.

Mackay, Charles   Extraordinary popular delusions and the madness of crowds. Harrap, 1956.

Magazine a la Mode, March 1777.

Mansel, Philip   The court of France 1789-1830. Cambridge U.P., 1988.

Masters, Brian   Georgiana, Duchess of Devonshire. Hamish Hamilton, 1981.

McIntyre, Ian   Garrick. Allen Lane, The Penguin Press, 1999.

Namier, Lewis and Brooks, John   The House of Commons 1754-1790. HMSO, 1964. (The history of Parliament)

Nouvelle Biographie Universall

O'Toole, Fintan   A traitor's kiss: the life of Richard Brinsley Sheridan. Granta, 1997.

Oxford companion to French literature; compiled and edited by Sir Paul Harvey and J.E. Heseltine. Oxford, Oxford University Press, 1959.

The Oxford companion to the theatre. Oxford University Press, 4th edition, 1985.

Penny, Nicholas   Reynolds; edited by Nicholas Penny. Royal Academy of Arts/Weidenfeld and Nicholson, 1986.

Pope-Hennessy, James   Lord Crewe: the likeness of a Liberal. Constable, 1955.

Pope-Hennessy, James   Monckton Milnes. Constable, 2 vols, 1949-51.

Ribeiro, Aileen   The dress worn at masquerades in England, 1730 to 1790, and its relation to fancy dress in portraiture. New York, Garland Publishing, 1984.

Rizzo, Betty   Companions without vows: relationships among eighteenth-century British women. Georgia U.P., 1994.

Rose, Hugh James   A new general biographical dictionary. 12 vols, 1850.

Schama, Simon   Citizens: a chronicle of the French revolution. Viking, 1989.

Sheridan, Betsy   Betsy Sheridan's journal: letters from Sheridan's sister 1784-1786 and 1788-1790; edited by William LeFanu. Eyre and Spottiswoode, 1960.

Sheridan, Richard Brinsley   The letters of Richard Brinsley Sheridan; edited by Cecil Price. Oxford University Press, 3 vols, 1966.

Stevens, William Bagshaw   The Journal of the Rev. William Bagshaw Stevens; edited by G.Galbraith. Oxford, 1985.

Summers, Judith   The empress of pleasure: the life and adventures of Teresa Cornelys – queen of masquerades and Casanova's lover. Viking, 2003.

Summers, Judith   Soho. Bloomsbury, 1989.

Thomas, R. G.   The House of Commons, 1790-1820. Secker and Warburg, 1986. (The history of Parliament)

Thorne, R.G.   The House of Commons, 1790-1820. Secker and Warburg, 1986. (The history of Parliament)

Tillyard, Stella   Aristocrats. Chatto and Windus, 1994.

Vigée le Brun, Elisabeth Louise   The memoirs of Elisabeth Vigée-le Brun; translated from the French by Siân Evans. Camden Press, 1989.

Vulliamy, C.E.   English letter writers. Collins, 1945.

Walpole, Horace   Horace Walpole's correspondence. Oxford University Press and Yale University Press, 48 volumes, 1937-1983.

Watson, J. Steven   The reign of George III. Oxford University Press, 1987.

Webster, Nesta H   The Chevalier de Boufflers: a romance of the French Revolution. Murray, 1917.

Williamson, George C.   Life and works of Ozias Humphry R.A. John Lane, The Bodley Head, 2 vols, 1918.

Windham William   Miscellanies of The Philobiblon Society, Vol.9. Printed by Whittingham and Wilkins, 1865-6.

Windham, William   The diary of the Right Hon. William Windham, 1784-1810; edited by Mrs Henry Baring. Longmans Green, 1866.

Windham, William   The Windham papers: the life and correspondence of the Rt. Hon. William Windham 1750-1810; with an introduction by the Rt. Hon. The Earl of Rosebery. Herbert Jenkins, 2 vols, 1913.

Wraxall, Sir N. William   Historical memoirs of my own time. Kegan, Paul, Trench, Trubner, 1904.

Picture Credits

(frontis) Frances Anne Crewe by Sir Joshua Reynolds: Private collection. (page 21) a) Sir Ranulphe Crewe by Henry Weekes: a sculpture at Crewe Hall, Cheshire; photograph by Michael Allen. b) Crewe Hall in the 18th century, from *Barthomley* by Edward Hinchliffe. (page 22) a) Frances Anne Crewe by Daniel Gardner: Private Collection. b) John Crewe, 1st Baron Crewe of Crewe, by Daniel Gardner: Private Collection. (page 23) a) Costume for a masquerade, from *Magazine a la Mode*, March 1777. b) The Crewe family at Crewe Hall by Arthur Devis. (page 24) Master Crewe as Henry VIII (i.e. John Crewe, 2nd Baron Crewe of Crewe) by Sir Joshua Reynolds: Private Collection. (page 45) a) Richard Brinsley Sheridan by Sir Joshua Reynolds: Wikimedia Commons b) William Windham 1787 by Sir Joshua Reynolds: National Portrait Gallery, London, ref NPG 704. (page 46) a) Fulke Greville by Ozias Humphry: from *Life and works of Ozias Humphry, R.A.*, by George C. Williamson. b) Lay episcopacy (i.e. Hungerford, 3rd Lord Crewe of Crewe) 1882 by Spy (Leslie Ward): Vanity Fair. (page 47) The Marquess of Crewe by Arthur Ambrose McEvoy: Guildhall Art Gallery, Corporation of London – Collage ref 14048. (page 48) Crewe Hall 1992; photograph by Michael Allen. (page 70) Frances Anne Crewe by John Downman: formerly Scottish private collection, now dispersed, Scottish National Portrait Gallery Reference Section, ref B6858. (page 119) a) Galeries du Palais Royal 1800: Wikimedia Commons. b) Count Alessandro di Cagliostro: Wikimedia Commons. (page 120) a) Frances Greville by Ozias Humphry: Private Collection. Photograph: Photographic Survey, Courtauld Institute of Art; Courtauld negative number 583/1(8). b) Frances Fortescue, Countess Clermont by Sir Joshua Reynolds, from *A History of the family of Fortescue* by Thomas (Fortescue) Lord Clermont. (page 121) a) Mlle Raucourt as Medea. b) Lady Clarges 1790 by John Downman: Tate, London 2006. (page 122) Comedie Francaise, 18th century: Wikimedia Commons. (page 169) Emma Crewe by Thomas Gainsborough: Private Collection. (page 170) a) The Palace of Versailles. b) Portrait of Madelin Rose Bertin by Jean-Francois Janinet: Wikimedia Commons. (page 171) a) The Marquis de LaFayette. b) Self-portrait by Elisabeth Louise Vigée Le Brun, c.1781; Oil on canvas; 64.8 x 54.0cm. In recognition of his service to the Kimbell Art Museum and his role in developing area collectors, the Board of Trustees of the Kimbell Art Foundation has dedicated this work from the collection of Mr. And Mrs. Kay Kimbell, founding benefactors of the Kimbell Art Museum, to the memory of Mr. Bertram Newhouse (1883-1982) of New York City. (page 172) A Half length portrait of a young lady (i.e. Frances Anne Crewe) by Nathaniel Dance-Holland: Courtauld Institute of Art Gallery, London.

All Reasonable efforts have been made to trace those with rights in the illustrations used in this book. If any further rights are brought to the attention of the author he will be pleased to recognise them in future editions or printings.

Index

Boufflers, Madame de 78, 192, 207
Bouille, Francois Claude, Marquis
  de 28, 106, 107, 111, 163, 167
Bouillon, Duchesse de 108, 109
Boulainvillers, Marquise de 50
Boulogne, France 205, 209
Bouverie, Harriot 20, 26, 33
boxing matches 195
Breteuil, Louis, Duc de 110, 111
Breteuil, France 206, 207, 209, 215
Bretonne, Retif de la 52
Brissac, Adelaide Diane, Duchesse
  de 111, 116, 117
Bristol, John, 2nd Earl of 33
British Embassy, Paris 27, 134
British Library 3, 30, 34, 36, 59,
  90, 174
British Museum 3, 30
Broglie, Comte de 80
Brooks's Club 9, 142
Bruce, Mr 200, 201
Brussels 1, 4, 28, 29, 32, 72, 73, 93,
  94, 97, 139, 142, 163, 189,
  217, 232
Buckinghamshire, George Hobart,
  3rd Earl of 124
Bullock, Colonel 209
Bunbury, Sarah - see Lennox, Lady
  Sarah
Bunker Hill, USA 42
Burke, Edmund 4, 16, 43, 94,
  142, 174, 182, 185
Burke, Richard (son of Edmund)
  4, 83, 94, 95, 107, 109
Burke, Richard (brother of
  Edmund) 94
burlesque theatre 168, 173
Burney, Charles 11-13, 25, 138, 139
Burney, Fanny 1, 2, 12-13, 14, 18,
  25-26, 38, 134, 138
  Evelina 3, 10, 26
Bussy, Madame de 27, 96, 97, 231
Bussy, Charles Joseph, Marquis de
  96
Butterbrodt, Paul 54
Buxton, Derbyshire 136, 137
Byng, George 81, 142, 143
Byron, George Gordon, 6th Baron
  186
cabriolet 67, 164, 165

Café Chartres 54
cafés 53-54
Cagliostro, Count Alessandro di
  49-51, 82-83, *119*, 189
Calais Road 201
Calais, France 67, 203
Calmic 42
Cambis, Gabrielle Francoise de
  78, 79, 85, 93
Cambridge University 35, 40
  Trinity College 7, 186, 193
Canada 42
Canning, George 3, 90, 114, 138
Canning, Joan 32
Canterbury, Kent 211, 213, 215, 217
Caraman, Marie Ann, Comtesse de
  27, 78, 79, 96, 114, 115, 135,
  231
Caraman, Victor Maurice, Comte
  de 63, 66, 78, 96, 111, 114,
  135, 141
card playing 11, 17, 62, 63, 111,
  114, 138, 192, 197, 200, 201
Carlisle House 17-25
carnival 52, 129, 193, 195
Caroline of Brunswick, Princess 186
carriages 20, 57, 67, 68, 139, 159,
  164, 165, 202, 209, 213, 215
Carrington, Baron - see Smith,
  Robert
Carter, Mary 78, 79, 87, 90, 91,
  111, 123, 128, 138, 141, 143,
  173, 199
Carter, Thomas, 90
Casio (from Shakespeare's *Othello*)
  175
Casanova 20
Castries, Armand Charles, Duc de
  28, 43, 64-65, 76, 77, 81,99
  117, 153, 157, 197
Castries, Marie Louise, Duchesse de
  64-65, 76, 77, 81, 105, 131,
  197, 205
Cave Castle, Yorkshire 140
Cavendish, Elizabeth 204, 205
Cavendish, George Augustus Henry
  204, 205
chaise 67, 68, 99, 202, 203, 207,
  209, 214, 215
channel crossing 211

CPSIA information can be obtained at www.ICGtesting.com
Printed in the USA
LVOW101916190112

264656LV00018B/71/P